SPHOṬA, PRATIBHĀ AND DHVANI

By

Dr. Ajodhya Nath Hota
Reader in Sanskrit
M.P.C. (Autonomous) College,
Baripada. (ORISSA)

BOOK EASTERN EBL LINKERS

Eastern Book Linkers

DELHI : : (INDIA)

Publishers :
EASTERN BOOK LINKERS
5825, New Chandrawal, Jawahar Nagar,
Delhi-110007
Ph. : 23850287, 32919869
e-mail : ebl@vsnl.net

First Edition : 2006

Price : 500.00

ISBN : 81-8754-110-6

Sphoṭa, Pratibhā and Dhvani
Dr. Ajodhya Nath Hota

Printed at : **R.K. Print Service,** Delhi

Preface

In the ninth Century Ānadavardhana had established *Dhvani* concept taking cue from the grammarians who were masters of the language. Modern research is committed to constantly exploring different facets of language. But it appears, no one has seriously tried to provide a linguistic status to the *dhvani* concept of Ānandavardhana. *Dhvani* concept is nothing but a linguistic theory whose origin goes back to Shpoṭāyana and Vārtākṣa. Bhartṛhari, the great grammatical philolopher, gave concrete shape to it. It is an object language which is developed from metalanguage. It is a mode of communication in common and poetic speech. In this century when Information Technology has taken giant strides in the field of communication skills, the analysis of *dhvani* language should not lag behind. An intensive study shows the development of this language from phonetic level to semantic level. As the bosom of the Ganges swells by various tributaries, the *dhvani*-semantics has similarly absorbed thoughts of many scholars through different ages. This book is an humble attempt to bestow semantic status to Ānandavardhana's language theory.

It was presented as a dissertation under the guidance of Dr. S.D. Joshi, Director and Professor in the Centre of Advanced study in Sanskrit, University of Poona, Pune. Dr. Joshi is a leading figure in grammar and linguistics. In the course of my investigation, he had constantly offered new insights and novel ideas. I convey my deep sense of gratitude to him for his generous guidance.

I am thankful to authorities of Poona University who have kindly given permission to publish this book. I also remember the scholarly assistance of my wife Pranati and inspiration of my daughters Shraddha and Payal. They have helped me to prepare the manuscripts and to correct the proofs. My friend, Dr. Madhusudan Mishra, who has taken a lot of trouble to bring this work to limelight, deserves thanks for his help.

I am thankful to Mr Deepak Malhotra and Ravi Malhotra, the proprietors of Eastern Book Linkers, Delhi who have published this book.

A.N. Hota

Abbreviations

Abh	Abhinavabhāratī.
ABORI	Annals of Bhandarkar Oriental Research Institute.
ALB	Adyar Library Bulletin.
AORM	Annals of Oriental Research, Madras University.
BDCRI	Bulletin of Deccan College Research Institute, poona.
BJA	British Journal of aesthetics, London.
BSOAS	Bulletin of the school of Oriental and African Studies, University of London.
BV	Bhāratīya Vidyā, Bombay.
DL	Dhvanyāloka
IHQ	Indian historical quarterly, Calcutta.
JDL	Journal of Department of Letters, University of Calcutta.
JGJRI	Journal of Ganganath Jha Research Institute, Allahabad.
JOI	Journal of Oriental Institute, Baroda.
JOR	Journal of Oriental Research, Madras.
JRAS	Journal of Royal Asiatic Society of Great Britain and Ireland, London.
KĀ	Kārikā

KD	Kāvyādarśa of Daṇḍin
KL	Kāvyālaṁkāra of Bhāmaha
KLR	Kāvyālaṁkāra of Rudraṭa
KLSS	Kāvyālaṁkārasārasaṁgraha of Udbhaṭa.
KLSV	Kāvyālaṁkārasūtravṛtti of Vāmana.
KM	Kāvyamīmāṁsā of Rājaśekhara.
KP	Kāvyaprakāśa of Mammaṭa.
KSH	Kāvyānuśāsana of Hemacandra.
LOC.	Locana
Mbh.	Vaiyākaraṇa Mahābhāṣya
NBH	Nyāyabhāṣya
Nir	Nirukta
NM	Nyāyamañjarī
NŚ	Nāṭyaśāstra
NS	Nyāyasūtra
NV	Nyāyavārtika
NVTT	Nyāyavārtika Tātparya Ṭīkā
OH	Our Heriage, Calcutta.
OS	Orientalia Suecana, Uppsala.
P	Pāṇini
POC	Proceedings of Oriental Conference
PLM	Paramalaghumañjuṣā of Nāgeśabhaṭṭa
PWISM	Proceedings of winter Institute of Sentence Meaning, C.A.S.S. University of poona.
Ṛg.	Ṛgveda
RG	Rasagaṅgādhara.
sb.	Śābarabhāṣyam
SD	Śāstradīpikā
Sphot	Sphoṭavāda
SS	Sphoṭasiddhi

Sva	Ślokavārtika
SVUJ	Śrī Veṅkaṭeśvara University Journal, Tirupati
TPS	Transactions of Philological Society, Oxford.
VBS	Vaiyākaraṇabhūṣaṇasāra.
VJ	Vakroktijīvita
VSLM	Vaiyākaraṇa Siddhānta Laghu Mañjuṣā

Contents

Introduction

In recent years the rapid growth in linguistics and semantics as academic subjects has led to the study of earlier works in the fields of linguistics and semantics in ancient India. On the basis of such a study one can argue that the achievements of earlier generations may be a source of new theories, procedures and applications developed later. Ānandavardhana's *dhvani* theory is not an exception to this. The emergence of the *dhvani* theory is not a sudden phenomenon, but a product of the past. Ānandavardhana did not start form scratch; he inherited many concepts and ideas from his predecessors. He concentrated on the earlier theories like *sphoṭa* and *pratibhā* which are significantly relevant to the *dhvani* approach to semantics. It is difficult to believe that Ānandavardhana suddenly introduced a new theory unrelated to insights form earlier works. The early grammatical works were the foundation of all the later works in India. What was said in the expression plane by the grammarians has been applied to content plane by Ānandavardhana. The present book seeks to evaluate the earlier theories of the grammarians against the later developed *dhvani* theory of Ānandavardhana. I have selected basically two theories in earlier grammatical works, namely *sphoṭa* and *pratibhā* that can be brought into an organised relationship with the *dhvani* theory. I wish to highlight in this book that without the development of the theory of *sphoṭa* and *pratibhā* in early grammatical works, the *dhvani* theory of Ānandavardhana would be poorer in content and less advanced in techniques. The *sphoṭa* and *pratibhā* theories provide a starting point on which the edifice of the *dhvani* theory has been built up later on by Ānandavardhana.

Vedic wisdom contributes many things towards the development of Sanskrit poetics. The definition of various figures of speech composed by rhetoricians can be applied to the hymns of the *Ṛgveda* and other Vedic literatures,[1] though the names of those figures do not occur in them except *upamā*.[2] The idea of similitude which is responsible for the figures of speech of the common class of *upamā* occurs in a number of places in the Vedic *Saṁhitās*, *Brāhmaṇas* and earlier *Upaniṣads*.[3]

Different philosophical systems contribute the idea of reality of language to poetics. Almost all systems deal with the ordinary speech. Some hold that meaning belongs to phonemes and others say it is found in the sentence. Various questions involved in understanding the nature of word and sentence meaning were discussed from different points of view. Much thought was given to the variable nature of meaning. They paid attention to the primary meaning of a word *(abhidhā)* and various meanings arising from its metaphorical use *(lakṣaṇā)*.

The early philosophers actually set up the pedestal for the *dhvani* theory by their subtle analysis of ordinary meaning. The earlier important contributions to Sanskrit poetics are the different interpretations of grammarians' *sphoṭa* theory. They are the idea of manifestation *(abhivyakti)*, the idea of causation,[4] the idea of *'mokṣa'* and *'ānanda'* of *Vedānta*, the theories of semantics (i.e. *abhidhā, lakṣaṇā, tātparya, arthāpatti* etc.), the concept of genus *(jāti)*, individual *(vyakti)* and quality *(guṇa)*. More of less, the *dhvani* theory is based on all these elements.[5] But the detailed study of all these aspects is beyond the scope of the present work.

In contrast to the contributions of other systems to Sanskrit poetics, the contributions of grammar and grammatical philosophy are more significant. The *Nighaṇṭu* provides a list of particles of comparison comprising twelve varieties (iii. 13). The *Nirukta* explains them (i. 4, iii. 13-18, ix. 6).[6] Yāska mentions certain similes namely *karmopamā, bhūtopamā, siddhopamā, luptopamā* and *arthopamā* etc.

P uses some technical terms of poetics namely *upamāna,*[7] *upamita,*[8] *sāmānya,*[9] *upamā,*[10] *aupamya,*[11] *upamārthe,*[12] *sudṛśya.*[13] He discusses the idea of similitude in not less than fifty *sūtras* dealing with feminine *kṛt, taddhita,* and *samāsāta* suffixes,[14] compounds[15] and accents.[16] Both Kātyāyana[17] and Patañjali[18] consider the meaning of these forms in some detail.

The idea of similitude generates many figures of speech in rhetoric. These figures are external decorations of poetic speech which owe their origin to grammar. But there is one element which brings internal charm to poetic speech. This element is suggestion. Ānandavardhana find its source in grammar and develops it. Thus both external and internal elements of poetic speech analysed in the works of rhetoric are originally inspired by the findings of grammarians.

While grammarians deal with the correctness of speech, the theorists of poetics deal with its literary embellishment. But all literary embellishments can work only through language. The basic structure of a language is analysed by the grammarians. Theorists of poetics take all the aspects of grammar into account in order to study suggestive values of speech. Thus the *dhvani* theory forms a branch of linguistic or grammatical science. P's *Aṣṭādhyāyī* does not make any explicit statement regarding the concept of meaning. But the procedure of derivation outlined in the *Aṣṭādhyāyī* involves a complete description of a basically semantic relationship. So meaning plays a crucial role in the derivation. The meanings *Aṣṭādhyāyī* refers to are of two types, namely, lexical meanings given in the *Dhātupāṭha* and the *Padapāṭha* and categorical meanings like *vartamāna* 'present', *bhūta* 'past', *anadyatana* 'not pertaining to this day'. These categorical meanings which are not defined by grammar are taken as basic meanings out of which the system of grammar is constructed. Though varieties of meanings like attitudinal meaning, implicative meaning, pre-suppositional meaning, and referential meaning[19] can be traced to the Aṣṭādhyāyī, the grammarians mainly take into account the lexical or denotative meaning of the expression. It is highly controversial whether P was aware of metaphorical meaning *(lakṣyārtha)*, since he has made no special provision for examples like *siṁho māṇavaka* or *agner māṇavaka.*[20] The secondary function comes into play only later, after the derivation of *agner* and *māṇavaka*, when they have been joined together. It is due to *ākāṅkṣā* which is a feature belonging to the meaning of a sentence. Therefore, as far as the addition of the nominative endings after the stems *agni* and *māṇavaka* is concerned, the *lakṣyārtha* is something external. It need not be taken into account during the process of derivation. But P takes into account suggested or implicative meanings. The notion of implicative meaning rests upon the distinction between what is actually said and what is intended by the expression. For instance, if somebody says *anu śākaṭāyanaṁ vaiyākaraṇāḥ*, the literal meaning of the expression will be "all grammarians are after Śākaṭāyana". But the implied meaning is something more than the literal meaning. The speaker wants to convey the inferiority of all other grammarians to Śākaṭāyana. So this additional meaning is the implied meaning and *anu* which indicates this meaning is called *karmapravacanīya* according to P. 1.4.86.

The grammarians are certainly aware of, suggested meaning. Bhartṛhari deals with some examples which depend on the speaker's intention (*VP*. II.310, 311, 321 etc.). This intended meaning of the speaker is different from linguistic meaning. According to Ānandavardhan a, this intended meaning is *dhvani* meaning. Thus the fact that grammarians are aware of the suggested meaning cannot be ruled out. If grammatical works do not make any explicit statement regarding the nature of *vyaṅgyārtha*, it should not be taken to mean that grammatical works have nothing to do with suggestive meaning. Although the grammarians do not give any explicit theory of semantics, yet the entire structure of the derivative system is based on it.

Rhetoricians of different schools consider grammarians as their God- fathers. Bhāmaha analyses the correctness of poetic speech in the sixth chapter of his KL. Vāmana elaborates them more vividly in the fifth *adhikaraṇa* of his *KLSV*. Further Bhoja discusses the peculiarities of grammar and theories of meanings in the first eight chapters of his *Śṛṅgāraprakāśa*. All these are evidences that rhetoric is sky dew without grammar.

On these pieces of evidence, an attempt is made to show that the philosophy of grammar has inspired the *dhvani* theory of Sanskrit poetics.

Ānandavardhana deals with the post-denotative function of language. Before him poetic language is analysed as an external entity. The poetic figures, styles, metres, poetic merits are attached to the external entity in different respects. For the first time, Ānandavardhana investigates the inner significance of poetic language. It is comparable to the grace of a beautiful lady. Ornaments are external appendage to her. This inner significance of language known as *dhvani* is marked by the capacity of language to employ the suggestion in place of implicit statement. It represents the deeper structure of poetic language which rests on the surface structure as the grace of a lady rests on her body, but the former overpowers the latter. This is a objective part of the language.

Ānandavardhana's cryptic declaration of his debt to grammarians may suggest many things, since he speaks little and suggests a lot. The present work attempts an evaluation of the earlier theories to indicate the continuity of thought in the grammarianś *sphoṭa* and *pratibhā* with Ānandavardhana's *dhvani* doctrine.

Scope of the work

It has been stated that the aim of the present work is to trace the source of *dhvani* theory of poetics in the early works on grammar. So far my investigation goes, there is no systematic and intensive study carried out on these lines except some stray remarks. Among the ancient authorities Abhinavagupta[21] draws our attention to this fact and later Mammaṭa tries to elucidate it. Both of them agree that the source of the *dhvani* theory is the *sphoṭa* theory of the grammarians. Abhinavagupta's analysis will be discussed in the fourth chapter of this work in adequate detail.

Mammaṭa's view regarding the influence of the grammatical philosophy on Ānandavardhana's aesthetic philosophy is noteworthy in this respect: "by the learned that is by the grammarians that word is called *dhvani* which suggests *sphoṭa* which is all important (in as much as it is through this *sphoṭa* that a word conveys its meaning); others carry this theory of grammarians further still and apply the word *dhvani* not only to the words, but also to senses, capable of suggesting meaning other than those directly expressed ones.[22]" In this translation[23], the term *pradhāna-bhūta* is rendered as 'meaningfulness' which is attached to the term *sphoṭa,* and accordingly, the *sphoṭa, the* auditorily perceived sound, stands for the meaning bearing segment of language. This is objectionable.

Mammaṭa neither uses the term *'artha'*, nor do we find any latent hint to this effect in this passage. He only mentions that *sphoṭa* is suggested and *dhvani* (articulated sound) is suggester of the word. Nowhere in this passage is the idea of *sphoṭa* as the latent word *(pradhānabhūta)* and *dhvani* as external word hinted. Whether *sphoṭa* stands for the meaning element is a different question which will be discussed in the first chapter of this book.

Māṇikyacandra (1159-1160 AD/Saṁvat 1216), one of the earliest commentators of *Kāvyaprakāśa,* interprets the above passage of Mammaṭa differently. He states[24]: "the articulated air *(dhvani)* suggests the secret *sphoṭa* before pronunciation ; then the previous dispositions reveal the external *sphoṭa* which is perceived in the form of various modes of utterance *(prayatna)*. It is like the denotative words and senses that are subordinated by suggested meaning. It is *(dhvani)* which is the suggested (meaning). Those words and senses empowered by suggestion are called *kāvya,* and on the similarity of suggestion *dhvani* is used in poetry. The author of *Hṛdaya Darpaṇa* holds that *(dhvani)* is the outcome of suggestion which is brought about when the denotative word and sense become secondary. But Mammaṭa holds that the suggestive meaning activated by the function of suggestion is *(dhvani),* which is the actual import".

This passage refers to the non-articulated sound *(dhvani)* which is considered to be the inner *sphoṭa,* whereas the articulated sound is regarded as an outer *sphoṭa.* This view favours the interpretation that *sphoṭa* is sound-image in its non-articulated form. Apart from the above statements no other attempt in this regard is made by ancient authorities.

In recent times no sincere attempt has been made to bring out a special relationship between the *(dhvani)* theory of Ānandavardhana and the *sphoṭa* theory of the grammarians. However, in almost every edition of the *Dhvanyāloka,* an attempt has been made to connect the *dhvani* concept with the *sphoṭa* concept without giving objective standards to judge the evolution of the past into the present one. Thus so far this comparison is concerned, all these attempts are unsatisfactory, because the later scholars read the later developed theories in the earlier works and read the past work through the eyes of later ones without probably assessing the contribution made in each work. Some scholars present superfluous and forced analogies without showing a continuous line of development between the works to be compared. Some of them have touched this subject briefly. Whatever help we get from these works should be gratefully accepted.

The present work deals with some basic problems common to both the traditions, namely grammarians and *dhvani* school of rhetoricians. This work seeks to trace the mutual relationship, influence, continuance and critical thought of works belonging to two different fields. In order to keep the inquiry within limits I have discussed mainly the more important theories in both the traditions namely, *sphoṭa, pratibhā* and *dhvani*.

Ānandavardhana proposes the theory of *dhvani* in order to account for the universal aesthetic experience. This doctrine of *dhvani* deals with the problems of meaning of poetic language and its aesthetic experience. In Indian semantics and philosophy, the meaning is defined in terms of relation.[25] This relation is a power which remains in the object signified and in the word which signifies it. It is through cognition of this relation these denotative words have a direct reference to the objects they denote. In other words, the relation between the denoting word and denoted sense is called *abhidhā*. Sometimes words fail to convey the primary sense. In such a situation words may convey the secondary meaning which is called *lakṣyārtha* 'secondary meaning'. The relation between the *lakṣaka* word (indicative word) and the object indicated *(lakṣyārtha)* is called *lakṣaṇā* 'secondary function'. This secondary should be connected to the primary in some way or other.

But words sometimes communicate something more than the primary and the secondary meaning. When the primary and the secondary functions of language fail to reveal the intended meaning, the function of suggestion comes to the rescue. It is variable and is based on the intention of the speaker. Suggestion deals with the inner meaning or secret meaning of the language. Ānandavardhana calls it *dhvani* language. An element which gives rise to a suggested meaning is called *vyañjaka* and the suggested meaning is called *vyaṅgyārtha*.

Patañjali and Bhartṛhari treat the term *dhvani* as an attribute of the word. It is characterised by resonance or re-sounding. The suggestive semantics of Ānandavardhana follow this nomenclature. The real content of a poem is not the sum total of lexical meaning of the words. When the lexical meaning spreads like resonance it continues to manifest the meaning. So the *vyaṅgyārtha* which is over and above the denoted meaning is pure resonance. It is to be congnised again and again. Probably owing to this generative power of language, Mukula Bhaṭṭa concludes that the suggested meaning appears as the extended meaning of denotation. The *dhvani* theory takes into account all the aspects of language in order to study the suggested value of speech. Therfore the *dhvani* theory deserves a place on par with phonetics, morphology, syntax and grammar etc. Thus *dhvani* theory forms the branch of linguistic science.

Generally it is believed that Ānandavardhana builds up the suggestive semantics on par with *sphoṭa* of Bhartṛhari. This is because :

(i) Ānandavardhana declares his indebtedness to the grammarians.

(ii) There is no other ancient work which deals with the nature of *sphoṭa* as satisfactorily as does Bhartṛhari in his *Vākyapadīya*.

(iii) Kumārila Bhaṭṭa and his followers, Śaṅkara, Maṇḍana Miśra, Kauṇḍa Bhaṭṭa, Nāgeśa Bhaṭṭa etc. read later developed theories in the *sphoṭa* doctrine of Bhartṛhari.

(iv) Abhinavagupta who is close to Ānadavardhana in time as in his thinking argues that the source of the *dhvani* theory of Sanskrit poetics is the *sphoṭa* theory of Bhartṛhari.

But my investigation reveals that both the *sphoṭa* and the *pratibhā* concepts of Bhartṛhari are real sources of the *dhvani* theory of Ānandavardhana. I have tried to establish this item in the fourth chapter of this book. Since Ānandavardhana has mentioned that his source of the *dhvani* theory is the works of grammar, the relevant concepts that come to our mind are the *sphoṭa* and *pratibhā* as developed by Bhartṛhari. Abhinavagupta himself states that the *sphoṭa* concept is the source of the *dhvani* theory. Thus my assumption agrees with Abhinavagupta.

Sphoṭa

The theory of *sphoṭa* has been discussed by the ancient and modern scholars alike. It has undergone two different interpretations : phonetic and semantic. The *Mīmāṁsakas*, headed by Kumārila Bhaṭṭa, the *Vedāntins* specially Śaṅkara, and the *Naiyāyikas* like Jayanta Bhaṭṭa vehemently refute the *sphoṭa* theory. They criticise the doctrine of *sphoṭa* put forth by the later grammarians. According to them, postulation of *sphoṭa* as meaning conveying entity is not necessary. Maṇḍana Miśra, Kauṇḍa Bhaṭṭa and Nāgeśa Bhaṭṭa support *sphoṭa* to explain unitariness of word and sentence as a meaning conveying units. Ānandavardhana's *dhvani* theory is based on both the earlier and later interpretation of *sphoṭa*. According to Ānandavardhana, just as the sounds reveal meaningful entities so in poetry words and their meanings reveal suggested sense. Just as the *sphoṭa* theory takes into account both the sound element and the meaning element, similarly Ānandavardhana's *dhvani* theory says that sounds reveal suggested sense. Thus we find a striking parallel of *dhvani* theory of poetics with the grammarian's *sphoṭa* theory.

Modern scholars, namely Prabhatcandra Chakravorty (1925), Siddheswar Verma (1925), S.S. Suryanarayan Sastri (1932), V. A. Ramaswami Sastri (1932), K. A. S. Iyer (1935, 1969 etc.) T. Burrow (1936), John Brough (1951, 1953), Gaurinath Sastri (1959, 1980), K.K. Raja (1963) and Harold G. Coward (1976, 1980) consider that the chief characteristics of *sphoṭa* are meaningfulness and indivisibility, a theory which own the recognition of later grammarians. An attempt was made by Heimann Betty (1941), R.E. Srikrishna Sharma (1980-81) and others to interpret the doctrine of *sphoṭa* in terms of the metaphysical aspect of word-doctrine (*Śabdabrahman*).

But the most startling departure from the traditional interpretation of *sphoṭa* is in the introductory chapter of *Sphoṭa Nirṇaya* (1967) by S. D. Joshi. He traces the evolution of the *sphoṭa* concept from Patañjali to Nāgeśa and points out the basic difference among them.

Patañjali's and Bhartṛhari's concept of *sphoṭa* deal with the feature level of language, whereas the *Mīmāṁsakas*, *Vedāntins*, *Naiyāyikas* and later grammarians have shifted the earlier concept of *sphoṭa* from the feature level of language to the semantic level.

According to Patañjali and Bhartṛhari, the term *sphoṭa* stands for the sound auditorily perceived but not necessarily understood semantically. According to the later grammarians, *sphoṭa* deals with the significative level of language. And, finally the later grammarians have attributed the metaphysical aspect to the doctrine of *sphoṭa*. This has been discussed in detail in the first chapter of my work.

Pratibhā

In both grammatical and poetic tradition *pratibhā* is a kind of divine gift. It has been interpreted by both ancient and modern scholars philosophically, psychologically as well as linguistically. Gopinath Kaviraj (1924) discusses it philosophically ; K.A. S. Iyer (1940, 1980-81), S. D. Joshi (1977) analyse it linguistically; and Elizabeth Christie (1979) presents it in mixed way. I have discussed the relevant views and I venture to conclude that the *pratibhā* enables the poet to present the familiar things in a striking way.

According to Bhartṛhari, the scope of *pratibhā* extends over all the aspects of activities. But according to Ānandavardhana, the scope of *pratibhā* is restricted to the poetic imagination.

Dhvani

Ānandavardhana's *Dhvanyāloka* is the most outstanding work in the history of Indian literary criticism. He developed the idea of *rasadhvani,* according to which, aesthetic experience is realised through the suggestive function of language. What he claims is that the *rasadhvani* is not beyond the realm of speech. The unique beauty of meaningful words consists in suggestiveness. The literal meaning aims at suggestiveness. The *dhvani* theory is the positive discipline of language and *dhavni*-meaning is an element of communication which is not beyond the province of language.

With this aim in view, I venture to point out that the theories, namely *sphoṭa* and *pratihbā,* provide a starting point for the *dhvani* theory. The study of these theories will help to discover the common undercurrents running through all of them. On the basis of the common similarities it can be concluded that the *dhvani* theory of poetics is born of the concept of *sphoṭa* and *pratibhā* of grammarians, especially of Bhartṛhari.

Plan

This book is organised in the following way :

Chapter 1 : The evolution of *sphoṭa,* Patañjali's views

on the nature of *sphoṭa*, Bhartṛhari's concepts of *sphoṭa*, *sphoṭa* and its relation with *dhvani*, three views about the nature of *sphoṭa*, the process of comprehension of *sphoṭa* according to Bhartṛhari, *sphoṭa* and meaningful unit, the two-sidedness of word, the word is without differentiation, the nature of *śabda* in the *Vākyapadīya*, *sphoṭa* as a symbol, *sphoṭa* as an auditory image, distinctive and significative levels of language, the Mīmāṁsakaś, the *Naiyāyikaś* and the later grammarians' view on *sphoṭa*, conclusion.

Chapter 2 : The concept of *pratibhā* according to Bhartṛhari, *pratibhā* as *paśyantī* form of speech, semantic and psychological study of *pratibhā*, Ānandavardhana's concept of *pratibhā*, the nature of *pratibhā* and *prajñā*, *pratibhā* and *rasa*, *pratibhā* and poetic theme, causes of *pratibhā*, later rhetoricians' concept of *pratibhā*, conclusion.

Chapter 3 : Hints about *dhvani* in earlier works *dhvani* theory of Ānandavardhana, nature of *pratīyamānārtha*, suggestion and denotation, process of manifestation of suggestion, suggestive elements and poetic speech, *pratīyamāna* and *vyñjanā*, genesis of *dhvani*, mediums of *dhvani* language, monistic concept of *rasa*, speaker's intention and *vyañjanā*, conclusion.

Chapter 4 : Synthesis.

Chapter 5 : Conclusion.

Anandavardhana's *dhvani* theory and its historical background

In recent times, keen interest has been shown in the study of *dhvani* semantics, both by Indian and foreign scholars. In this book I have attempted to present the views of Bhartṛhari and Ānandavardhana in a historical perspective. It is my endeavour to set forth the *sphoṭa*, *pratibhā* and *dhvani* theories using modern terminology to the extent possible and necessary.

Suggestive semantics of Ānadavardhana

It is a new inquiry into the study of semantics which the general linguists avoid. Karl Vossler points out this lacuna.[26] Though Pāṇinian grammar deals with lexical and categorical meanings for derivative purpose, it does not say anything on semantics[27] which Bhartṛhari extends and expounds. P's commentators believe that the attitudinal meaning is a property which remains in the speaker.[28] The word has a natural capacity to convey the denotative and indicative meaning. But this power cannot work in the case of attitudinal meaning. Words do not convey any meaning unless we intentionally use them to signify certain things. Contextual factors including speaker's intention determine the special meaning of speech. Bhartṛhari enumerates such contextual factors in a number of verses. The meaning of a word used in a secondary sense cannot be fixed without its context. In the case of polysemic words the meaning cannot be fixed apart from the context. For example, the meaning of the sentence *saindhavam ānaya* differs in different contexts, It means 'bring a horse' when used in the context of a battle and it means 'bring a salt' when used in the context of food. Bhartṛhari also distinguishes between the two kinds of meaning of words, 'primary' *mukhya* and 'secondary' *gauṇa*. The meaning of the word *go* is primary in the sentence *gām ānaya* 'bring a cow' and secondary in *gauḥ vāhīkaḥ*. Here the word *go* secondarily stands for a studied person. Here the meaning which is determined with the help of context or speaker's intention is secondary. Thus the speaker's intention plays a considerable role in determining the meaning of a word. Bhartṛhari quotes the view that if the word *go* denotes a thing that has *gotva* it is its primary usage. But if the word *go* is used for denoting a thing which has no *gotva* but which is similar to a cow in some respects, it is considered to be a secondary use. The secondary meaning of a word is fixed with the help of the speaker's intention.[29]

Ānandavardhana inducts this concept of speaker's intention to frame his suggestive semantics. In suggestive semantics the denoted meaning is always subservient to the suggested sense. The speaker's intention which gives rise to the suggested sense is always supreme. The expression in literature has reference mainly to speaker's intention. The referential meaning does not contradict the poetic meaning. It is not inadequate for poetic feelings. It is a power of words fully realised, projecting a suggestive meaning. The words denotatively used are soaked into the emotional reactivity so that they can generate the miracle of their activities.[30]

Ānandavardhana adopts the principle of compromise. He concentrates on poetic constructions which have both a denotative and suggested meaning. Where suggested meaning is less relevant, denotative meaning (direct meaning) conveys poetic intention and that become an inferior type of poetry.

Essentially both ordinary and poetic speech have one similarity. In both the cases, the meaning is determined by speaker's intention. The grammatical tradition is the upholder and bearer of this idea. Bhartṛhari explains it in detail. Ānandavardhana finds it useful to the suggestive semantics. In this respect he is indebted to grammarians.

Principle of two levels of language

Ānandavardhana assimilates one more important concept of the philosophy of language through Bhartṛhari.

P's rule 1.1.68[31] indirectly indicates two levels of language. It says that 'a word (in grammatical rule) which is not a technical term, denotes its own form'. On this Kātyāyana comments, *śabdapūrvako hy arthe saṁpratyayas tasmād arthanivṛttiḥ* (*Mbh.* Vol. I, p. 176). It means, 'the understanding of the thing meant is preceded by the comprehension of the word form. In a grammatical context, the thing meant is not important but the word-form. That is to say the thing meant is subservient to the word-form. Therefore utterance signifies priority of its own form as connected with the thing meant by it. The word-form is the name of which *saṁjñīn* is the object meant by it. The *saṁjñā* represents the word form and *saṁjñīn* represents the context. Thus the word has two sided entity. Always we first recognise sounds which provide information. That is to say first we identity sounds. The sound factor is so basic that we cannot overlook its importance. Once sound is grasped the second factor is of getting meaning. Meaning cannot appear independently of sound. These above two factors are the basic conditions which are responsible for verbal communication.[32]

In social discourse, the speaker first conceives the correct form of the word and then comprehends meaning. In the same process the listener understands the linguistic form first, and then the meaning (*VP*. I.53). Unless the linguistic form is cognised meaning cannot be understood (*VP*. I. 56). That is why the listener fails to understand the meaning when the linguistic form is not apprehended, and he asks the speaker as to what he has uttered (*VP*. I.57) Thus in social communication the meaning is predominant and linguistic form is subservient. (*vṛtti* of *VP*. I.53), whereas in grammatical operations the linguistic form is primary and the meaning is secondary.[33]

John Brough has presented lucidly the ideas of Bhartṛhari in this regard. He say, "just as a technical term like *vṛddhi* which, linked with its own form, is also attached to what is named by it, viz. the speech entities symbolised by *ādaic* (i.e. *ā*, *ai*, *au*) so likewise this word *agni* (in every day use, i.e. the meaning fire), is also attached to the sound *agni* which (in this context) has the word *agni* as the thing expressed. The word which is uttered (in ordinary uses) is certainly not the one which partakes of the opertion (of adding the suffix). But in conveying is other sense, its power (to convey the normal sense) is not impeded.[34]

Bhartṛhari explains this two sidedness of language by offering analogies. Language can be compared with light and knowledge, because it can reveal itself at the same time revealing others. As knowledge reveals its own form while revealing the object of knowledge (*VP.* I. 50), and just as light reveals itself while revealing other objects, similarly each word has the power to be the object of apprehension *(grāhyatva)* and the power to convey the meaning *(grāhakatva)*.[36]

These two levels of language may be interpreted in favour of meta-language and object language. Meta-language is a language consisting of expressions which refer to expressions in an object language. In the interpretation of P. 1.1.68, the term *vṛddhi* (P. 1.1.1) and the term *agni* to which the suffix *ḍhak* (P. 4.2.33) is to be added are meta-languages, whereas the *ā ai, au* and the object fire represent the object language.

Ānandavardhana receives inspiration in this regard form Pāṇinian tradition, especially from Bhartṛhari. He forms this *dhvani* language which has two levels, i.e. the denotative level *(vācya)* and the suggestive level *(pratīyamāna)*. The suggestive level cannot operate without denotative level. The denotative level which functions by the symbolic powers *(saṁketagraha)* of the language, is utilised to comprehend the suggestive level which depends on the suggestive power of language. But both are distinct. This problem is discussed elaborately in the third chapter of this book.

In a way, denotative level may be called the metalanguage and the suggestive level may be called object language. It is because through the physical medium of denotation,the suggestion is expressed. Then a speaker speaks about language he speaks in meta-language. Similarly when communication (through denotation) speaks about communication (suggested sense) then it can be termed as meta-communication.The denotative meaning expresses the suggestive meaning. Following the grammarians analysis on the expression side Ānandavardhana offers parallel analysis of content side.

On this background it seems that Ānandavardhana follows the footsteps of the grammarians to shape his *dhvani* theory.

Ānandavardhana utilises the *Vedānta* metaphysics and the grammatical metaphysics of Bhartṛhari for the exposition of his *rasadhvani.* From the arguments arrayed in favour of *Śāntarasa* (*DL*.IV), one can understand the tremendous influence of monistic *Vedānta* on him. Not only has he borrowed the ideas, but also the terms from *Vedānta,* namely *avidyāprapañcarūpam, paramārtha satyasvarūpam* (*DL*. IV. 276,8), *mahāmohamagna* (*DL*. IV.274,8), *vimalajñāna* (*DL*. IV. 274,9), *paraṁbrahmaṇ, paraṁbrahmaprāpti* (*DL*. IV. p. 278,1,3) etc. All the rhetoricians did not resist the temptation of comparing the process of *rasāsvāda* with *brahmāsvāda.*

Details of this aspect have been discussed in the third and fourth chapter of this book.

In the comparative study of the *Dhvanyāloka* and the *Vākyapadīya* mention should be made of the revealer and the revealed, and the outer and the inner relations. Just as *dhvani* reveals *sphoṭa* according to Bhartṛhari, similarly the parts (i.e. suffix, phonemes, ideas, figures, *dhvani* and suggesters) reveal the whole *rasadhvani.* Just as Bhartṛhari holds that the sentence is over and above the phonemes and words, and the sentence-meaning is over and above the word-meaning, similarly Ānandavardhana holds that the meaning of a poem is not equivalent to the meaning of words and sentences in it. Again just as the inner level of language *(paśyanti)* is superior to the outer level of language (*madhyamā and vaikharī)* similarly the suggestive level of language (inner) is superior to denotative level (outer) of language. Ānandavardhana clearly distinguishes the denotation of words and expression from what might be called the suggested meaning.

The emergence of the *dhvani* theory in Sanskrit poetics is considered to be an epoch making event. The meaning of a string of denotative words *(dhvani)* reveals the beauty of language *(dhvani)*. But it is very difficult to tread on this path of *dhvani*. Even opponents of the stature of Mahima Bhaṭṭa admits this fact.[36] It is wrong to believe that such famous and creative theory is imitated from the principle of grammar. K. Krishnamoorthy seems to be correct in believing that Ānandavardhana forms his new theory and looks towards the authority of language (grammarians) for approval.[37] However, we cannot deny that Ānandavardhana's *dhvani* theory belongs to the province of language as a whole. The *dhvani* theory deserves a place on par with phonetics, grammar, *sphoṭa* and *pratibhā*. Ānandavardhana shows that the *dhvani* theory forms a branch of linguistics and semantics. The facts of expression convey suggested sense and not the external objects referred to. The facts of expressions convey ideas, sentiments of the speaker, and other implications. The *dhvani* meaning is accessible to linguistic expression. The term *dhvani* is specially chosen by Ānandavardhana. Just as linguists pay attention to the data of sound, so also the data of *dhvani*-meaning is accessible to the linguistic explanation. *Dhvani*-phonetics and *dhvani*-semantics constitute two components of language. This approach of Ānandavardhana provides a kind of model that can be directly connected with suggestive meaning which language conveys. Since previously no sincere attempt has been made in this regard, the present book aims at justifying the declaration of Ānandavardhana that for the formation of the *dhvani* theory he is indebted to the grammarians. Keeping in view all these facts, I attempt a comparative study of Bhartṛhari, the grammarian philosopher, and Ānandavardhana, the semanticist, to measure the debt of the latter to the former.

REFERENCES

1. Prahallad Kumar, *Ṛgvede'laṅkārāḥ*, Munshiram Manoharlal, Delhi,1977
2. *Ṛg*. V. 34.9; 1.31.15.
3. For detail see, P.V. Kane, *History of Sanskrit Poetics*, Delhi, 1971, pp.326-341; S.K.De, *Sanskrit Poetics*, Vol.I, Calcutta, 1960, p.2
4. *Sāṁkhya Sūtra*, 1-117-118
5. S.K.De, *op. cit.*, pp. 9-11.
6. Also see *Nirukta*, Laksman Swarup, i.19, ii.6, iii.5, iv.11, v.22, vii. 13 etc.
7. P. 2.1.55, 3. 1. 10, 2. 79, 4.45; 5.4.97, 137; 6.1.204, 2.2, 72, 80, 127, 145, 169.
8. P. 2.1.56
9. P. 2.1, 55, 56; 8.1.74.
10. P. 2 3.72.
11. P. 1.4.79; 4.1.69; 6.2.113.
12. P. 8.2.101.
13. P. 2.1.6-7; 6.2.11.
14. P. 1.4.79; 2.3.72; 3.1.10, 2.79, 4.45; 4.1.69, 4-9; 5.1.115-116, 2-39, 3.96, 106, 4.97, 137.
15. P.2.1.7, 31, 55-56; 6.2.11.
16. P. 5.1.18; 6.1. 204, 2.2, 11, 72, 80, 113, 127, 145, 169, etc.
17. *Mbh*. on P.1.3.21, 2.1.55, 2.24, 4.71, 3.1.10 etc.
18. *Ibid*. Vol.I, p. 397:
    tat samīpe yaṁ nātyanta ya mimīte tad upamānaṁ gaur iva gavya iti ।
19. Dinabandhu Kar, *Semantic basis of the Aṣṭādhyāyī, unpublished Ph. D these submitted to* University of Poona, 1980, pp. 29-45.
20. See S.N. Dasgupta, S.K. De. *History of classical Sanskrit Literature*, Calcutta University, 1962, pp. 514-517; also K.K. Raja, "*Pāṇini's attitude towards Lakṣaṇā*", ALB, Vol.XXIX, 1965.
21. *Locana* on *Dhvanyāloka*, ed. J. Pathak, Varanasi, 1965, pp.138-142.
22. *Kāvyaprakāśa* of Mammaṭa, ed. Vamancharya Jhalakikar, BORI, Poona, 1965, p.19 ;
    budhair vaiyākaraṇaiḥ pradhānabhūtasphoṭarūpavyaṅgyavyañjakasya śabdasya dhvanir iti vyavahārah kṛtaḥ tatas tan matānusā-

ribhir anyair api nyagbhāvita vācyavyaṅgyavyañjanakṣamasya śabdārthayugalasya ।

23. Ganganath Jha, english traslation of Mammaṭa's *Kāvyaprakāśa*, Bharatiya Vidya prakashan Varanasi, 1967, p. 6.

24. *Kāvyaprakāśasaṁketa* of Māṇikyacandra, ed. Vasudev Shastri Abhyankar and Vinayak Ganesh Apte, Anandashram Sanskrit Series, 1921, p. 8.
śruyamāṇasya śabdasya prāk pratyekam eva tat tat varṇātmatayā sphoṭam asphuṭaṁ vyañjayataḥ pūrvapūrvaviṣayasaṁskāra sācivyāt paścād ante sphuṭaṁ sphoṭam ābhāsayataḥ prayatnabhedānupātino vāyavīya dhvanir ity arthaḥ ।
tau śabdārthan vācyonyakgbhāvitāvupasarjanīkṛtyo yena vyaṅgyenār-thena sa tathā sa cāsau vyaṅgyaś ca tasya vyañjane kṣamasya śabdārthayugalasya kāvyam iti vyapadeśyasya vyañjakatvasāmyād dhvanivyavahāraḥ hṛdayadarpaṇakṛtā nyagbhāvita śabdārthasva-rūpatā vyañjanavyāpārasyocye mammṭena tu vyañjanavyāpāra-viṣayasya vyaṅgyasyeti tātparyārthaḥ ।

25. Siddheswar Verma, "Analysis of Meaning is Indian Pholosophy of language", *JRAS*. London, 1925, p.21 "Analyais of Meaning in Indian Semantics", *JDL*, Calcutta, 1926, pp. 1,37.

26. See in V.K. Gokak, *The poetic approach to language*, Oxford University Press, 1952, p. ix; also I.A. Richards, *Principles of literary Criticism*, 1925, pp.267,273; The Geneva School of Linguistic Science, notably Charles Bally, emphasised the emotive use of language for the first time; also see MacDugall who discusses suggestion in *Social psychology*, 1908.

27. Dinabandhu Kar, *op. cit.*, pp.29-45.

28. *Kāśikā* on P.8.1.8, 8.1.10 etc.;
prayoktṛdharmo nābhidheyadharmaḥ

29. *VP*. II. 399-400
aslo, K. A. S. Iyer, "Bhartṛhari on the primary and secondary meanings of words", *S. M. Katre's felicitaion Vol.* part I, 1968, p.101, 102-3,

30 cf, Louis Hjelmslev, *Prolegomena to a theory of language*, tr. F. J. Whitfield, 2nd edition, The University of Wisconsin Press, 1963, pp.47-60.
The suggestive semantics of Ānandavardhana has striking

similarites with Hjelmslev's conception of stylistic analysis as the treatment of the content plane and the expression plane of a natural language in some specific usage as themselves together forming the expression plane of a higher order 'Connotative Semiotic'.

31. *svaṁ rūpaṁ śabdasyāśabdasaṁjñā.*
32. *VP.* I.50; *VP.*III.1.6;
also cf. K.K. Raja, *Indian Theories of Meanings* 1977, p.118.
33. cf. M. Suryanarayan Murti, "Bhartṛhari on *svaṃ rūpaṁ śabdasyāśabdasaṁjñā, ALB*, Vol.44-45, 1980-81, pp.602-13.
34. John Brough, *"Theories of general linguistics* in the Sanskrit grammarians", *TPS*, 1951, p.30; cf. K.K. Raja, *op.cit.*, p.118; Vol. I.59-61.
35. *VP.*I.55; for Buddhist idea of two-fold power of words, See K.K. Raja, *op.cit.*, p.119.
36. *Vyaktiviveka* of Mahima Bhaṭṭa, ed. Rewaprasad Dwivedi, Varanasi, 1964, p.4 :
dhvani vartmayatigahane skhalitaṁ vāṇyaḥ pade pade sulabham ।
37. K. Krishansmoorthy, *Dhvanyāloka and its critics*, Kavyalaya Publishers, Mysore, 1968, p.32.

1

The Evolution of Sphoṭa

The question regarding the semantic relation that exists has not yet been solved between a sentence and its component words. Sentences are clearly more than the sum-total of their constituent elements, whether considered from the semantic or the grammatical point of view. Indian philosophers have debated the question extensively. The followers of the *abhihitānvayavāda* maintain the view that the sentence is built up of words each contributing its meaning to the total meaning of the senteance. But Bhartṛhari regarded the sentence as a single undivided unit which conveys its meaning as a flash *(pratibhā)*. In this connection Indian grammarians developed the *sphoṭa* theory. This theory of *sphoṭa* was formulated differently by different scholars. According to this theory, sound has two aspects : actual event or individual realisation (*dhvani*) and the actualised entity *(sphoṭa)*. Later grammarians state that the sentence *sphoṭa (vākya-sphoṭa)* as a single meaningful unit actualised by a succession of articulate sounds conveys meaning. Further Bhartṛhari has used two terms, *prākṛta-dhvani* and *vaikṛta dhvani*. The actualised sound in which the individual variations have been elaminated *prākṛta dhvani* and *vaikṛta-dhvani* that which has individual variations. A further development of *dhvani-sphoṭa* relationship is seen in Ānandavardhana's theory of poetic language. Just as the sounds reveal the meaningful entity *(sphoṭa)* so in poetry the words convey their primary meaning and reveal further suggested meaning and the beauty of the *kāvys* as a whole. The close connection betweeen thought and language, the content (*dhvani* of Ānandavardhana) and the form of language (*dhvani*-sound) have been accepted by the philosophers. Thus the expression and content together give rise to the realisation of *rasa*. The present work attempts to find out the origin and evolution of the past into the present as far as the *dhvani* theory of Ānandavardhana is concerned. The growth of *dhvani* theory can be traced back to a number of theories like *sphoṭa, pratibhā* etc. Therefore this work begins with the evolution of the earlier theories, namely *sphoṭa* and *pratibhā*.

Sphoṭa before Patañjali

The doctrine of *sphoṭa* is a phantom concept in Sanskrit grammatical philosophy. It is devised to exlplain certain intricate aspects of speech. Its nature is some what indistinct. On the one hand it is related to the sound aspect of speech and on the other hand it is also related to the meaning aspect of speech. In order to accommodate later developed doctrines neo-philosophers interpret it variously. Its mythic founder is Sphoṭāyana. But the indirect reference to it is found for the first time in the view of Audumbarāyaṇa as mentioned in the *Nirukta*. It is not unlikely that Yāska has given his own views on *sphoṭa* while classifying words into four categories which are different from the sound units of words.[1] Audumbarāyaṇa holds that speech is eternal. It remains in the auditory organ[2] of the speaker as well as the listener. But Yāska disagrees with this view. According to him speech is all pervasive.[3] The meaning of the speech is comprehended form the utterance because of its all pervasiveness. John Brough interprets this line of Yāska with the help of Bhartṛhari (*VP* II.342-43). According to Brough, in this aphorism, Yāska wants to suggest that a sentence is a fundamental linguistic unit bereft of any obstruction.[4]

In contrast to the interpretation offered by Brough, Simonsson suggests that in the present context, Yāska refers to the two dimensions of sound occurring in the speech unit. The sound may be utterly small *(aṇiyas, Nir.* p.8) or 'transcendental' *(vyāptimat, Nir.* p. 7). The first attribute represents the pure phonetic aspect in its individual capacity whereas the second one brings the meaning into account, and therefore represents the semantic aspect of speech.[5]

Durgācārya, the commentator of the *Nirukta,* is more influenced by the post-Bhartṛhari grammarians while interpreting Yāska. According to him, speech grasped through the intellect remains indivisible in form. It is manifested by the efforts of the speaker and enters the ear of the listener. When it is translated into thought it reveals its meaning (*Nir*. p. 7). As to how meaning comes form the sound, it is thought that *sphoṭa* auditorily grasped conveys meaning.[6] According to this view, Yāska considers *sphoṭa* as meaning conveying unit of speech. Simonsson interprets the term *'vyāptimat'* in the sense of all pervasive meaningful segment of the speech and connects it with *sphoṭa* which represents the significative level of language.[7]

But strictly speaking it is difficult to come to the conclusion that *sphoṭa* represents the meaning conveyer word, because Yāska did not use the tera *sphoṭa* and seems to have known little about it. Audumbarāyaṇa also does not mention the term *sphoṭa* directly. His awareness of *sphoṭa* is speculated on the basis of the *sphoṭa* concept of Bhartṛhari. Brough goes to the extent to state that Audumbarāyaṇa is the founder of *sphoṭa* theory and Vārtākṣa knew it (*VP*. II. 342,343).[8] Some other scholars attribute the origin of *sphoṭa* to Sphoṭāyana[9] which means a remote descendant of *sphoṭa*. However, this does not mean this doctrine goes back to Sphoṭāyana.

From the foregone discussion it can be concluded that pre-Patañjalian concept of *sphoṭa* is somewhat opaque in nature. It is related to the two sided entity of speech which is popular among grammarians before. Nothing positive can be speculated on the nature of *sphoṭa* in pre-Pāṇinian age, because we do not find even the word *sphoṭa* in pre-Pāṇinian literature representing something similar to the *sphoṭa* doctrine developed later.

Patañjali's concept of *Sphoṭa*

Why is *sphoṭa* concept introduced in grammar?

The grammerians hold that *śabds* is eternal. Each *śabda* is a chain of different sound units. The word *'gau'* comprises three different sound units, i.e. *g*, *a* and *au*. when *g* sound is uttered, the other two *a* and *au* sounds do not exist. When the *a* sound is uttered, the *g* sound vanishes and an sound is yet to come into existence. Again when *au* sound is pronounced, the preceding sounds i.e. *g* and *a* have already perished as soon as they are uttered. So the combination of sounds itself is impossible. Since we cannot account for the simultaneity of sounds, we cannot explain the units of word or sentence. To solve this difficulty, the later grammarians devised the theory of *sphoṭa* which states that the *sphoṭa* as a single meaningful entity is over and above the disjoined elements of different sound units which constitute complete utterance. But *sphoṭā* as the indivisible unit is nowhere suggested in Patañjali's *Mahābhāṣyā*.

For the first time we find the discussion of *sphoṭa* in the *Mahābhāṣya* of Patañjali under P.1.1.70 and 8.2.18. According to him, there are two aspects of *śabda*, i. e. *sphoṭa* and *dhvani*.

Sphoṭā and *dhvani* according to Patañjali

Patañjali dwells on *sphoṭa* and *dhvani* while explaining P.1.1.70: *taparas tatkālasya*. The *sphoṭa* is a permanent element of *śabda* whereas *dhvani* represents its non-permanent aspect. The *sphoṭa* is not audible like *dhvani*.[10] But it is not identical with the *śabda*. The *sphoṭa* is manifested by articulated sounds. The *dhvani* elements of speech may differ in phonetic value with reference to the variation in the utterance of different speakers. Difference in speed of utterance and time distinctions are attributes of the *dhvani* which cannot affect the nature of *sphoṭa* revealed by sound. When a sound passes from the speaker's lips, *sphoṭa* is revealed instantaneously. But before the listener comprehends anything, *dhvani* elements manifest the permanent element of the *śabda*. So *sphoṭa* comes first and the manifesting *dhvani* also continues to exist after the revelation of *sphoṭa*. That is why Patañjali remarks that *dhvanis* are the attributes of *sphoṭa*.[11]

Patañjali points out that the *sphoṭa* which is revealed by the articulate sounds can be presented through phonemes only. A phoneme (vowel) which represents *sphoṭa* remains the same in three different modes of utterance, whereas *dhvani* (articulate sounds) differs in different utterances.[12] It is just like the distance which remains the same even if it is covered by various means which travel slow, fast and faster. Patañjali gives the analogy of a drumbeat to explain the unaffacted nature of *sphoṭa*. When a drum is struck it produces a chain of various sounds whose pitch can be observed by the distance it covers. The generated sounds may be of different sonorousness and durations. Hearing the sound of drumbeat one may travel twenty feet, another thirty feet and still another travel forty feet and so on. Though the sounds produced by beating of the drum differ, the drumbeat remains the same. Likewise the variations of sounds do not affect *sphoṭa*.[13]

But the term *sphoṭa* may stand for a single phoneme according to Patañjali, but this should not be taken as the final verdict.[14] It represents the phonetic species of phonetically different sounds. While interpreting P.8.2.18, *kṛpo ro laḥ*, Patañjali states that the *l* (with all its phonetic species) is substituted for *r* (i.e. to all its phonetic species).

The consonantal *l* and vocalic *l* come under l̲-*sphoṭa*., and consonantal *r* and vocalic *ṛ* come under *r-sphoṭa*. Though phonetically *l* and *r*, *r* and *ṛ* are different, *l-sphoṭa* includes all varieties of l̲-sounds and all varieties of *r-sounds* belong to the single *r-sphoṭa*.This *r* sound which is replaced by *l-sound* also means that the vocalic *ṛ* is also replaced by vocalic *l*. Thus according to Patañjali the single class of various articualted sounds which may not be comprehended by the listener is called *sphoṭa*. But the articulated sounds as members of the single class-phoneme which may differ in phonetic values (like tempos and various modes of utterances) are known as *dhvani*.[16] Here *sphoṭa*s stands for the phonematic pattern of the word.[17]

Thus according to Patañjali, *sphoṭa* is a conceptual entity or generic feature of articulated sounds, either in the form of isolated phonemes or a series of phonems. It is a permanent element of physical sounds which are transitory in nature, and which vary in length, tempo and pitch of the speaker. It is an actualised replica of ephemeral sounds, to which S.D.Joshi says as 'auditory image of varied articulated sounds' or 'sound image auditorily perceived'.[18]

Sphoṭa and meaning conveying expression

J. Brough, K. K. Raja, K. A.S. Iyer, G. Sastri and H. G. Coward believe that the *sphoṭa* theory is adhered to by the grammarians to explain how meaning is understood from the sound. According to the later grammarians, there are two aspects of the word, i.e. the sound aspect and the meaning aspect. When the sound is uttered *sphoṭa* word is cognised through which the meaning is conveyed. But this proposition is not accepted by Patañjali. He does not state that *sphoṭa* -word conveys meaning. The *sphoṭa* concept is restricted to the distinctive level or phonemic level of language. It is an auditory impression of the uttered sounds which stand for a class sound. It does not necessarily represent the significative or semantic level of language.

To support this I offer the following arguments.

Phonemes as the smallest distinctive units

Accounting to Patañjali, if a particular word is an instrument of a particular sense, then the sense conveyed by a word is the meaning of the said word.[19] In the *pratyāhārāṇika* of the *Mahābhāṣya, Śivasūtra*. 5 *(Ha, ya, va, rat)*, Patañjali stated his view on identification of phonemes. According to him, the phonemes may be meaningful or may not be meaningful under different conditions.[20] A single phoneme in the form of roots (ex.√ *i, eti, adheti, adhīte* etc.) noun bases or declinables (ex. *a* in *ābhyām, ebhiḥ, eṣu*), affixes (ex. *a* in *aupagavaḥ, kāpaṭavaḥ* etc.), *nipātas* (ex. *a* in *apeti, i* in *indraṁ paśya* and *u* in *uttiṣṭha* are meaningful.[21] Again the meaningfulness of the phoneme is confirmed from the fact that if a phoneme disappears the sense of the word is lost.[22]

But a single phoneme is meaningless if it is separated from the word.[23] Sometimes the transposition, disappearance, addition and mutilation of phonemes cannot change the sense of the word. So a single phoneme belonging to a word which consists of many phonemes is not considred to be a meaning-bearing-unit.[24]

Saṁghāta, a single entity as meaning-bearing-unit

According to Patañjali, the concept of *saṁghāta* (as a single entity) is an essential feature of meaningfulness. Sometimes while the phonemes belong to a single phoneme word in their individual capacity convey meaning. But in most cases the phonemes which make up a word and when they are not isolated from a word convey meaning. This is to say *saṁghāta* as a whole conveys meaning. It is an entity which blends isolated phonemes into a single structure to convey meaning. so by virtue of *saṁghāta* isolated phonemes grouped together can only be meaningful.

Logically it may be argued that if the whole *(saṁghāta)* is meaningful the parts (isolated phonemes) may be also meaningful. For instance, if one having eyes can see, a group of persons having eyes can also see. If a sesame seed yields oil, a collection of sesame seeds can also yield oil.[25] If one blind person cannot see, a group of blind persons cannot see either. This would mean that if the whole is meaningful its parts (phonemes) are also meaningful.

But this logic does not hold good in case of *saṁghāta* which is a structured force of the phonemes. Here the whole is to be regarded as a different unit from a mere collection of parts.

To explain the concept of *saṁghāta* Patañjali gives the analogy of a chariot. A chariot when its parts are put together is capable of moving. If the parts are disconnected the chariot cannot move. So also the phonemes separated from the whole (*saṁghāta*) do not convey any meaning. Thus *saṁghāta* is an unitary, sequenceless entity which conveys meaning.[26] Regarding the role of unity *(saṁghāta)* Patañjali further remarks that when a word is uttered, different sounds of individual phonemes do not remain together. They remain in the mind of the speaker and listener in a particular order, as they have been uttered. It is the simultaneous cognition of phonemes explaining the unitary notion of the word which conveys meaning.[27]

Patañjall has used the term *śabda* in three different senses i.e. *arthasaṁpratyāyakaḥ śabdaḥ, dhvni śabdaḥ* and *sphoṭa śabdaḥ.*[28]

To begin with, the term *śabda* in one definition bears the nature of *saṁghāta*. In this view *śabda* stands for meaning which can be divided into phonemes.[29]

In the alternative definition of *śabda* Patañjali points out that it is the name given to the articulate sound. This second definition lays emphasis on the phonetic character of a word.[30]

Patañjali makes another important statement about the nature of a word. According to this statement, *śabda* represents the auditory image of the sound revealed by the articulatory movements. So here *śabda* stands for auditory sound.[31]

Sphoṭa as *śabda* in the *Mahābhāṣya*

It is generally misunderstood that Patañjali has used the term *śabda* in the sense of meaning bearing element which represents the chief charater of *sphoṭa*. But recent studies reveal that Patañjali has used the term *śabda* in three different contexts. In one context (ch. I, fn. No. 29) he says that if an utterance brings about cognition of an object having dewlap, tail, humb, hooves, horn, then it is known as a word, a cow. In this definition two terms, i.e. *uccārita* (uttered) and *sampratyaya* (cognition, knowledge) are important. The definition indicates that a word has a two sided identity. One side represents the sound and the other meaning. Thus according to this definition when the *śabda* is uttered, it brings the idea of the thing meant. Here Patañjali defines word as a meaningful sound.

According to the second definition, any vocal sound is called *śabda* which may or may not be meaningful. The term *śabda* is a popular term *(pratītapadārtha)* and it stands for any articulate sound whether meaningful or meaningless.[32]

Joshi argues that Patañjali believes in two levels of language, i. e. morphemic level and phonetic level. The first definition refers to the morphemic character of the word whereas the second definition refers to the phonetic character of the word.[33]

There is one more aspect of *śabda* given in the *Mahābhāṣya* which is altogether different from those stated earlier. This is an important feature of *śabda* which is perceived as an auditory image of the sound. According to this view, *śabda* is that which is perceived by the ear, comprehended by the mind and manifested by the sound.[34] On this view each of the three adjectives reveals three different aspects of the word. The phrase,' *śrotropalabdhiḥ'* refers to the auditorily grasped pure sound, *'buddhi-nirgrāhyaḥ'* refers to the mental or physical aspect, and *'prayogeṇābhijvalitaḥ'* revealed by the sound suggest the *sphoṭa* aspect of the word. Thus *śabda* is 'auditory impression of the sounds grasped through the intellect'.[35]

Thus *sphoṭa* of Patañjali does not necessarily stand for meaning the bearing aspect of *śabda*. According to Patañjali, sphoṭa is manifested by *dhvani* and it is an auditory impression of the *dhvani* which is grasped by the intellect. It is the sound image or conceptual entity of the sound. According to another view the term *sphoṭa* is used to perceive sound which remains the same in all different modes of utterances, whereas the term *dhvani* stands for the speech-sound which is associated with individual peculiarities. Thus it appears that Patañjali does not identify *sphoṭa* with the meaning bearing aspect of the word.[36]

While Joshi thinks that the *sphoṭa* of Patañjali is an auditory image of the sound, Raja believes it to be a unit of sound as either an isolated phoneme or series of phonemes which can be examined as a succession of sound-units.

Virendra Sharma in his *Vākyapadīya Sambandha Samuddeśa* criticises Joshi's view on *sphoṭa*. On the basis of the interpretation of Kaiyyaṭa and Bhartṛhari, he tries to justify that the first definition of *śabda* of the *Mahābhāṣya* is identical with *sphoṭa* which conveys meaning.

The second definition of *śabda* as *dhvani* also deals with meaningful sound.[37] He firmly believes that *sphoṭa* of Patañjali stands for meaningful indivisible sound.[38]

From the above discussion the following conclusions emerge.

Patañjali has not used the term *sphoṭa* while discussing meaning. Kaiyyaṭa and other later grammarians try to read into Patañjali's statement the theories developed later.

According to them, Patañjali's first definition refers to a single indivisible meaning-bearing-unit called *sphoṭa*.

But in fact this *sphoṭa* of Patañjali is an intermediary between sound and sense. The sound elements uttered have a unified image of their own before their actual manifestation. This unified image or conceptual entity of the sounds uttered is *sphoṭa*. It can be heard by the auditory organs, but can be grasped by the intellect. Though in existence, *sphoṭa* precedes the sounds revealed to the listener's ears in manifestation it follows the sounds. It works as a channel in between thought and sound *(dhvani)*. But it is more akin to the sound and hence its nature is phonetic and not semantic.

This *sphoṭa* is fixed in nature in contrast to the sounds which are associated with individual peculiarities. It stands for a class of sounds of particular phoneme (phonetic-pattern). As it is bereft of sequence *(saṁghāta)*, it cannot be associated with meaning. It is the conceptual form of the physical sound which operates in phonetic level of language. Patañjali's concept of *sphoṭa* is altogether different from those of later grammarians[39] who consider *sphoṭa* as meaning- conveying word.

Bhartṛhari's Concept of *Sphoṭa*

After Patañjali, Bhartṛhari discussed the concept of *sphoṭa* exhaustively. In the *Vākyapadīya* he has stated his own view alongwith the views of others without mentioning their names.

The term *sphoṭa* occurs nine times in the *Vākyapadīya* (kāṇḍa-I).[40] Since mystic and linguistic philosophy move hand in hand there, one finds it difficult to demarcate the actual nature of *sphoṭa*. The use of the term *śabda* in different senses[41] namely *pada, vākya, sphoṭa, dhvani, nāda, prākṛtadhvani* and *vaikṛtadhvani* pose certain difficulties to determine the actual nature of *sphoṭa*. Out of nine times, only once *(VP.* I.49) the term *sphoṭa* is used in relation to the term *śabda* (word). However, in the *VP* I. 47, the term *śabda* is identified with *sphoṭa*.[42] Both ancient and modern scholars have identified the meaningful *śabda* with *sphoṭa*. Bhartṛhari never does this. In interpreting *sphoṭa* he follows the tradition handed down by Patañjali. He seems to borrow it from the lost work of Vyāḍi. However, Bhartṛhari develops it in greater detail. The actual nature of *sphoṭa* of Bhartṛhari can be determined by carefully studying his statements in the *Vākyapadīya*. In the succeeding sections a detailed account of Bhartṛhari's view on the nature of *sphoṭa* is projected.

Sphoṭa and its relation with *dhvani*

Sphoṭa, according to Bhartṛhari, is always intimately related to sound *(dhvani)*. We cannot have *sphoṭa* without sound. The sounds which are produced at the contact of articulatory organs manifest *sphoṭa*. As soon as the sounds are produced the *sphoṭa* is cognised instantly. Since the sounds reveal *sphoṭa,* they are manifesters and *sphoṭa* is manifested *(VP.* I. 97). Bhartṛhari speaks of two types of sounds, i.e. 'primary sound' *prākṛtadhvani* and 'secondary sound' *vaikṛtadhvani*. *Sphoṭa* is manifested by primary sounds which have temporal distinctions (i.e. *hrasva, dīrgha* and *pluta)*. The primary sound and *sphoṭa* are simultaneously cognised and therefore sound is wrongly identified with *sphoṭa*. But in reality sound and *sphoṭa* are different things *(VP.* I. 76, 77).

The initial vibration of articulatory organs produced primary sounds which in turn reveal *sphoṭa*. But when vibration stops, the production of sounds does not cease. At this stage, a series of sounds come out from the initial sounds which are identified as *vaikṛtadhvani* 'secondary sounds'. These secondary sounds help in the continued perception of *sphoṭa*. It is explained by the analogy of a flame. As one flame lights another flame and that flame still another, and the process goes on, similarly one sound which manifests *sphoṭa* produces another sound and that sound produces still another sound. Each subsequent stage in the chain of sounds continues to reveal the same *sphoṭa* *(VP.* I. 106). The secondary sounds which cause the continued manifestation of *sphoṭa* are affected by the difference in the speed of utterance. They have either short, middle or longer duration. But *sphoṭa* remains unaffected by such differences *(VP.* I. 77).

The idea is, when the speaker engages in the phonetic act it produces some sounds. The sounds belonging to the first moment are primary sounds. As soon as the listener hears the primary sound he perceives the *sphoṭa.* But the perception dose not stop abruptly. It lasts for a short time in quick speech, a little longer in speech of medium speed, and still longer in slow speech. The sounds in the succeeding moments *(vaikṛtadhvani)* which have the same duration of the sounds of first moment continue to reveal *sphoṭa.* The duration of perception of *sphoṭa* through secondary sounds depends upon the difference in the speed of utterance. The continued perception of *sphoṭa* through the secondary sounds cannot be explained unless we assume that the manifesting sounds also continue in the succeeding moments. But, the difference in speed (slow, medium, and rapid) associated with the secondary sounds is not even falsely attributed to the *sphoṭa.*

Sometimes it appears that *sphoṭa* has temporal distinctions *(kālabheda).* But this is not correct. The primary sound varies. Its utterance may take either less or a little more or still more time on the basis of which it can be either short, long or prolated respectively. In reality the temporal distinction belongs to the primary sound. But as primary sounds and *sphoṭa* are produced simultaneously, the difference is not conspicuous. Therefore, the property of primary sound, such as length, pitch, etc. are wrongly felt to be associated with the manifested *sphoṭa* which is in reality free from such distinction (*VP.* I. 75).

Bhartṛhari elucidates the nature of *sphoṭa* with the help

of an analogy (*VP*. I. 49). The image of the moon appears to be reflected on the water. Though in reality it is immovable its reflection seems to have movement because of the movement in the water. Here the property of the water, i. e. movability is superimposed on the reflected image of the moon. But the moon is immovable, only its reflection on the water is movable. The *sphoṭa* is immovable like the moon and *dhvani* is movable like the reflected image of the moon on the water. The temporal distinction (*VP*. I. 75) and variations in the speed of utterance (*VP*. I. 77) are the properties which provide many varieties and thereby they explain continuity of the perception of the *sphoṭa*. But the properties of the secondary sounds do not belong to *sphoṭa*. As movement is the quality of the water, vibration is the quality of *dhvani*. The quality of vibrations in the form of temporal distinctions is superimposed on *sphoṭa* which in reality does not belong to it.

Thus *sphoṭa* is free from variation like the original image. It is an entity which is not influenced by the properties of *vaikṛtadhvani*. It is the articulate sound which gives rise to the reflection in the listener's ear in the form of the *sphoṭa* word. To put it differently it is a replica of *dhvani* having phonetic features. That is why S.D. Joshi thinks it to be an 'auditory image of the sound'.[43]

Three different views about the nature of *sphoṭa*

Bhartṛhari has referred to three views about the nature of *sphoṭa* in the *Vākyapadīya*.

The first view is that the initial sounds produced by the conjunction and disjunctions of the articulatory organs are themselves *sphoṭas* and the sounds which are produced from the initial sounds that spread in all directions in gradually decreasing strength are *dhvanis* (*VP*. I. 102). According to this view, both the initial and subsequent sounds are transitory in nature. As the initial sound is momentary, *sphoṭa* is also momentary. The subsequent sounds are reverberations of the initial sounds which spread like waves form the centre (initial sounds) in a series. The chain of sounds which are produced form the sounds (*śabdajā śabdāḥ*) lose their strength gradually. As *sphoṭa* gives rise to the chain of sounds, it is said that *sphoṭa* produces *dhvani*.

In this connection *vṛtti* refers to two views on the nature of *sphoṭa*. According to the first view, *sphoṭa* is manifested by the sounds produced by contact and separation of the articulators with the point of articulation.[44]

According to the second view, *sphoṭa* is revealed by resonance of the initial sounds. *Dhvani* manifests *sphoṭa* and gives rise to the variations in the speed of utterance and ultimately disappears.[45]

According to another view, *sphoṭa* and *dhvani* are produced at the same time. There is no time gap in between the production of the sound and manifestation of *sphoṭa*. It is just like a flame and the light which appear at the same time. When a flame is lit, immediately light moves in all directions. Similarly, when *sphoṭa* is revealed the *dhvanis* (other sounds) spread everywhere.[46] Both these views emphasise the ephemeral nature of *dhvani*.

Still another view is that *sphoṭa* stands for the class of individual sounds (*dhvani*). The *sphoṭa* represents the universal and individual sounds are its units. The individual sound units constitute the class nature of *sphoṭa*.[47] It is believed that the present view belongs to Bhartṛhari himself which is also corroborated by Bhaṭṭoji Dīkṣita.[48] Joshi identify *sphoṭa* with 'phonetic pattern of sound' because of this class-nature.[49]

The sounds (*dhvani*) manifest *sphoṭa*. Bhartṛhari has recorded three alternative views in this respect.

According to the first view, some think that both *dhvani* and *sphoṭa* appear to be identical. If a red flower is placed near a crystal, the crystal seems to absorb the red colour of the flower. Similarly, the *sphoṭa* which is manifested by the sound appears to absorb the properties of the sound and appears to be identical with it *(VP.* I. 81).[50]

The second view holds that when *sphoṭa* is revealed, the sound is not perceived at all. It is just as the senses without being perceived cause the perceptions of their objects. So also *dhvani* causes the perception of *sphoṭa* without being cognised. For instance, when some objects are seen or some sounds are heard, the respective sense organs and their attributes do not come into the picture. Similarly, the sounds which cause the perception of *sphoṭa* are not perceived.[51]

According to the third view, *sphoṭa* and *dhvani* are distinct. It sometimes happens that the sounds are heard but the *sphoṭa* cannot be comprehended.[52]

Bhartṛhari's views on the process of revelation of *sphoṭa*

The sources remain in the intellect before their production.[53] As soon as the sounds are produced by the articulatory organs *sphoṭa* is revealed. But the listener cannot understand *sphoṭa* immediately. Each individual sound unit contributes something to the total perception of *sphoṭa*. The first sound unit reveals *sphoṭa* vaguely, next unit a little more clearly, still next more clearly. This process continues till the last sound perceives *sphoṭa* absolutely. Thus *sphoṭa* is progressively revealed by each successive sounds.[54] The process of comprehension of *sphoṭa* has been compared to a student's attempt who tries to memorise a Vedic verse by heart. This first recitation provides a vague impression of the verse and the subsequent recitation gives a clearer impression. The last recitation fixes the verse fully in memory.[55] Similarly, the perception of each sound unit progressively reveals *sphoṭa*. When the final sound is uttered it leads to the cognition of the *sphoṭa* word.[56]

Sphoṭa and meaning bearing aspect of the word

It is a difficult problem to ascertain whether the *sphoṭa* represents the meaningful aspect of the word. There are two groups of scholars holding different views on it. G. Sastri (1959, 1981), K. K. Raja (1963), and K.A.S. Iyer (1969) are prominent among those who believe that *sphoṭa* represents a meaningful aspect of the language. According to these scholars, *sphoṭa* stands for the meaning bearing value attached to the speech units. But S.D. Joshi (1967) holds an opposite view. According to him, the *sphoṭa* concept of Bhartṛhari represents the auditory level of language. The *sphoṭa* stands for auditorily grasped speech units which may or may not be semantically understood.

In fact, Bhartṛhari nowhere relates *sphoṭa* with the meaning. He never uses the meaningful *śabda* (word) as a synonym of *sphoṭa*.[57] Sastri, Iyer and Raja etc. identify *śabda* with *sphoṭa*. It has generated much controversy. They depend on the commentaries of Kaiyyaṭa, Nāgeśa Bhaṭṭa, Harivṛṣabha and Maṇḍana Miśra etc. for their interpretation. These commentators are greatly influenced by the interpretations of *sphoṭa* later developed by the Mīmāṁsakas headed by formidable Kumārila Bhaṭṭa and the neo-*Naiyāyikas*. The followers of both these systems explain the *sphoṭa* concept of Bhartṛhari in the light of meaning conveying speech unit.

It is very difficult to say why these great traditional commentators jumbled up the meaningful *śabda* with *sphoṭa*. Probably the confusion has arisen in the mind of the later scholars because they identify Bhartṛhari's concept of *sphoṭa* with meaningful *śabda*.

It is a fact that every new interpretation indicates the development of a concept. Thus various interpretations of *sphoṭa* seem unavoidable. Thus the *sphoṭa* which is manifested through the articulate sounds, according to Bhartṛhari, has undergone different interpretations in the works of the opponents. The statements having phonetic or distinctive level of language in Bhartṛhari's work are metamorphosed into semantic level in their works. This metamorphosis is due to the varying nature of the term *śabda*. To make my statements clear, I will discuss Bhartṛhari's views on the nature of *śabda* in the following section.

Śabda as a two sided entity

The term *śabda* is used in different contexts to represent different aspects of a word. But *śabda* is essentially a two sided entity. It is related to the sound aspect and meaning aspect. One side of it represents 'sound' and the other, the content of speech unit.[58] The sounds which the speaker utters manifest meaning conveyer speech unit. It is indivisible and sequencesless. It also absorbs the reflection of the object.[59]

When a word is used to refer to a thing meant, the word reveals the thing meant and at the same time reveals its own form. For instance, when the word *'agni'* is uttered it refers to the thing meant fire as well as the phonetic form *a-g-n-i* after which the suffix *ḍhak* has been prescribed (P. 4. 2. 33).[60] Similarly, the term *'vṛddhi'* when uttered conveys its own form, and also stands for grammatical technical meaning, namely *āt*, and *aic* etc.[61] So when the words *'agni'* and *vṛddhi'* stand for their own form, they are known as *'saṁjñā'* and when both the terms stand for the thing meant they are known as *saṁjñīn* 'the object to which the designation is given'.[62]

K.K. Raja and S. D. Joshi analysed this two sidedness of the word from the linguistic point of view. Every linguistic expression, they hold, has two levels, i.e. phonetic and semantic. This phonetic level is the external aspect of the word. This is produced by the vocal organs in the form of sound-pattern known as *prākṛtadhvani* 'primary sound'. This *prākṛtadhvani* has time sequence. Raja thinks that the sound-pattern is one side of the word whose other side is *sphoṭa*.[63] Here Raja identifies *dhvani (prākṛta)* with the sound pattern which manifests *sphoṭa*. But, according to Joshi, the sound-pattern is different from the phonemic-pattern of the sound which remains the same in all different modes of utterances and it is identical with *sphoṭa*.[64]

The internal *śabda* which is the mental equivalent of an articulate sound, conveys meaning and it is called *sphoṭa*. It is an internal linguistic symbol.[65]

Both Iyer and Raja hold the same view with regard to the twin aspect of *śabda* (word). What Iyer refers by 'sound', Raja explains it as sound-pattern. But both believe that the meaningful aspect of the word is *sphoṭa*.

Word is without differentiation

The twin aspects of the word remain in the intellect in an undifferentiated state.[66] Just as a full grown peacock remains in the egg in potential stage contracting its peculiarities, similarly the twin manifestation of the word is essentially one in unmanifested form. The unified word is revealed through a series of sounds. The process of emergence of the word has been compared with the painter's vision before he paints a picture. At first he has a vague idea of the picture. In this stage parts of the picture are differentiated. Then he has a mental vision of the whole picture. After that he paints it part by part. Similarly, the hearer perceives the word differentiated when the last sound in the series is heard. The *sphoṭa* is cognised progressively by the perception of each sound. The cognition of series of sounds finally leads to the full perception of the word.[67]

Iyer thinks that *sphoṭa* is identical with the word in its meaning bearing capacity which is taken as a unity.[68] Kaiyyaṭa interprets Patañjali's definition of *śabda* in the light of the doctrine of *sphoṭa*. He holds that *sphoṭa* is sometimes known by the term *śabda (VP*. I. 77), *pada* and *vākya*. All of them stand for meaning bearing unit (*VP*. I. 88).[69] The *vṛtti* possesses the same view.[70] The concept of *sphoṭa* emerges as a solution to the problem as to how meaning comes from the articulated sounds. The sounds uttered by the speaker manifest *sphoṭa* which conveys meaning.

Bhartṛhari's view on the nature of *śabda*

Iyer's attempt to identify *śabda* with *sphoṭa* appears to be incongruous that Bhartṛhari has used the term *śabda* in different senses. In one case only, amongst all of them, dose the term *śabda* bear the traits of *sphoṭa*.

(i) In some cases the term *śabda* represents the ultimate reality.[71]

(ii) Again in other cases the term is used to denote meaning conveying unit. The *śabda* stands for the conceptual word which remains in the intellect (*buddhistha śabda*).[72] In this capacity *śabda* is an undivided single speech unit[73] which is used to communicate sentence that cannot be broken into smaller linguistic units so far as its meaning conveying aspect is concerned. The term *śabda* here represents the significative or meaning bearing aspect of language.

(iii) In some other contexts again Bhartṛhari has used the term *śabda* to represent distinctive aspect of language. Here *śabda* stands for auditorily grasped sound by a listener.[74] The *śabda* which is auditorily perceived may be identified with *sphoṭa* but not in all respects as Iyer thinks. The term *śabda* is a two-sided entity. One side of it represents phonemic sound-pattern which may be identical with *sphoṭa* whereas the other side represents the meaning.[75]

Thus we have two different words: *dhvani śabda* 'sound word' and *arthasaṁpratyāyakaśabda* 'meaning conveying word'. *Sphoṭa* is related to *dhvani* but not necessarily to the communicative aspect of language. The *sphoṭa* represents a class of universal sounds where as *dhvani* represents a particular sound. The relation between *dhvani* and *sphoṭa* is that of manifester and manifested - *(vyaṅgyavyañjaka bhāva).*

Sphoṭa as a symbol

On the basis of modern linguistic findings Brough has given a strikingly new interpretation to the *sphoṭa* concept of Bhartṛhari eliminating altogether the mystical ghost of *śabda Brahman*. He also things the term *śabda* is mistranslated as sound.

Brough claims that Bhartṛhari describes language in its three aspects, i.e. *prākṭadhvani, vaikṛtadhvani* and *sphoṭa*

(i) The *prākṛtadhvani* is a stage before the articulated sound comes into existence. It is associated with temporal distinction. It represents the phonological structure, or the sound pattern of the norm. It may also represent class sounds of which individual sounds are members.

(ii) The *vaikṛtadhvani* is a sound of individual instance, which is actually spoken by the speaker and heard by the listener. It includes all sorts of differentiations in the speed of utterance.

(iii) The *sphoṭa* aspect of language is an integral linguistic symbol. It conveys meaning, though it can neither be pronounced nor written, only we can name it as *sphoṭa*.[76]

Though Brough emphasises that the *sphoṭa* of Bhartṛhari deals with the description of the semantic aspect of language, his stand is different form that of Iyer. Iyer believes that when the speaker utters sounds the *sphoṭa* is revealed which conveys meaning.[77]

But according to Brough, *sphoṭa* is a symbol of meaningful segment of the word.[78] He holds that a word, as a collection of phonemes in particular order, cannot express meaning, because the sounds have no function to connect themselves with the meaning. So to represent a meaning bearing aspect of language a separate entity is required which should not be identified with the group of sounds. This entity which is manifested by the group of sounds, convey meaning. This is *sphoṭa*. When one utters sounds by the articulatory organs, the sounds fade away leaving a conceptual entity as a whole which is single and indivisible. It is not an 'hypostatization of sounds'. Among the two aspects of the word of Bhartṛhari *(VP*. I. 44) the first aspect represents the sound-pattern (which according to Joshi is *sphoṭa*)and the aspect which is revealed by the actual utterance is *sphoṭa*. It conveys the meaning.[79]

Raja has been greatly influenced by Brough's interpretation. He concentrates on the *sphoṭa* aspect of the word which has further two aspects, namely significant (that which means) and signifie (that which is meant). These two aspects are dependent on each other. Among these two aspects of *sphoṭa* the significant one represents the phonematic pattern (acoustic image or physical entity or auditory image or la-langue). This acoustic image or phonematic pattern of the sounds are the conceptual entity of the actual uttered sounds.[80] The term 'signifie' represents the idea or the meaning. Thus both the 'acoustic image' and the idea, constitute the superstructure of *sphoṭa* collectively. But Raja is not satisfied treating *sphoṭa* as a sign. He adds that the *sphoṭa* is somewhat different from the sign. It is a timeless, indivisible, meaning-bearing symbol. The features of the sounds are super-imposed upon the *sphoṭa* because of our inability to distinguish between sound and symbol.[81]

Sphoṭa as an auditory image

Joshi interprets *sphoṭa* altogether differently form others. His analysis of *sphoṭa* is based on nine verses of the *VP* in which the term *sphoṭa* occurs. According to him, nowhere in the *VP* is it stated that *sphoṭa* is indivisible and is without inner-sequence. It does not stand for the meaning-bearing aspect of the word. It is not over and above the sound. The term does not occur in connection with the sentence and word in the second and third *kāṇḍas* of the *Vākyapadīya*. It is always related to the sound *(dhvani)*.[82]

Bhartṛhari does not say that *sphoṭa* is an indivisible entity. He dose not treat it as a meaningful segment of language. Later grammarians see *Sphoṭa* as meaning-conveying power of language. The idea of indivisibility of *sphoṭa* can be traced in the *VP*. I. 73. Accordingly, 'there are no phonemes in the word nor are their parts in the phoneme. There is no absolute difference of the words form the sentence'.[83] Joshi understands from the verse that significative units cannot be broken into parts. But the phonemes have no relation with the meaning. He thinks that an indivisible nature is assigned to *sphoṭa* by the later grammarians which goes against the intention of Bhartṛhari. They have deliberately interpreted the term *varṇasphoṭa* in the sense of stems, roots, suffixes etc. to justify the indivisibility and meaningfulness of *Sphoṭa*. They have imposed their own idea on Bhartṛhari.[84]

Bhartṛhari's statement pointed out that the *śabda* is self-revealing, i.e. it reveals its own phonetic form as well as meaning. This self-revealing character of a word has been wrongly applied to *sphoṭa* by the later grammarians. But Bhartṛhari does not say that *sphoṭa* is self- revealing.85

According to Joshi, the *sphoṭa* is comprehended by the listener through the sound produced by the speaker (*VP*. I. 81). The *sphoṭa* represents a class of individual sounds, wheras *dhvani* represents a particular sound. The *sphoṭa* is a sound or a type of scund which may or may not be meaningful. The meaning-conveying nature of the word in the *VP*. I.44 has been wrongly identified with the feature of *sphoṭa* by the later grammarians and some modern scholars.

Distinctive and significative levels of language

Joshi, in order to explore the real nature of the *sphoṭa* concept of Bhartṛhari, has analysed the language situation.

He has followed the method of Brough[87] but form a different angle. His classification can be put in the following manner.[88]

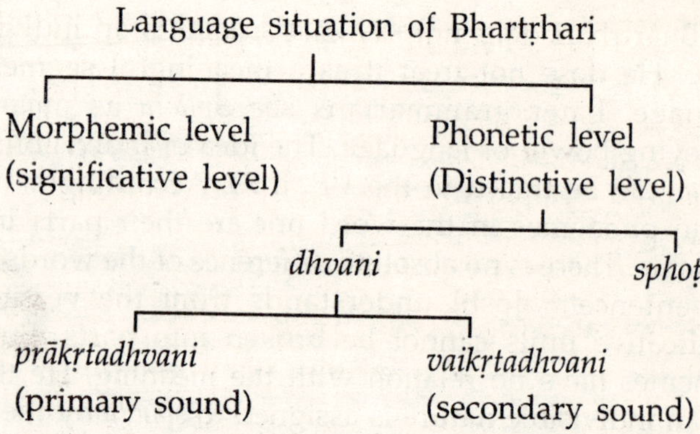

Joshi hold that language may be brought under two levels, i.e. significative level and distinctive level. The significative level includes meaningful elements of language in the forms of words, sentences, suffixes and roots etc. Bhartṛhari's statement in the *VP*. I.73 suggests that when one hears or speaks a sentence in ordinary conversation, a sentence is not taken into account in terms of a series of meaningful units. These units only complete the sturcture of the sentence and the sentence as an absolute linguistic unit brings meaning to comprehension through the sounds (of the sentence) uttered by the speaker.[89] The listener in the reverse process, first receives the sounds and then translates the sounds into linguistic thoughts. The significative level deals with morphemic structure of the language which is constituted of smaller meaning bearing elements. Later grammarians identified this level with *sphoṭa* which, according to them, is the meaning bearing speech-unit of language.[90] Joshi believes that *sphoṭa* does not represent the semantic aspect of the word.

The distinctive aspect deals with the phonetic or sound features of the language. The *sphoṭa* of Bhartṛhari operates in this level. Bhartṛhari's concept of *sphoṭa* emerges in the context of how the language utilises the sound-matter. The *sphoṭa* is a type of sound or phonematic pattern of sounds which has neither temporal distinction nor difference in the speed of utterances.[91] The *sphoṭa* cannot be auditorily perceived.[92] It is revealed by the sounds only. The *sphoṭa* is manifested and the *dhvani* is the manifester (*VP*.1.97). It represents the distinctive class feature of the individual sounds.[93]

The *sphoṭa* is the auditory impression or acoustic image of the actually uttered sound. That is why only when the sound is uttered the *sphoṭa* is manifested. It is the conceptual entity or conceptual replica of the uttered sound. Brough has suggested this idea, instead of the fact that his *sphoṭa* operates on semantic level in contrast to Joshi's view.[94] Joshi holds that occasionally the term *śabda* stands for the distinctive nature of *sphoṭa*. In those cases cases *śabda* represents the sound-pattern of language. Bhartṛhari in his *Mahābhāṣyadīpikā* points out that *śabda* in its distinctive aspect is *sphoṭa*.[95]

Thus, according to Joshi, the *sphoṭa* of Bhartṛhari stands for an auditory image of the sound or sound-pattern or phonetic pattern of the sound. Meaningfulness has been attributed to it by Kaiyaṭa, Maṇḍana Miśra, Kauṇḍa Bhaṭṭa, Nāgeśa Bhaṭṭa and Śeṣakṛṣṇa. Modern scholars follow the controversial *vṛtti* of Bhartṛhari while interpreting *sphoṭa*. Therefore the real nature of *sphoṭa* remains elusive.

Assessment and conclusion

According to the aforesaid discussion, modern scholars differ on the nature of *sphoṭa*.

Iyer, Brough and Raja are unanimous on the point that *sphoṭa*, according to Bhartṛhari, represents a meaning converyer unit, but their approaches are not similar. Iyer strictly follows the tradition that has firmly been established since the days of the *vṛtti*, the *Mahābhāṣyadīpikā* and the *Pradīpa* which state that meaningfulness, eternality and indivisibility are chief characteristics of *sphoṭa*.[96] One cannot separate the concept of *śabda* from *sphoṭa*. Probably Iyer thinks that the word in the intellect (*buddistha śabda, VP*. I.46,47, 53) is nothing but *sphoṭa*. It is the mental and psychic aspects of *sphoṭa*. The *sphoṭa* is a concept which links sound with meaning. Iyer, following the commentators, has identified Bhartṛhari's concept of *śabda* with the concept of *sphoṭa*. Often, however, the commentators impose their own view on Bhartṛhari. For the interpretation of the *VP* we cannot do without the help of commentators. But the opinion of commentators cannot replace our independent judgement. Iyer sees the *VP* through the eyes of the commentators. Therefore he interprets the nature of *sphoṭa* in the light of the *śabda Brahman* doctrine.

Brough has given a new direction to the traditional interpretation of *sphoṭa* which has been elaborated by his student Raja. According to him, both *sphoṭa* and *prākṛta-dhvani* are mental. The *Prākṛtadhvani* represents 'sound pattern of the norm'.[97] It is not perceived by the auditory organ of the hearer but comprehended by the consciousness. But it is different from *sphoṭa*.[98]

This interpretation goes against Bhartṛhari since he has not suggested anywhere that *prākṛta-dhvani* is a mental affair. His *prākṛta-dhvani* as a sound-pattern does corroborate neither Patañjali nor Bhartṛhari. Brough has identified the concept of *prākṛtadhvani* with the concept of *sphoṭa* as they cannot be divorced from each other.

Iyer has criticised[99] this view of Brough and states that *prākṛta-dhvani* is actually uttered sound which reveals *sphoṭa* and the *dhvanis* which are produced from *prākṛta-dhvani* of reverberation type are known as *vaikṛtadhvani*.[100]

Another inconsistency in Brough's view is that he believes *sphoṭa* is meaning-conveying unit of language. This is what Maṇḍana Miśra and others have attributed to *sphoṭa*. Bhartṛhari does not attribute semantic function to *sphoṭa*.[101]

Joshi has isolated this 'sound pattern' from *prākṛtadhvani* as understood by Brough and has given a new interpretation of *sphoṭa* which is the acoustic image of the uttered sounds. In this respect his interpretation is an extension of Brough's phonological findings.

Joshi has isolated the *sphoṭa* concept of Bhartṛhari from the concept of meaningful *śabda* and establishes with evidence that *sphoṭa* is the auditory impression of the sound which has nothing to do with meaning. It is a sound-pattern.

Two more interpretations of *sphoṭa* may be referred to which add a little to the earlier interpretation given by Brough. Gaurinath Sastri is one among them. Using a Greek name he identifies *sphoṭa* with logos. According to him, each significative word has two elements, i.e. element of sound and element of logos. Appropriate sound reveal the logos which is the real word. As soon as the word is revealed it denotes meaning automatically.[102]

Still another interpretation is given by S.K. Verma. But his view is a misinterpretation which Iyer has severely criticised. Verma[104] holds that when words or sentence become audible, meanings are comprehended from them. This comprehended meaning is *sphoṭa.* He wants to state that *sphoṭa* conveys meaning.

Among all these interpretations, the interpretation of Joshi seems to be most empirical one. Instead of following blindly the *vṛtti* of the *VP* and views of later interpreters, he has used his own independent judgement to determine the nature of *sphoṭa* of Bhartṛhari. He isolates the metaphysical and semantic concepts of the *śabda* from *sphoṭa.* According to him, *sphoṭa* is sound-image. In other words it is the conceptual impression of the actually articulated sound auditorily perceived.

But the phonetic nature of *sphoṭa* of Bhartṛhari is changed into semantic nature by the *Mīmāṁsakas,* the *Naiyāyikas,* the *Vedāntins* and the later grammarians. They have popularised *sphoṭa* and they have tried to link grammar with the metaphysical doctrine of *śabda-brahman*. Their views are used to be understood as the views of Bhartṛhari. But the real nature of *sphoṭa* of Bhartṛhari is side-tracked and a great deal of unnecessary mystification has been introduced.

The views of those later writers are considered in the succeeding sections. It will help to compare their views with that of Bhartṛhari and will give a complete picture of the evolution of the *sphoṭa* doctrine.

The Mīmāṁsakas' view on *sphoṭa*

The *sphoṭa* doctrine put forth by the grammarians influenced the propagators of different disciplines. Kumārila Bhaṭṭa was one among the *Mīmāṁsakas* who has refuted the views of the grammarians on *sphoṭa* in his *Śloka vārttika*. Kumārila interprets that the grammarian's *sphoṭa* is a mystical entity which conveys meaning. When a speaker makes an utterance, the sounds of the preceding phonemes die as soon as the sounds of the succeeding phonemes come into existence. Each dying sound leaves a residual trace behind before its extinction. When the utterance is completed, the residual traces of individual sounds give vent to an indivisible entity which conveys meaning. This is *sphoṭa*. The non-eternal sounds (*nāda*) manifest the eternal indivisible *sphoṭa*.[105] Pārthasārathi Miśra rebuffs the meaning conveying aspect of *sphoṭa* of the grammarians.[106]

The *Mīmāṁsakas'* non-acceptance of *sphoṭa* stems from the controversy regarding the real nature of *śabda*.

According to Śabara phonemes constitute a word. The '*gau*' is a *śabda* which is constituted of three phonemes i.e. *g*, *au* and *visarjanīya*.[107] A *śabda* is that which is audible to the ear and which conveys meaning. But since individual phonemes cannot convey meaning, the *Mīmāṁsakas* maintain that word is an aggregate of sounds and it conveys meaning. The *Mimāṁsakas* admit that the simultaneous existence of phonemes cannot be accounted for because they die away when the succeeding phonemes are uttered. The cognition of the last phoneme alongwith the remembrance of the preceding phonemes cannot be presented in the mind of the listener because phonemes are momentary. So the *Mīmāṁsakas* postulate *saṁskāra* or residual trace. The cognition of each phoneme though momentary in nature leaves a lasting impression. In a word, the last phoneme when uttered carries the impression of earlier phonemes and produces a joint effect which conveys the meaning.[108] Kumārila defines *śabda* as that which is perceived by the auditory organ, no matter whether it conveys or does not convey any sense. In this respect phoneme is also *śabda*.[109]

The Nature of Phoneme

By means of speech organs the speaker brings forth *dhvanis*. It has neither parts nor it is the part of any entity.[110] Either inference or simile or *arthāpatti* can prove the divisibility of phoneme.[111] The sounds *'nādas'* are manifester of phonemes.[112] It is beyond the perception of senses.[113] According to Kumārila[114], the temporal distinction *(Kālabheda)* really belongs to the sound. The attributes of temporal distinction are wrongly superimposed upon the *sphoṭa*. Similarly the difference in the speed of utterance (*vṛttibheda*) are the attributes of sound.[115] In reality the attributes of the sounds are reflected on the phoneme. Explaining this point Pārthasārathi says that the size of the image may be small or big. It depends on the size of the mirror. But the size of the image remains unaltered. Similarly, the sound becomes variable and not the phoneme. The nasal pronunciations etc. are attributes of the sound and not of the phoneme.[116]

Phonemes convey meaning

In order that phonemes should convey meaning, the

Mīmāṁsakaṣ postulate the four typical features, i.e. coexistence, sequence, remembrance and *apūrva*.[117]

The phonemes in their individual capacity cannot convey meaning. To do so they are to be grouped in the form of a word.[118]

The phonemes of a word cannot be uttered all at a time. They are uttered in sequence. But phonemes uttered in sequence cannot constitute a word. When succeeding phonemes are uttered, the preceding phonemes are no longer there. So no relation can be established between the existent and nonexistent.

In order to avoid this difficulty, the *Mīmāṁsakas* assume a new concept called *saṁskāra*. They hold that each phoneme when uttered leaves a lasting impression. When the last phoneme is uttered its impression alongwith the impressions of the preceding phonemes convey the meaning.[119] This impression is identified as *vāsanā*.[120] This impression has two powers i.e.

(i) The power of productive remembrance,

(ii) The power to convey and make understand the meaning.

Here another difficulty arises. As the sounds of the preceding phonemes of a word are momentary, their impressions should also be momentary. To get rid of this diffuculty Kumārila postulates *smṛti* 'remembrance'. Accordingly, every preceding impression remains in the memory of the speaker. It is awakened when the last phoneme sound is perceived.[121] The cause of this *smṛti* is *adṛṣṭa*. The cognition of the phoneme in the form of remembrance is gradually perceived.[122] This remembrance can work only when impressions are taken as a whole.[123]

Kumārila explains it with an analogy. In a painting various colours submerge to give the cognition of a whole picture. Similarly, in a word various sound impressions of phonemes are grouped as a whole to convey the idea of remembrance.

But this impression cannot convey meaning directly. As phonemes are permanent, they cannot coexist. In collective remembrance, all the impressions of the phonemes do not figure in particular sequence. So how can the same phonemes in different order not convey the same meaning.[124] For instance, *nadī* and *dīna* would convey the same meaning.

The *Mīmāṁsakas* postulate *apūrva* to solve this problem. It is a kind of potency which is brought about by the cognition of phonemes pronounced in a fixed order by a particular speaker and leading to the understanding of meaning. The idea is, in a Vedic sacrifice various acts performed in a particular order bring a joint potency called *apūrva*.[125] Similarly, in the case of a word, the phonemes are to be uttered in a particular order by the same speaker, and the listener cognises it in the same order. In this way the impressions in particular order can convey the meaning.

According to the *Mīmāṁsakas,* every phoneme has semantic function. Each of them contributes some meaning to the word. When all phonemes are taken as a whole meaning of the word emerges. It is just like the parts of a chariot when put together can carry the load and when dismantled cannot do that work.[126] This is similar to *saṁghāta* of the grammarians.

From the above discussion it is obvious that phonemes are external and meaningful. Each of them contributes something to the exposition of meaning of the word. The last phoneme of a word, accompanied by the impression of previous phonemes in particular order as they have been uttered, give rise to a particular potency like *apūrva*. This potency conveys the meaning of the word.

Kumārila argues that grammarians' *sphoṭa* concept suffers form the following defects :

(i) They postulate an unseen entity called *sphoṭa*

(ii) Phonemes are different from it so far as the meaning conveying nature is concerned.

(iii) A non-existent *sphoṭa* is contemplated in place of cognised *śabda*.[127]

Kumārila claims that grammarians postulate a concept called *vāsanā* to preserve the impressions of dying phonemes. The *sphoṭa* cannot be the denoter of meaning because it is different from phonemes.[128] So if instead of *vāsanā, saṁskāra* is postulated, then the meaning conveying problem would have been easily solved.[129] To explain this particularly, Kumārila says that, of what use is the *sphoṭa* when *varṇas* would explain the constituents of speech. How could it be possible that there can be such a thing like a *sphoṭa* which on the one hand is manifested through successive phonemes and on the other hand is utterly different from the manifesting phonemes? How could the *sphoṭa* be indivisible when a meaning is revealed through the utterance of successive phonemes? Everybody feels that meaning arises from *śabda*. From this it is clear that *śabda* is the cause of understanding meaning. The *sphoṭa* doctrine would introduce a third element between a *śabda* and *artha*.

Pārthasārathī states that the idea that *dhvani* manifests *sphoṭa*, is vague. In fact *dhvani* manifests the phoneme which conveys the meaning. Apart from this, there is nothing called *sphoṭa*.[130]

Vācaspati Miśra in his *Tattvabindu* defends the unity of word and sentence without accepting *sphoṭa*. He maintains that the experience of unitariness of word is due to the association of the two external adjuncts. According to him, the unitariness of word and sentence is based on the idea conveyed by it. The word and the sentence cause the cognition of a single idea and therefore they are regarded as one. Criticising the *sphoṭa* concept of the grammarians, he argues that if a phoneme is identical with *sphoṭa* it can convey meaning. Again if it is different, the phonemes cannot manifest *sphoṭa* Further the *sphoṭa* cannot be indivisible and partless where phonemes reveal *sphoṭa* successively. The manifestation of phonemes in succession suggests the divisibility of *sphoṭa*.[131]

Maṇḍana Miśra, though a *Mīmāṁaska,* refutes the views of Kumārila in his work *Sphoṭasiddhi.* He argues in favour of the grammarians' view.[132] According to him, *sphoṭa* conveys meaning. Ordinarily the *Mīmāṁsakas'* concept of *sasṁkāra* and the grammarians' concept of *vāsanā* or *bhāvanā* (pre-disposition or impulse) serve the same purpose. But when *saṁskāra* groups the single phonemes, *vāsanā* brings *sphoṭa* into cognition which conveys meaning. So *sphoṭa* does not postulate something unknown as the *Mīmāṁsakas* think. It refers to known things only in contrast to *apūrva.*[133]

The Naiyāyikas' non-acceptance of the *sphoṭa* theory

Like the *Mimāsaṁkas,* the *Naiyāyikas* also level their criticism against the grammarian theory of *sphoṭa.* Vācaspati Miśra (976-77 A.D.) refers to this context while commenting on the word and its meaning of the *Nyāya Sūtra* 11.2, 60-71. He holds that according to the grammarians the phonemes do not signify objects either singly or collectively. It is not the fact that things can be signified by the last phoneme when added by the impression of the preceding phonemes, because the impressions can produce remembrance of only those objects which pertain to their own objects of experience (that generate the impression), and not to other things. Here the impression of phoneme can produce only the cognition of phoneme but not of other things, namely, the objects referred to by those phonemes.[134] But in actual experience, when the phonemes of a word, namely *ghataḥ,* are uttered there is a cognition of the jar. The grammarians argue that the concerned phonemes produce the manifestation of an entity which is called *sphoṭa.* This *sphoṭa* in its turn conveys the thing meant *ghataḥ.* The several phonemes produce a kind of conglomeration of sounds namely *sphoṭa* which is just like several words consisting a sentence. So the grammarians conclude[135] that phonemes, when uttered, only serve to manifest *sphoṭa.* This *sphoṭa* is *vācaka* and it conveys the meaning. The physical sounds reveal this *sphoṭa* entity.

Commenting on the grammarians' view, Vācaspati remarks that the word (*śabda*) by which things are denoted, is constituted as phonemes only. Apart from it there is nothing called *sphoṭa.* When the speaker speaks, phonemes only are perceived. As phonemes are many in number and word is only one, the name applies to the collection of phonemes only. These phonemes produce the cognition of a single thing. As long as the problem of verbal cognition can be explained on the basis of directly perceived phonemes, there is no justification for postulating a supernatural and purely hypothetical entity called *sphoṭa,* which is beyond our perception.[136] Vācaspati interprets the grammarians' *sphoṭa* as a semantic unit of speech. The meaning emerges when individual phonemes coexist in the form of the word. As to the question whether sound is identical with *sphoṭa* or different, Vācaspati does not accept any of the alternatives.[137] He seems to hold *sphoṭa* as a species of sound which has the quality of sound but not identical with physical sound.

The Nature of sound

The *Naiyāyikas* hold that sound *(nāda)* is non-eternal in nature. Every sound consists of a series of sounds.[138] According to Gautama, sound is non-eternal firstly because it has a beginning. Vātsyāyana explains that non-eternality refers to the things which have origination, existence and destruction. Absence is not a criterion of non-eternality.[139] Udyotakara thinks that non-eternality is conditioned by two limits, i.e. beginning and end.[140] Sound is non-eternal because it is apprehended through the contact of sense organ. It refers that sound is a product and not a manifestation. It is in the form of reverberation *(anuraṇana-rūpā).* When one cuts the wood from a distance the sound of cutting is heard by a person remaining at a distance even if the hammering ceases. The impact of the axe produces the initial sound which again produces a series of sounds and when the last one reaches the ear, the sound is actually heard.

This concept of sound is analogous to the sound in *VP*. 1.102. Bhartṛhari quotes the opinion of some scholars according to whom the sound floats in the form of reverberation from the actual source till it reaches the ear. The initial sound is *sphoṭa* and the series of sounds produced from it *(sphoṭa)* is called *dhvani.*

This view on sound suggests its non-eternal nature.[141] Vātsyāyana (*Nbh*. II.2.14) in this respect holds the similar view as referred to by Bhartṛhari.

Udyotakara gives the analogy of *Kadamba koraka* to explain the resonance nature of the sound.[142] The initial sound which is produced by the conjunction and disjunction of articulatory organs, produces other sounds which spread in all directions, just as the filament of a *kadamba* flower blooms in a circulatory fashion from the centre. From each of the succeeding sounds some other sound comes. From that sound still another sound is produced and so on. When this process goes on, the succeeding sounds become duller than the preceding ones. The series continues to produce other sounds till one gets an obstruction in the air. When the last sound becomes too weak to produce more sounds, the chain breaks. If this last sound reaches the ear, then it is heard. This sound of reverberation type is named by Bhartṛhari as *'śabdajā śabdāh'*.[143] Again the *Naiyāyikas* claim that the sound is a product.[144]

All these features of sound which claim its non-eternal nature are hinted in the *VP*. I.102. Iyer connects this view with the *locana* which I will discuss in different contexts.

Jayanta Bhaṭṭa holds that *sphoṭa* of the grammarians is an entity which conveys the meaning. It is different from phonemes individually and collectively. The grammarians postulate *sphoṭa,* because the parts in a sentence being fictitious fail to convey the meaning. It is eternal and appears in the form of word.[145] The term *śabda* is used to denote *sphoṭa*[146]. It is a partless whole and without sequence.[147]

Jayanta states that *sphoṭa* is manifested by phonemes gradually. When the first letter is heard *sphoṭa* is manifested. The consecutive letters add something in their respective capacities to manifest *sphoṭa*. This is just like the activity of a goldsmith who looks at the precious stone repeatedly to determine its real nature.[148]

Referring to the views of the grammarians, Jayanta says that *sphoṭa* is manifested by articulated sounds. At the initial stage *dhvani* manifests partless *sphoṭa*. When a *sphoṭa* is manifested it comes in contact with the organs of speech which are the sources of phonemes. The phonemes are mere appearances and they cannot manifest *sphoṭa*. The phonemes are different media in which the nature of *sphoṭa* appears to be variant. They are just like swords and mirrors in which the image looks different.[149] These phonemes are only fictions wheras *sphoṭa* conveys the meaning. This *sphoṭa* may either be word or sentence. The *pada sphoṭa* and *vākya sphoṭa* are partless in so far as their meaning conveying function is concerned. Their parts are imaginary which are to be used for grammatical purposes only.[150]

Refutation of the *sphoṭa* concept

The *Naiyāyikas* refute *sphoṭa* on the same lines as the *Mīmāṁsakas*. Jayanta states that the existence of *sphoṭa* cannot be proved either on the basis of inference or of *śabda*. It is beyond perception. That *sphoṭa* is indivisible, is absolutely groundless. The phonemes in their non-eternal capacity communicate the meaning. The phonemes constitute the words and words build the sentence. The *sphoṭa* which is different from phonemes cannot convey meaning. It is beyond auditory perception.[151]

The phonemes individually do not convey meaning,

unless they are put in a collected form.[152] The phonemes come into being in succession but they produce a joint effect conjointly. This is compared to the feeling of satisfaction in which various actions contribute to achieve a common goal.[153] In a word, though the phonemes are perceived one after another, there arises a recognitive judgement of inner perception like an introspection. This recognitive judgement (cf. *saṁaskāra*) carries the memory impression of orderly perished phonemes.[154] Ultimately it conveys the meaning of the word as a total effect.[155] The *Mīmāṁsakas* are of the opinion that the function of *saṁskāra* is to revive the memory and not to convey the meaning. Jayanta does not agree with this view. According to him, *saṁskāra* not only generates recollection, but is also capable of producing the apprehension of an object.[156] Each phoneme represents a class. The difference in utterance (*udātta* etc.) do not hamper their communicative ability.

Though the *Naiyāyikas* and *Mīmāṁsakas* claim that the grammarians postulate *vāsanā*, similar to *saṁskāras*[157], there is no evidence to it in the works of Patañjali and Bhartṛhari. In short, the *Naiyāyikas* understand the grammarians' concept of *sphoṭa* as an entity of the speech which conveys the meaning. But basically they oppose this doctrine.

Kauṇḍa Bhaṭṭa and Nageśa Bhaṭṭas' interpretation of *sphoṭa*

Kauṇḍa and Nageśa tried to answer some of the objections raised by the *Naiyāyikas* and the *Mīmāṁsakas* on *sphoṭa*. The *sphoṭa* theory of the grammarians faced a lot of criticism at the hands of *Mīmāṁsā* and *Nyāya* system of thought. Both of them have justified *sphoṭa* because the meaning bearing aspect of a word cannot be dispensed with as regards the notion of phonemes and their sequence.

According to Kauṇḍa Bhaṭṭa, the *śakti* (communicative power) is the capacity of the word which conveys the meaning.[158] This *śakti* is based on the *vṛtti* or function of the word, and the substratum of the *vṛtti* is *sphoṭa*.[159] The *sphoṭa* is a form of *vāk* (speech). It is what we contemplate in our intellect. It comes into existence by the sound. Nāgeśa states that gross sounds *(nāda)* are originated from *madhyamā vāk* and *vaikharī vāk* at a time. The sounds originated from *madhyamā vāk* manifests *sphoṭa*. It is a subtle form of the sound. The articulated sounds are *dhvanis*.[161] Sometimes this *sphoṭa* is perceived as articulated sounds which are produced from the convulsion of the articulatory organs.[162] The *sphoṭa* is indivisible. But it appears to have parts because of the divisibility of *dhvani*. All attributes of *dhvani* are super imposed upon it.

According to Nāgeśa, the *sphoṭa* has two aspects in relation to *dhvani*, i.e. the *āntarasphoṭa* 'inner *sphoṭa* ' and the *vāhya sphoṭa* 'outer *sphoṭa*'. The inner *sphoṭa* conveys the meaning. The outer *sphoṭa* which is in the form of *vaikṛtadhvani* is the cause of variations in the speed of utterance *(vṛttibheda)*.[163] Just as a crystal appears to have absorbed the colours of a flower placed near it though it is without any colour, similarly *sphoṭa* seems to have part in relation to *dhvani*; but in reality it has no parts.

Nāgeśa Bhaṭṭa states that *sphoṭa* is the manifestation of inner *praṇava (āntarapraṇavarūpa)*.[164] Similarly the *śabda* is all pervading[165] and remains in the intellect of the speaker. In this stage sound and meaning are indistinguishable. When there is ejaculation of articulatory organs the sound aspect in the shape of phoneme is conspicuous. In reverse process the sound enters into the ear of the listener. Then it passes through the intellect. The sound is transformed into phoneme in the intellect, and then phonemes conjointly convey the meaning. The action *(prayatna)* of the speaker may die but the *śabda* remains.[166]

This process of communication may be shown in the following diagram :

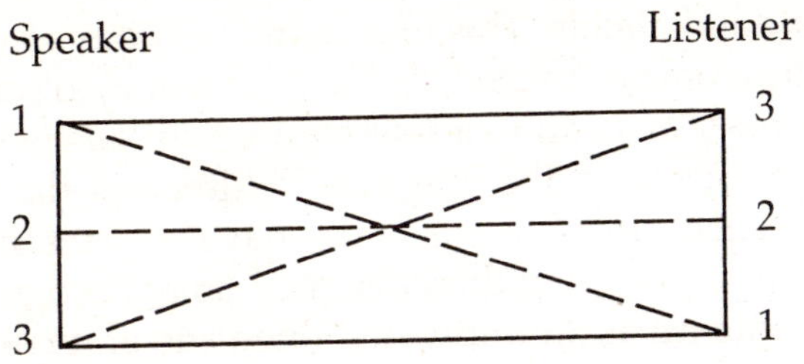

1. The *sphoṭa (śabda)* in the intellect which conveys the meaning.
2. Transformed into linguistic units, i.e. phonemes etc.
3. Expressed by articulated sounds.

According to Nāgeśa, meaningful *śabda* is *sphoṭa*.[167] The *sphoṭa* is manifested by sounds. It may take the shape of a word or a sentence.

Though a staunch follower of Bhartṛhari, Nāgeśa has his independent view on *dhvani.* According to him, *prākṛta dhvani* is derived from the word *prakṛti* which refers to the unit uttered to convey meaning. Thus *prākṛta dhvani* is that sound which is produced out of the natural urge of the speaker. It manifests *sphoṭa* which conveys meaning.[168] The temporal distinction is the attribute of *prākṛta dhvani.*[169] As soon as the *prākṛta dhvani* is produced *sphoṭa* is perceived. The *vaikṛta dhvani* is produced from the *prākṛta dhvani.* The difference in various speed of utterance are its attributes. It remains permanently and never dies.[170] Thus according to Nāgeśa the *prākṛta dhvani* gives power to *sphoṭa* to convey the meaning, and the *vaikṛta-dhvani* has permanent existence. In these two points Nāgeśa does not follow Bhartṛhari. He follows Bhartṛhari so far as the *prākṛta dhvani* reveals *sphoṭa.*[171]

Nāgeśa states that *sphoṭa* is indivisible. It assumes various forms because of the sounds in the form of phonemes, words and sentences which manifest it. The *sphoṭa* appears to have various forms because it is felt to be associated with manifester's attributes. In reality, it is integral and indivisible. This idea of indivisibility of *sphoṭa* probably has come from the *VP*.I.73.[172] According to Nāgeśa, the phoneme-*sphoṭa* and word-*sphoṭa* are fictitious whereas the sentence *sphoṭa* is the real one.[173] Although the parts of the sentence are fictitious, they have a place in the grammatical process, and therefore they cannot be ignored. Thus the sentence as an undivided linguistic unit conveys meaning.

The later grammarians hold the same view through different analogies as to how *sphoṭa* is comprehended. Maṇḍana Miśra states that *sphoṭa* is manifested by sounds.[174] But it is not immediately perceived. It is perceived gradually. The vague perception of residual impressions of the sounds is gradually crystallised and reveals *sphoṭa*. This is analogous to the perception of a gem by a goldsmith.[175] In course of the examination some vague ideas contribute to the totality of correct perception until he arrives at a final conclusion. Maṇḍana Miśra has also given an analogy popular in the Vedānta. When one looks at a tree in the darkness, it appears like an elephant. But when he looks at it again and again, his false notion is changed and ultimately he knows it to be a tree.[176] Similarly, the *sphoṭa* grasped in final cognition accompanies the residual memory impressions of earlier vaguely perceived sounds. These sounds progressively reveal the form of *sphoṭa*. In this respect Śeṣakṛṣna mentions that when one utters the word *'kamala'* he utters each syllable one after another. When he utters *ka* nothing is clear. But when he utters *ma* it brings some apprehension of the forthcoming. And when the last syllable *la* is uttered, the listerner clearly grasps the *sphoṭa*-word.[177]

The *sphoṭa* concept of grammarians faced a lot of trials in the hands of the *Mīmāṁsā* and *Nyāya* scholars, and came down to Ānandavardhana with a lot of modification. The *sphoṭa* has been described in terms of revealed sound in the *VP*. But it has been related to the semantic features by the later grammarians. Even opponents treat it as an entity which conveys meaning. Bhartṛhari does not identify the *sphoṭa* with the meaningful *śabda*. His *sphoṭa* is manifested by sounds, and so it is *śabdavyaṅgya* and not *arthavyañjaka*. The opponents and later proponents of *sphoṭa* consider it to have *arthavyañjakatva*. Nowhere in the *VP is* it treatd as an *arthapratyāyaka*.

Before Ānadavardhana (9th Century A.D.) *sphoṭa* has already undergone sufficient interpretations. Its *śabdavyaṅgyatā* with Bhartṛhari has already been metamorphosed into *arthavyañjakatva* by Kumārila Bhaṭṭa and Maṇḍana Miśra etc. Ānandavardhana has picked up the latter interpretations of *sphoṭa*. That is why, he has classified *dhvanikāvya* not only on the basis of *śabda*, but also on the basis of *artha*.

Every concept is prone to certain changes at the hands of great scholars. The *sphoṭa* concept is not an exception to it. It has undergone a change from the distinctive level of language to the semantic level of language. This is the history of evolution of the doctrine of *sphoṭa* of the grammarians.

The works on *sphoṭa* deal with the problems in the philosophy of language which are interrelated with the problems in semantics. The present work includes the material from various disciplines that deal in several ways with one or another aspect of meaning. I have tried to interrelate the views from early writings of philosophers whose theory deal with semantics in the narrower sense. There is a considerable volume of literature dealt with in this section on the problem of how the speech act is related to the meaning. Grammar deals with systems of relations which join the units in the sentence. But the meaning of a sentence hits over and above the constituent meanings and their relation. The sentence communicates something more than the mere logical or grammatical relations conveyed by the items. What is additionally communicated is *dhvani* 'emotional overtones'. The grammatically similar or the same sentences are found to differ in effectivity or emotiveness. An expression totally devoid of motion is rare in ordinary language. But the effectivity or emotiveness may be correlated with the speech act. The whole material of language has to be studied from the new point of *dhvani*, because effect may be due to choice of sounds or words or the grammatical order, etc.

The *dhvani* theory of Ānandavardhana deserves a place on par with *sphoṭa*, phonetics, vocabulary and grammar. It takes all these aspects into consideration in order to study effectivity and emotiveness.

Thus the *dhvani* theory of Ānandavardhana is a branch of a linguistic science and it is related to the earlier theories, although from a special angle. The features of language are an important aid to the appreciation of literary values. According to Ānandavardhana, *dhvani* conveyed by the expression is the systematic nature of literary science. The present book attempts to show a close relation between *dhvani* of the grammarians and *dhvani* of the *ālaṁkārikas* because both of them are enclosed in the speech act.

References

1. K. Madhavakrishna Sharma, "Vāk before Bhartṛhari", *poc* Vol. VIII, 1943, pp. 21-36; John Brough, "Audumbarāyaṇa's theory of language", *BSOAS*, Vol. XIV, 1952, pp. 73-77; R.S. Bhattacharya, "Some broad aspects on Indian Grammar and the theory of sphoṭa " *JGJRI*, Vol. XV, 1957-58, p. 91; Nils Simonsson, "Audumbarāyaṇa's theory of sound", *OS*, Vol. X, 1962, pp. 22- 30.
2. *Nirukta*, ed. Mukunda Sharma, New Delhi, 1982, p. 6: *indriya nityavacnam.*
3. *Ibid.*, p. 7 : *vyāptimatvāt tu śabdasya*
4. J. Brough, *op. cit.*, pp. 74-76.
5. Nils Simonsson, *op. cit.*, p. 27.
6. P. C. Chakravorty, "Linguistic speculation of the Hindus", JDL, Vol. XII, 1925, pp. 61, 139.
7. Nils Simosson, *loc. cit.*

8. J. Brough, *op. cit.*, also K. K. Raja, *Indian Theories of Meaning*, Madras, 1977, p. 99
9. P. 6. 1. 123; *Padamañjarī* on *Kāśikā* on it; Nāgeśa Bhaṭṭa, *Sphoṭavāda*, Madras, 1977, p. 102
10. *Mbh.* Vol. I, p. 181 : *dhvani sphoṭa' ca śabdānāṁ dhvanis tu khalu lakṣyate*
11. *Ibid., evaṁ tarhi sphoṭaḥ śabdaḥ dhvani śabdaguṇah*
12. *Ibid., ,katham avasthitā varṇā drutamadhyavilambitāsu kiṁ kṛtas tarhir vṛttiviśeṣaḥ vaktus' cirāciravacanād vṛttayo viśiṣyante ı vaktā kaścid āśvābhidhāyī bhavati ı āśu varṇān abhidhatte kaścic cireṇa kaści ciratareṇa tat yathā tam evādhvānaṁ kaścid āśu gacchati kaścic cireṇa gacchati kaścic ciratareṇa gacchati rathika āśu gacchati āśvikas cirena padātiś ciratarena ı viṣama upanyasaḥ adhikaraṇa mātrādhvā vrajati kriyāyāḥ tatra āyuktaṁ yadadhikaraṇasya vṛddhihrāsau* **syātām** ı
13. S. D. Joshi's interpretation with a little modification is accepted here; See *Sphoṭa Nirṇaya*, Poona, 1967, p. 14
14. K.K. Raja, *op. cit.*, p. 102
15. S.D. Joshi, *Sphoṭa Nirṇaya*, p. 15.
16. *Mbh.* Vol. I, p. 26 : *athavobhayataḥ sphoṭamātraṁ nirdiśyate, r- śruter l- śrutir bhvati;* also S.D. Joshi, *op. cit.*, p. 16; J. Brough, "Theories of general linguistics in the Sanskrit grammarians", *Tps*, 1951, p. 37
17. J. Brough, *Ibid.*, p. 34; also S. D. Joshi, *op. cit.*, p. 15
18. S. D. Joshi, *op. cit.*, pp. 10-11.
    NB. K. K. Raja in his *Indian Theories of Meaning*, p. 102, claims that *Sphoṭa* is a unit of sound, but his view is untenable because Patañjali nowhere mentions or indicates that *Sphoṭa* is identical with sound *(dhvani)*. In fact, the *Sphoṭa* is a conceptual form of the physical sound.
19. *Mdh. vol. I,* p. 175 : *asty anyāt rūpāt svaṁ śabdasyeti kiṁ punas tat arthaḥ.......śabdenoccāritena artho gamyate gām ānaya dadhy aśānety arthānīyate' rthas' ca bhujyate;* also *Ibid.*, p. 176: *śabdapūrvakohyarthasya saṁpratyaḥ*
20. K.K. Raja, *op. cit.*, p. 108.
21. *Mbh.* Vol. I, p. 30: *dhātava eka varṇā arthavanato dṛśyate.......*
22. *Ibid. varṇavyatyaye cārthāntaragamanān manyāmahe' rthavanto varṇa iti .....varṇān upalabdhau cānarthagater manyāmahe' rthavanto varṇā iti*
23. *Ibid.*, p. 31: *na hi prativarṇam arthā upalabhyante.*

24. *Ibid., varṇa vyatyayāpāyopajana vikāreṣvarthadarśanān manyāmahe' narthakā varṇā iti* ।
25. *Ibid.*, p. 30 : *saṁghātārthavatvāc ca manyāmahe' rthavanto varṇā iti......*
26. *Ibid.*, p. 220 : *ime punar varṇā atyantāyaivānarthakāḥ vathā tarhi rathāṅgāni vihṛtāni pratyekaṁ vrajikriyāṁ praty asamartrāni bhavanti tat samudāyaś ca rathaḥ samartha evam eṣāṁ varṇānāṁ samudāyā arthavanto' vayavā anarthakā iti;* also S. D. Joshi, *op. cit.*, pp. 5-11-13, 18-19; R.S. Tripathy, *Saṁskṛta Vyākaraṇa Darśana*, Delhi, 1972, pp. 81-82.
27. *Mbh.* Vol. I p. 356 : *buddhau kṛtvā sarvāś ceṣṭāḥ kartā dhīras tatvannitiḥ* । *śabdenārthān vācyān dṛṣṭvā buddhau kuryāt paurvāparyam* । also *Ślokavārttika, Sphoṭa-vāda*, V. 113; *Yoga Sūtra Bhāṣyam* 111. 17: *tad eteṣam arthasaṁketā vacchinānāṁ......* Though Vyāsa does not admit *Sphoṭa* here he approves the sequence of phonemes as a unity. P 1. 4. 109: *paraḥ sannikarṣaḥ saṁhitā*
28. S. D. Joshi, *op. cit.*, p. 18
29. *Mbh.* Vol. I, p. 1: *yenoccāritena sāsnālāṅgulakakudakhuraviṣāṇināṁ saṁpratyayo bhavati sa sabdaḥ*
30. S. D. Joshi, *op. cit.*, pp. 8-9
31. *Ibid.*, pp. 10-11
32. *Mbh.* Vol. I p. 1 : *athavā pratrtapadārthako loke dhvaniḥ śabda ity ucyate tad yathā śabdaṁ kuru, śabdaṁ mā kārṣīḥ, śabdaṁ kārlyaṁamāṇavaka iti* । *dhvaniṁ kurvan nevam ucyate, tasmād dhvanīḥ śabdḥ*:also S. D. Joshi, *op. cit.*, p. 32: *Ibid.*, "Patañjali' s defintion of a word, an interpretation", BDCRI, poona, 1966, pp. 66-67.
33. S. D. Joshi, *Sphoṭa Nirṇaya;* Poona, 1967, pp. 9, 32.
34. *Mbh.* Vol. I, p. 18 : *śrotropalabdhir buddhinirgrāhyaḥ prayogeṇābhijvalitaḥ ākāśadeśaḥ śabdaḥ ekaṁ ca punarākāśam*
35. S. D. Joshi, *op. cit.*, pp. 10-11; also see footnote of *Mahābhāṣya*, ed. K. A. Abhyankar and J. M. Joshi, BORI, Poona, 1975, p. 67.
36. S. D. Joshi, *op. cit*, p. 10; also K.A.S. Iyer, Bhatṛhari, Poona 1969, pp. 156-157; K.K. Raja, *Indian theories of meanings*, p. 103: "Patañjali" conception of the *Sphoṭa* was entirely different from that of the later grammarians. To him, the *Sphoṭa* is not a single indivisible symbol considered as the meaning-

bearer, but only the unchanging sound unit, or a time-series pattern of such units."

37. Virendra Sharma, *Vākyapadīya Saṁbandha Sammuddeśa: A Critical Study*, Hoshiarpur, 1977, pp. 33, 35 also *Mahābhāṣyadīpīkā*, ed. *Abhyankar* and *Limaye*, poona, 19, p. 4 : *śabda ity etasya...*
38. Virendra Sharma, *Ibid.*, pp. 42-46; also Harold G. Coward, *The sphoṭa theory of language*, Delhi 1980, p. 73. NB Coward believes that *sphoṭa* of Patañjali represents the *śabda* proper. It represents the internal aspect of the word which conveys the meaning. It is revealed by the external aspect of the word that is sound.
39. John Brough, *op. cit.*, p. 34.
40. *VP*. I.49, 75, 77, 81, 83, 97, 102, 103, 106.
41. K.A.S. Iyer, *op. cit.*, pp. 156-157.
42. *VP*. I.44, 55, 59; also S.D. Joshi, *op. cit.*, p. 51
43. S.D. Joshi, *op. cit.*, pp. 15, 51.
44. *Vṛtti* on *VP*.I.102 : *nityapakṣe saṁyogajā vibhāgajā dhvani vyaṅgyaḥ sphoṭaḥ*
45. *Ibid.* : *ekesāṁ saṁyogavibhāgajā dhvani saṁbhūtā nādābhivyaṅgyāḥ*
46. *VP*. I. 104 : *dūrāt prabheva dīpasya dhvani mātraṁ tu lakṣyate* ।
47. *Ibid.*, I. 93.
48. K.K. Raja, *op. cit.*, pp. 115-116
49. S.D. Joshi, *op. cit.*, p. 51
50. *Vṛtti* on *VP*. 81:
śabdena saṁsṛṣṭo dhvanirūpāśrayānurāgaiva sphaṭikādīnāṁ vibhakta upalabhyate
51. *Ibid.* : *keṣāṁcit tu yathendriyāṇindriyagunāś ca saṁvedyarūpā eva viṣayopalabdhihetavas tathāyaṁ dhvaniranugṛhyamāṇarūpaḥ śabdagrahe nimittaṁ bhavati*
52. *Ibid.*, *dṛṣṭā kevalasya dhvaneḥ sphoṭarūpānavadhāraṇe dūrād upalabdhiḥ*
53. *Mbh.* Vol. I. p. 18 : *śrotropalabdhiḥ buddinirgrāhyaḥ* ... also, *VP*. I. 84 : *buddhau śabdo'vadhāryate; VP*. I.46 : *tadvac chabdo'pi buddhisthaḥ;*
VP. I.47 : *vitarkitaḥ purā buddhyā kvacid arthe niveśitaḥ* ।
VP. I. 53 : *yathā prayoktuḥ prāg buddhiḥ śabdeṣveva pravartate*
54. *VP*. I. 83 : *pratyayair anupākhyāir grahaṇānuguṇais tathā*
55. *Idid.*, I. 82.

56. *Ibid.*, I.84.
57. S.D. Joshi, *op. cit*,. p. 39.
58. *VP*.I.49
59. K.A.S. Iyer, *op. cit.*, p. 152.
60. *VP*.I. 60
61. *VP*.I. 59, also K.K.Raja, *op. cit.*, p. 118
62. See for details, J. Brough, "Theories of general linguistics in the Sanskrit grammarians, *TPS*, 1951, pp. 28-31; Srimannarayana M.Murthi, "Bhartṛhari on *svaṁ rūpaṁ śabdasyāśabdasaṁjñā*, *ALB*, Vol.44-45,1980-81, pp. 602-613;K.A.S. Iyer, *op. cit.*, p. 155
63. K.K.Raja, *op. cit.*, pp. 116-117.
64. S. D. Joshi, *op. cit.*, p. 20
65. K. K. Raja, *op. cit.*, p. 117
66. K.A.S. Iyer, *op. cit.*, p. 151 ; also *VP.I*.45-47, 53, 84, 90.
67. *VP* .I. 52
68. K. A. S. Iyer, *op. cit.*, p. 157
69.(i) *Pradīpa* on *Mahābhāsyam* ed. Rudradhar Jha, Varanasi, p. 11 : *iti tad vyatiriktaḥ sphoṭo nādābhivyaṅgyo vācako vistareṇa vākyapadīye vyavasthāpitaḥ*
(ii) *Mahābhāṣyadīpikā*, P. 4.1.3-4, p. *etaccārthasvarūpaṁ sphoto'yam eva śabdātmā nityaḥ ye tu kramajanmāno yugapat-kālā vyaktayo dhvanyātmānāte.*
70. *Vṛtti* on *VP*. I.82 : *varṇapadavākyaviṣayāḥ prayatnaviśeṣasādhyā dhvanayo varṇapadavākyākhyān sphoṭān punaḥ punar āvirbhāvayanto buddhisvadhyāropayanti.*
71. *VP*. I. 1-2.
72. *VP*. I. 46, 47, 53, 84.
73. *V.P*. II.1. : *eko navayavaḥ śabdaḥ kramo buddhyanusaṁhṛtiḥ*
74. *VP*. I. 44. 55, 58.
75. S.D. Joshi, *op. cit.*, pp. 47-48, 51.
76. John Brough, *op. cit.*, p. 40.
77. K.A. S. Iyer, *op. cit.*, p. 159
78. John Brough, *op. cit.*, pp. 33, 38.
79. *Ibid.*, p. 37.
80. S.D. Joshi Justifies this 'acoustic image' is *sphoṭa* itself. This term is borrowed form de *Saussure*. See K. K. Raja, *Indian theories* of *meanings*, p. 122. Raja holds that Saussure's la-*langue* can be compared with *sphoṭa* and *la-parloe* with *dhvani*

which is actual articulated sound (K.K. Raja, op. cit., pp. 104-5, 123).

81. K.K. Raja, *op. cit.*, p. 123; For *sphoṭa* as partless symbol see D.M. Datta, *The Six ways of knowing* ,George Allen, and Unwin, London, 1932, p. 250
82. S.D. Joshi, *op. cit.*, p. 35
83. K. A. S. Iyer, English trnaslation of *Vākyapadīya.* I. 73, poona, 1965, p. 77.
84. S.D. Joshi, *op. cit.*, p. 37
85. *Ibid.*, pp. 40-43.
86. *Ibid.*, pp. 37, 38, 46; Nāgeśa Bhaṭṭa, *Sphoṭavāda,* Madras, p. 9.
87. J. Brough, *op. cit.*, p. 40; also, K. K. Raja, *op. cit.*, p. 120
88. S.D. Joshi, *op. cit.*, p. 45
89. *Ibid.*, p. 52
90. Nāgeśa Bhaṭṭa, *op. cit.*, p. 52 : *tatra sphuṭatyartho 'smād iti sphoṭaḥ, vācaka iti yāvad evaṁ ca varṇasphoṭādipadānāṁ varṇādayo vācaka ity arthaḥ, sphuṭyate varṇaiḥ yaḥ varṇābhivyaṅgya*
91. John Brough uses the phrase, 'time-series pattern' to connote that *sphoṭa* has neither time nor parts. To him time-series pattern is the attibute of *dhvani* which is an abstract sound pattern of the utterance constituting the phonetic aspect of the word. But for Joshi, the sound-pattern is the other name of *sphoṭa.* He dose not believed in the semantic power of *sphoṭa* of Bhartṛhari.
92. S.D. Joshi, *op. cit.*, p. 38
93. *Ibid.*, pp. 26, 27, 53; *VP.* I. 93; also John Brough, *op. cit.*, p. 33.
94. S.D. Joshi, *op. cit.*, p. 51; *VP.* I.44, 55, 58.
95. *Mahābhāṣyadīpikā*, p. 20, 10-20: *tatra caitat* etc.
96. K.A.S. Iyer, *op. cit.*, pp. 157-159.
97. J. Brough, *op. cit.*, p. 40
98. *Ibid.*, p. 41
99. K. A. S. lyer, "Bhartṛhari on *Dhvani*", *ABORI,* Vol. XLVI, 1965, Poona, p. 63.
100. *Ibid.*, "who are *anityasphoṭavādins?*" *POC,* 1935. NB. The term '*anye*' in *VP.* I. 102 suggests that *vaikṛtadhvani* of reverberation type is not appereciated and supported by Bhartṛhari.

101. J. Brough, *op. cit.*, pp. 38, 41; also K.K. Raja, *op. cit.*, pp. 116, 120, 123.
102. G. Sastri, (i) *The philosphy of word and meaning*, Calcutta, 1959, pp. 102-103.
(ii) *Dialectics of sphoṭa*, Delhi.
103. K.A.S. Iyer, "Bhartṛhari on *Dhvani*" *ABORI*, XLVI, p. 65.
104. S. K. Verma, *Bhāṣātatva aur Vākyapadīya* (Hindi), Delhi, 1964, pp. 54, 55, 57.
105. *Sva sphoṭā.*, 91, ed. Durgadhar Jha, Darbhanga, 1967: *yasyānavayavaḥ sphoṭa vyajyate varṇabuddhibhiḥ*
106. *SD.* ed. Kishor Das Swami, Varanisi, 1977, p. 186 : *sphoṭasya ca śaśaviṣāṇāyamānasya dūranirastaṁ vācakatvam iti sambandha eva vācyavācakabhāvo nirādhāratvāt nasyānnatarāṁ । nityatvam iti...*
107. *SB.* Vol. I, ed. Yudhisthir Mimāṁsaka, Haryana, 1977, p. 35; also K.A.S. Iyer, "The doctrine of *Sphoṭa* " *JGJRI*, V. Part II, Allahabad, 1948, p. 125; *SS.* ed.K.A. S. Iyer, Poona, 1966,p. 4, *hā.* 3.
108. *SB.* p.36 · *pūrvavarṇajanitasaṁskārasahito' ntyovarṇaḥ pratyāyaka ity adoṣāḥ*
109. *Sva. Sphoṭa.*, 5-6:
tasmāc chotraparicchinno yadarthaṁ gamayen na vā । sarvathā tasya śabdatvaṁ loka siddhaṁ na hīyate ।। yadi tvarthagatau śaktir na syād asya tataḥ punaḥ । vastvantaraṁ prakalpyeta vinā śabdaprasiddhitaḥ ।। also *SD.* p. 186 : *varṇāḥ eva śabda ...*
110. *Sva. Sphoṭa.*, 10-11, 18; also, *VP.* I. 73.
111. *Ibid.*, 13.
112. *Ibid.*, 40.
113. *Ibid.*, 38.
114. *Ibid.*, 51.
115. *Ibid.*, 21-23.
116. *SD.* pp. 188-189 :
dhvanidharmas tv ete varṇe kevalam ābhāsante । yathā 'lpe mahati ca darpaṇe yugapad dṛśyamāne mukhe'lpatvaṁ mahtvaṁ ceti । tasmāt varṇasya vyaktyekatve'pi na virodha iti...
117. *Sva. Sphoṭa.*, 70.
118. *SS.* p. 9 :
nanu ca varṇā evābhidheyādhigamanimittaṁ svābhidheyāvabodhāvadhi labdhaparicchedāḥ padaparikalpanābhājaḥ ; also *Sva, Sphoṭa.*, 971;

119. *Sva.Sphoṭa.*, 97 : also *SS. kā.* 5.
120. *Ibid.*, 99
121. *Ibid.*, 100, 102.
122. *Ibid.*, 104.
123. *Ibid.*, 115.
124. *SS. kā.* 7.
125. *Ibid.*, p. 29 :
astu tarhi pūrvavarṅajanitasaṁskārasahito 'ntyo varṇo vācaka ity evaḥ । mā 'bhud eṣa jñānaprasavaḥ smaraṇanimittaṁ saṁskāraḥ । api tu yāgādikarmabhedopapādita iva svargādinimittam apūrvābhidhāno' nya eva niyatakarmakartṛbhedaprayuktavarṇavijñānopāhito'rthādhigamaphalaḥ ; also, Sva. Sphoṭa., 130.
126. *Sva.Sphoṭa.*, 89.
127. *Ibid.*, 94.
128. *Ibid.*, 133, 137.
129. *Ibid.*, 126, 129 ; also *SS. kā* 6.
130. *SD.* p. 195 :
evaṁ tarhi dhvanikramo yo varneṣvāropitaḥ । pratibhāsate so'ṅgam ity adoṣaḥ । tasmād vyañjakānāṁ dhvanīnāṁ krameṇa vyaṅgyeṣu samāropitena tadvantaḥ smaryamāṇā varṇā vācakāḥ । nānyaḥ śabdo'stīti, siddhaṁ ।
131. S.D. Joshi, *Sphoṭa Nirṇaya*, pp. 65-66, also S. S. S. Sastri, "Vācaspati's criticism of *sphoṭa-vāda*" *JOR*, Vol. VI, part IV, 1932, p. 313.
132. For detailed account see K. A. S. Iyer's "The dotrine of *sphoṭa*", JGJRI, Vol. V, part II, 1948, pp. 131-133; also for camparison of Kumārila and Maṇḍana Miśra's views on *sphoṭa* see *The sphoṭa theory of language* by H.G. Coward, Delhi, 1980, pp. 100-101.
133. *SS. kā* 10; also its *vṛtti* :
sphoṭopalabdhiḥnibandhanas tu bhāvanābhidhāna eva saṁskāra iti vakṣyate
134. S.S.S. Sastri, *op. cit.*, p. 312.
135. *NVTT.* on *NS* II.2.60 ed.
136. *Ibid.*, II.2.60.
137. S.S.S. Sastri *op. cit.*, p. 315.
138. *NS.* II. 2.14.
139 *NBH.* II. 2.14.16
140. *NV.* II.2.16.

141. For details see K.A.S. Iyer, "who are *anityasphoṭavādinaḥ?*" POC, VIII, Mysore, 1935.
142. *NV*. II.2.14.
143. K.A.S. Iyer, *Bhartṛhari*, p. 175 ; also *NBH*. II.2.35-38, 40.
144. *NBH*. II.2.14.
145. *NM*. Vol. I, p. 336 :
nanv etad eva na kṣamante na hi varṇānāṁ samūhaḥ kaścid asti vāstavaḥ tena kutas tat samūhaḥ padaṁ bhaviṣyati tad abhāvāc ca natarāṁ padasamūho vākyam avakalpate na ca varṇānāṁ vyastasamastavikalpopahatatvena vācakatvam upapadyate tasmād anya eva sphoṭātmā śabdo'rtha pratipādakaḥ iti partijānate sphoṭasya ca nityatvena āptapraṇītatvam ataś ca yasyānityatvaṁ varṇātmanaḥ śabdasya sādhitaṁ nāsāvarthapratītihetur ato na pramāṇaṁ yaścārtha pratītihetuḥ sphoṭātmā śabdaḥ ...
146. *Ibid*., p. 338 :
ataś ca sphoṭo 'rtha pratipādakaḥ tatra śabdād iti prātipadikạrtho 'pyupapannaḥ; also *Ibid., p. 339 : ... sphoṭa eva śabdaḥ.*
147. *Ibid*., p. 338 :
sa ca niravayavo nitya eko niṣkramaka iti ı
148. *Ibid*., p. 340 :
prathamavarṇaśravaṇavelāyāṁ sphoṭobhivyakto bhavati na ca dvitīyādivarṇa vaiphalyaṁ tad avagater evātiśayakaraṇād yathā ratnaparīkṣāṇāṁ prathamadarśane ratnarūpam amalam aprakāśamāṅam api punaḥ punaḥ parīkṣamāṇānāṁ carame cetasi cakāsti niravadyaṁ ratnatatvam, evam ihāpi prathamavarṇaśrutyā vyakte'pi sphoṭe sphuṭatarapratītyai varṇānarāṇi prayokṣyante iti; also *SS*. p. 43 :
yathā ratnaparīkṣiṇah parikṣamāṇasya .... ,VP.I.82, 89; K. K. Raja, *Indian Theories of Meaning*, p. 125; S. D. Joshi, *Sphoṭa Nirṇaya*, p. 58, K.A.S. Iyer, "Doctrine of *Sphoṭa*" *JGJRI*, Vol. V. p. 1, pp. 121 ff.
149. *NM*. Vol. I, p. 340 : *yathā kṛpāṇamaṇidarpaṇādi vyañjakabhedena śyāmadīrghādirūpaṁ vadanasya nādātmako hi śabdo vīṇāveṇumṛdaṅgapaṭahādivyañjakabhedena nānātvam upagacchan dṛśyate tasmān nuparamārthikā eva te varṇāḥ ...*
150. *Ibid*., pp. 341 ff.
151. *Ibid*., p. 355 :
iti vitatayā varṇā
ete dhiyā viṣayīkṛtām ı
dadhati padatāṁ vākyatvaṁ

vā ta eva ca vācakāḥ ।
na ca tadaparaḥ sphoṭaḥ
śrote vibhātyavabodhane । na ca vidhiheto vācye
buddhiṁ vidhātum asau kṣamah ।।

152. *Ibid.*, p. 344 :
varṇānāṃ samastā eva te vācakāḥ ।

153. *Ibid.*, pp. 344-345 :
yathā yugapadbhāvinaḥ samāstrayo etc.

154. *Ibid.*, p. 345 : *atha vā kramopalabdheṣv api varṇeṣu mānasam anuvyavasāyarūpam akhilavarṇaviṣayaṁ bhaviṣyati saṁkalanā-jñānaṁ yad upajāyate tadarthapratyāyanāṅgaṁ bhaviṣyati ...*

155. *Ibid.*, p. 346 :
tasmāt prathamāvagamanīyatānupūrvīkās te tadanantarabhāvisa-mastāvabhāsi saṁkalanāpratyayopārūḍhā varṇā arthapratītikāriṇa iti.

156. *Ibid.*, p. 346 : *hi smaraṇaśaktiḥ saṁskāraḥ kiṁ tvātmaguṇo vāsanākhyaḥ sa ca smṛtim ivārthapratītim api janayitum utsahate*

157. *SS.* p. 17 : *saṁskāraṁ tu vāsanādvitīyanāmānaṁ*, also foot note no. 156, Ch. I.

158. *VBS.* ed. S.D. Joshi, in the *Sphoṭa Nirṇaya*, p. 101, 4-5; *arthopasthāpakajñāna viṣayaśabdavṛttijñāna kāraṇatvasyaiva śaktitvāt yuktaṁ ca itat viṣayatā saṁbandhena śābdabodhamātre vṛttijñānasya lāghavena hetutve siddheh ।*

159. *PLM.* ed Alakhadeva Sharma, Varanasi, 1974, p. 60 :
nanu kas tarhi vṛttyāśrayaḥ śabdaḥ । sa sphoṭatmaka iti gṛhāṇa ।

160. *Ibid.*, p. 60;
tato hṛdayaparyantam āgacchatā tena vāyunā 'bhivyaktā tat tadarthavācaka sphoṭarūpā śrotragrahaṇāyogyatvena sūkṣmā japādau buddhinirgrāhyā madhyamā vāg ucyate; also *VSLM.* ed. Sabhapati Sharma Upadhyaya, Varanasi, 1973, p. 196; *VP.* I.134.

161. *Ibid.*, p. 61.

162. *VSLM.* pp. 194, 199 :
sphoṭa eva śrotṛa grāhyaḥ ... śrotrendriyagrāhyaḥ sphoṭanāmā padarthaḥ śabdaḥ ... dhvanirūpeṇā 'pi sphoṭa eva gṛhyate ।

163. *Ibid.*, p. 198 ; also *PLM.* p. 65.

164. *VSLM*, p. 369

165. *Nir.* p. 7, see foot note No. 3, Ch. I.

166. *VSLM.* p. 375
abhidhānābhidheyarūpā buddhir hṛdayākāśapratiṣṭhitā parbodhane-

cchayā puruṣeṇodryamāṇā kaṇṭhādiṣu varṇabhāvamāpakdya (māṇa) bāhyākāśasthaṁ śabdaṁ sva svarūpaṁ kṛtvā śrotradvāreṇa tatra sthitāṁ śrotur buddhim anupraviśya sarvārthasarvābhidhāna-rūpāṁ tadbuddhiṁ vyāpnoti ।

167. *Ibid.*, pp. 378, 195.
168. *PLM.* p. 66 : *prakṛtyā arthabodhanecchayā svabhāvena vā jātaḥ sphoṭa vyañjaka prathamaḥ prākṛtaḥ*
169. *VSLM.* p. 198 : *etena hrasvadīrghaplutair abhivyaktasphoṭe ...*
170. *PLM.* p. 66 : *tasmāt prākṛtāj jāto vikṛti-viśiṣṭa cirasthāyī nivarrtako vaikṛtikaḥ* ।
171. K.A.S. Iyer, "Bhartṛhari on *Dhvani*" *ABORI.* Vol. XLVI, 1965, Poona, pp. 62-63.
172. See S. D. Joshi's interpretation of indivisibility in the *Sphoṭa Nirṇaya*, pp. 35-37.
173. *PLM.* pp. 4-5 : *tatra vākyasphoṭo mukhyaḥ tasyaiva loke 'rthabodhakatvāt tenaivārthasamāpteśceti... tatra śāstraprakriyānirvāhako varṇa sphoṭaḥ* ; also *VBS*, 64, pp. 141-151, 175-176.
174. *SS.* 18, pp. 42-45.
175. *Ibid.*, p. 43; also *VP.* I.82-84.
176. *Ibid.*, p. 19 also, K. A. S. Iyer, *Bhartṛhari*, pp. 163, 165.
177. S. D. Joshi, *Sphoṭa Nirṇaya*, p. 59; also K. A. S. Iyer, *op. cit.*, pp. 162-163; *VP.* I.62; *VP.* II.238; *VBS.* 68.

2

Pratibhā

The concept of *pratibhā* according to Bhartṛhari

What is the *nimitta* of *śābdabodha* 'verbal knowlegde'? How does the listener grasp the meaning of a sentence? How is the meaning of a sentence communicated? Does the division of a sentence into words and that of words into their grammatical componets concern the listener? When the listener grasps the meaning of a sentence, does he take account of the inter-relation of the words in the sentence and of the phonemes constituting the words? Is a sentence to be regarded as the single meaning-bearing unit? These are the various questions which have puzzled the Indian philosophers for a long time and have been answered differently by Indian thinkers. In this connection Bhartṛhari holds the view that we understand the meaning of a sentence spontaneously. The meaning of the whole sentence appears as a flash of understanding *(pratibhā)*. Later on Ānandavardhana says that the speech act reveals the suggested sense and the beauty of the poem as a whole. Here we find a striking parallel between Bhartṛhari's conception of *pratibhā* Ānandavardhana's *dhvani,* although their approach is rather different. In this connection it would be worthwhile to study the concept of *pratibhā* as developed by Bhartṛhari in the *Vākyapadīya*.

Bhartṛhari in the *Vākyapadīya* discusses the concept of *pratibhā* in relation to the speech act. In a true Vedantin's spirit he proclaims that the entire cosmos is the outcome of *śabdabrahman* which is one and which manifests various forms because of its supreme power.[1] All cognitions spring from the *śabdabrahman*. The *pratibhā* as a type of cognition comes from the *śabdabrahman*.[2] The *pratibhā* is brought about by *śabdabhāvanā* which is abstract and emanates form residual impressions. When a child speaks, he inherits some residual impressions of actions from his previous birth.[3] These residual impressions inspire verbal behaviour in the new born child. But these impressions remain in a dormant stage in the new born infant. No instruction, but *pratibhā* activates these residual impressions which further put the verbal behaviour i.e. the movement of articulatory into motion.[4]

Pratibhā as *paśyantī* form of speech

The word principle is one. But for practical purposes it has a three-fold divisions, namely *vaikharī, madhyamā* and *paśyantī*. A fourth division, known as *parāprakṛti* is added to this list by the *vṛttikāra*.

The *vaikhrī* form of speech is that which is actually heard by the sense of hearing. It is manifested in the form of phonemes and heard in the form of sounds.[5] The *madhyamā* form of speech occurs in between *vaikharī* and *paśyantī*. It appears to have sequence. It is located in the mind, and must be assumed to be the cause of *lokavyavahāra* 'ordinary communication'. Sometimes it is accompanied by breath *(prāṇa)*.[6]

The *paśyantī* form of speech is the most obscure and the subtlest form of speech. The *vṛtti* states, 'the *paśyantī* is that in which sequence is merged and though it is one, the power to produce sequence has entered it. It is restless and also still in concentration, hidden and pure; the forms of object of knowledge have entered it or merged into it, or it has no form at all; it has the appearance of limited objects or of connected objects or the appearance of all objects has come to an end in it. Thus it has infinite variety'.[7]

Thus *paśyanti* is beyond ordinary communicaion, but even in this stage *yogins* have an understanding of division of words. It is also clear that the *Vākyapadīya* speaks of a division of speech into three and not into four elements.

The *vṛtti* again mentions, '(but) the supreme form of *paśyanti* is devoid of all correct forms, it is not mixed up and it is beyond worldly use.[8] Further the *vṛtti* defines, 'the *paśyantī* is indivisible and is entirely without sequence. It is the inner light, the subtle word, imperishable.[9]

Thus according the the *vṛtti*, the *paśyantī* stage of speech is abstract in nature. It has no sequence and no form. It is indivisible and beyond worldly use. One desirous of realising the *paśyantī* form of speech passes through various stages[10] and ultimately arrives at an undifferentiated state known as *pratibhā*. The *pratibhā* is a means to attain the supreme good. It is derived from word-principle. It is identical with the being. It is the source of modification. It has the power of accomplishment and things to be accomplished.[11] In an ordinary verbal communication one starts from *paśyantī* and goes upto *vaikharī*. But in *śabdapūrvayoga* or *vyāyoga* one has to commence from *vaikharī* and ascend upto *paśyantī*. The *vṛtti* states, 'after having reached the undifferentiated state of the word, *pratibhā*, he comes to the source of all differentiation. From that *pratibhā* in which all being is latent and which, due to the repetition of the union tends to produce its result, he (the aspirant) reaches the supreme source in which all differentiation is completely lost'.[12]

The *paśyanti* form of speech and *pratibhā* are literally the same. The *pratibhā* is undifferentiated form of speech. It is the source from which all differentiations of speech begin. It is identical with the *prakṛti* or *paśyantī* which is the subtlest form of speech.

But there is a difference between *paśyanti* and *pratibhā*. *pratibhā* is the means wheras *paśyantī* is the end. By virtue of *pratibhā*, the *paśyantī* form of speech is activated. H.G. Coward explains the difference as follows :

He says that the language passes through three levels. At the first level *pratibhā* as intuitive flashlike understanding operates. It appears in the form of the meaning of the sentence, or book, or poem as a whole. It is known as *paśyantī* (inner-speech). In the third level, the outer speech known as *vaikharī* constitutes the physical sound and reveals the phoneme-structure of the sentence or of the book etc. In between the first level and third level operates a second level which is known as *madhyamā vāk*. At the first level the word exists in the mind of the speaker as a unity or *sphoṭa.* At the second level (*madhyamā*) the unitary *sphoṭa* appears separated into sequence of thoughts, words and phrases none of which has as yet reached the level of uttered sounds.

At the third level, the speaker produces a sequence of different sounds, so that it appears to have differentiations. But though the listener hears a series of sounds, he perceives the utterance as a unity. In this way the speech (*vāk*) which is absolutely eternal and which is known as *pratibhā* or *paśyantī* in the begining becomes gradually externalised for the purpose of communication.[13]

Coward's explanation of the three levels of speech has been jumbled up, since in order to explain the *paśyanti* form of speech, he picked up the traits of *pratibhā* from the second *kāṇḍa* of the *Vākyapadīya*. *Paśyantī* is a mystical form of speech which is activated by still mystical *pratibhā* which is the source of differentiation. Both are abstaract in nature. In this respect K.A.S Iyer's speculation seems to be justified. He thinks that Bhartṛhari considers *pratibhā* from two angles. It may be the speaker's experience before he speaks. Again it may be the listener's experience after he hears the speaker's word. When the *Pratibhā* is analysed from the speaker's angle, the units of language in the form of words and sentences are not important. It is because at this stage *pratibhā* precedes the actual spoken language, and the language comes after *pratibhā* (*paśyantī*). This aspect of *pratibhā* is hinted in the *vṛtti.*[14] Again when the *pratibhā* is analysed from listener's point of view, it is absolutely related to the language, because it is occasioned by it. In the whole second *kāṇḍa* of the *Vākyapadīya*, Bhartṛhari has analysed this aspect of *pratibhā*.

Thus the *pratibhā* as *paśyantī* form of speech is mystic in nature. Its empirical traits are elaborated in the second *kāṇḍa* of the *Vākyapadīya*.

Semantic role played by *pratibhā* according to Bhartṛhari

In the first chapter, the *sphoṭa* is seen as the inner reality of speech. It is an image of the sound. It is manifested by the sound and it is of an integrated nature. The sentence-*sphoṭa* (*vākya- sphoṭa*) is the finest form of *sphoṭa* compared to that of phoneme-*sphoṭa (varṇa-sphoṭa)* and the word *sphoṭa* (*pada-sphoṭa)*. The sentence-*sphoṭa* of Bhartṛhari is unique in nature. In modern linguistics, the whole expression is taken into account when the meaning is to be conveyed. *Pratibhā* as meaning of the sentence is such a concept. According to Bhartṛhari, a sentence as a meaningful linguistic unit cannot be sub-divided further into smaller significant units. A sentence has parts which constitute its external structure. But all parts of a single integrated sentence do not convey the meaning of the sentence severally. The meaning of the sentence is something over and above the meaning of the parts. Thus the meaning of the sentence understood as a flash, according to Bhartṛhari, is *pratibhā*. Before the actual discussion begins on *pratibhā* we may refer to the closed frontier between *sphoṭa*, indivisibility of utterance and *pratibhā*. It has been stated that *sphoṭa* represents a sound-pattern i.e. phonetic level of speech. The *sphoṭa* as the indivisible meaning bearing unit is nowhere suggested by Bhartṛhari. It is developed by the later grammarians. It is based on a wrong interpretations of the text of Bhartṛhari and Patañjali. The identification of Bhartṛhari's concept of *śabda* with tha concept of *sphoṭa* on the part of later grammarians is the root cause of this confusion.

The *sphoṭa* is a subtle stage in between the actually uttered sound and meaning. It is an auditory image of the articulated sound. All the varieties of *sphoṭa* cannot work beyond the distinctive level of speech. Therefore, the phoneme-*sphoṭa* is an abstract image of the uttered sound of phoneme. The word-*sphoṭa* is an auditory impression of the articulated word. The sentence-*sphoṭa* is an auditory impression of the actually uttered sentence in its intergrated form. When a speaker makes a phonation act the sound produced by the vocal mechanism are heard. The auditorily perceived sound has two levels of existence. In the first level it is the sound which passes from the speaker's mouth and reaches the listener's ear. At this level the sound has the physical existence. In other words it is physical-sound. At the second level the physical-sound which dies away in the next moment, leaves an impression or idea of the uttered sound. This impression of the dying physical-sound is *sphoṭa*. It is an exact image or replica of the uttered sound. This is *sphoṭa* or sound-image.

Every expression consists of three elements i.e. the physical sound (*dhvani* or *nāda*), *sphoṭa* and the meaning. Bhartṛhari has treated the first two elements in the first *kāṇḍa* of the *Vākyapadīya*, and for the third element he has entirely devoted the second *kāṇḍa*.

According to him, the meaning of a sentence is *pratibhā*. When a speaker utters the sounds (*dhvani*) they die away in the next moment revealing the *sphoṭa* which is the auditory impression of the sound. Immediately thereafter *pratibhā* as a flash translates the impression of the sound into meaning. The gap between tha flash and understanding of the sentence meaning is not noticeable. Due to this, people think that both are identical. Sometimes the meaning of a sentence is understood even before the sentence is auditorily perceived.

The sentence-*sphoṭa* (*vākya-sphoṭa*) and the meaning of the sentence (*vākyārtha*)

The *vākyārtha (pratibhā)* and *vākya-sphoṭa* are two different concepts. The *vākya-sphoṭa* is a type of *sphoṭa* whereas the *vākyārtha* is the meaning of the sentence. The *vākya-sphoṭa* has to do with the auditory impression of articulated sentence whereas *pratibhā* connects the meaning conveyed by two different units of sentence. Thus auditorily sounds are first conceived and then their meanig is understood. In other words the *pratibhā* becomes activated only when the *sphoṭa* ceases to work.

The *vākya-sphoṭa* represents the auditory impression of uttered sentence. It does not necessarily represent the meaning conveying unit. If the *sphoṭa* doctrine arose as solution to the problem of the understanding of meaning, Bhartṛhari would not have introduced the additional doctrine of *pratibhā* to explain the process of understanding. The *sphoṭa* doctrine would have taken care of it. When Bhartṛhari postulates *pratibhā* for the meaning of the sentence, it is obvious that his *vākya-sphoṭa* is destined to explain some other things. According to him, the *vākya-sphoṭa* deals with how language is used and grasped rather than how language is understood. This sound-image of a sentence auditorily perceived is subsequently transformed into the meaning components in the mind.[16] The *pratibhā* arises spontaneously by virtue of which we cognise the meaning of the whole sentence. Bhartṛhari calls the flashlike working of *pratibhā* by the term *avicāritā. (VP*. II.144).

In this connection some leading scholars namely J. Brough, G. Sastri, K.K. Raja, K.A.S. Iyer and H.G. Coward hold contradictory views.[17] On the one hand they maintain that the *sphoṭa* in general and *vākya-sphoṭa* in particular has been assumed as a solution to the problem of the meaning of the sentence. On the other hand they argue that the *pratibhā* has the capacity to flash the meaning of the sentence, and on account of this, the *pratibhā* is the meaning of the sentence. This appears to be inconsistent. In this regard we find ample evidences. Some of them are quoted here.

Thus to the meaning bearing element which Patañjali calls *śabda*, Bhartṛhari applies the word *sphoṭa* and characterises it as eternal. Thus once more Bhartṛhari identifies the eternal meaning bearing unit *(śabda)* with *sphoṭa*.[18]

Contrary to the above view Iyer states, 'according to Bhartṛhari, the indivisible sentence is the unit of communication and that its meaning is understood in a flash (*pratibhā*). This meaning is also something indivisible, a complex cognition in which the central element is an action or process with its accessories closely associated with it.[19]

According to Iyer, if the *vākya-sphoṭa* theory is assumed to solve the process of communication, then *pratibhā* could not be assigned the same function. But Bhartṛhari clearly refers that *pratibhā* is the meaning of the sentence which is known by a flash of understanding (*VP*.II.143). In other words by a sudden flash of *pratibhā* the meaning of the sentence is comprehended.

Thus the *vākyārtha (pratibhā)* deals with how the language is understood and the *vādya-sphoṭa* deals with how the sounds are grasped. For the process of communication the impressions of the sounds of the sentence are to be transformed into semantic units in the mind by virtue of *pratibhā*.

Pratibhā as the meaning of the sentence

The *pratibhā* is the meaning of the sentence. It is indivisible. The sentence is the only means of communication. By communication, we mean, what the speaker transfers to the hearer. The linguistic communication is possible when the exprssion is indivisible. The worldly communication takes place through the sentence. According to Bhartṛhari, the concept of indivisibility refers to the unitary character of meaningful speech units. These speech units cannot be further subdivided into smaller meaningful units. So a sentence which is an indivisible speech unit cannot be further subdivided into parts. The division of a sentence into phonemes, stems, roots and suffixes from the point of communication is considered to be fictitious. But for grammatical use a sentence can be divided into constituent parts, and these parts connot be utilised for the purpose of communication. Bhartṛhari has this idea of indivisibility when he states that there are no phonemes in the word, and no words in the sentence (*VP*. I.73). Among the various interpretations of Bhartṛhri's idea of indivisibility, S.D. Joshi's interpretation seems to be convincing. He states that any meaningful speech unit in the form of a word or a sentence cannot be further divided into smaller meaningful units. In his own words 'however, Bhartṛhari's idea of indivisibility of *pada* and *vākya* is something else. He means that the significative level of language cannot be divided into smallest units i.e. phonemes, because phonemes have no correlation with meaning which is denoted by *saṁghāta* : 'whole'. He does not maintain that *pada* cannot be structurally divided into smaller differentiating units'.[20]

So far as the communication of meaning is concerned the whole expression is taken as a single indivisible unit. The phrases i.e. *eko'navayavaḥ śabdaḥ* 'the one indivisible word', *jātiḥsaṁghātavartinī* 'the universal inhering in the collection of words' and *buddhyanusaṁhṛtiḥ* 'the unification in the mind' support the above mentioned idea of indivisibility. [21] That is to say, in a sentence all parts merge themselves to bring out a single entity losing their separate identity.

Both the sentence and the meaning of the sentence are essential for communication. As the sentence is indivisible and without parts, so also the meaning of the sentence (*pratibhā)* is also indivisible and without parts. It cannot be split into smaller units in the form root-meaning, stem-meaning, suffix-meaning, word-meaning etc.

Adumbrating the idea of indivisibility, Bhartṛhari brings about an analogy of the cognition of a picture. He says, 'just as the picture is cognised through its different colours like blue etc. which belong to its parts, similarly, (the meaning of) the sentence absolutely self-sufficient and complete, is organised through (the meaning of) individual words which requires another'.[22]

The idea is, the cognition of a picture is a complex type of cognition which brings into its fold many objects. Every cognition is one. The *'citrajñāna'* as a cognition is also one. Though indivisible, there is a touch of multiplicity in it, because of the presence of many objects. A picture is a single entity, but the presence of different colours in it are signs of multiplicity which in fact do not affect the unity of colours.

Similarly, a sentence is a unity having words and phonemes with their diversity contributing something to the whole. Their presence does not harm the indivisible existence of the sentence. The words and phonemes merge into a single sentence leaving their multiple identities to build a single cognition. This single cognition of the sentence is different from the cognition of the picture which is different form the cognition of the colours used in it. In the same way, the cognition of the meaning of the sentence is one, and it is different from the parts. The phonomes, words etc. lose their individual meaning when they appear in the meaning of the sentence. Suggesting the oneness of sentence-meaning Bhartṛhari says, 'Just as the one entity, comprising the cognition of all objects is differentiated on the basis of distinction in what is cognised, so is the cognition of the sentence-meaning.[23]

Thus the 'sentence-meaning' *pratibhā* is a single cognition and it is indivisible. It is a single semantic unit of integrated languge which cannot be further divided into smaller semantic units. This is the idea of indivisibility of sentence-meaning *'akhaṇḍa vākyārtha'* of Bhartṛhari.

Pratibhā has no parts or sequence

The *pratibhā* is not only indivisible, but it has also no parts and sequence. It cannot be divided into word-meanings. The word-meanings separated form the sentence -meaning cannot be used for the purpose of communication. Keeping this view in mind Bhartṛhari analyses the views of the *Mīmāṁsakas* as *pūrvapakṣa,* and the views of the grammarians as *siddhānta-pakṣa.*

The old school of the *Mīmāṁsakas* maintain the *sakhaṇḍa pakṣa,* according to which, the sentence and the meaning of the sentence are the outcome of the coalescence of smaller units, namely, words and word-meaning. According to this view, a word is not a product of sentence analysis but an autonomous unit of meaning.

Bhartṛhari presents no less than eight different views on the nature of the sentence. Puṇyarāja says that five of these (i, ii, v, vii, viii) are based on the traditional *Mīmāṁsā* doctrine of the *abhihitānvayavāda* (the theory of mutual relation of separate word-meanings) which admits of the division of the sentence into parts, and the *anvitābhidhānavāda* (the theory of denotation of related word-meanings) which maintains that the meaning of words can be comprehended only as related to the sentence and that words have no independent meaning apart form the sentence. Strictly speaking the second view and the fourth view are based on the *abhihitānvayavāda,* while (i), (vii) and (viii) are based on the *anvitābhidhānavāda* The remaining three views (iii), (iv) and (vi) are based on the indivisibility of the sentence-meaning. Let us consider the eight theories on the nature of sentece in the order of enumeration.

(i) *ākhyātaśabdaḥ*'a verbal form' : According to this view, a sentence is defined by a verbal form. This view emphasised the fact that a verbal form is considered the most important element in the sentence, and it conveys its meaning as intimately related to other constituents of a sentence. This theory belongs to *anvitābhidhānavāda.*[24]

(ii) *saṁghātaḥ;* unified whole' : In accordance with this theory, a sentence, as a unit, conveys the meaning. This view is designated as *abhihitānvyavāda,* because it holds that the unified meaning of a sentence is always conveyed by the concentration of the word meaning.[25]

(iii) *Jātiḥ saṁghātavartinī* 'universal residing in the whole' : This generic view maintains that the listener is not concerned with the utterance of particular speakers, but with the type of utterance. The universal pattern of a sentence takes into account the whole structure and considers that the sentence is an undivided unit. Therefore this view represents the theory of indivisibility of a sentence.[26]

(iv) *eko,navayavaḥśabdaḥ* 'a single undivided utterance' : This view maintains that the sentence uttered by different persons at different times is in reality only one. The sentence-form is one, not because it belongs to the same class, but because it is essentially the same. This view also represents *akhaṇḍatva* of the sentence.[27]

(v) *kramaḥ* 'sequence': This view asserts that the sentence is regarded as a series of words. This view represents the *anvitābhidhānavāda.*[28]

(vi) *buddhyanusaṁhṛtiḥ* 'single conceptual unit': The unity of a sentence lies only in our mind. This notional form of a speech is regarded by Bhartṛhari as an internal word.[29]

(vii) *ādyaṁ padam* 'the first word' : The first word of a sentence may be looked upon as a sentence itself because it conveys its own meaning as well as its relation to the other words in the sentence This view belongs to the *anvitābhidhānavāda.*[30]

(viii) *pṛthak sarvapadaṁ sākāṅkṣam* 'all the words mutually expectant when taken separately'. This view asserts that the sentence is a collection of words which have expectancy for other words to complete their meaning. This view belong to *abhihitānvayavāda.*[31]

Bhartṛhari who is a staunch believer of indivisibility of sentence provides us with a number of arguments which support the theory of *akhaṇḍatva* 'indivisibilty'. To prove that the sentence-meaning is grasped as a unity, he takes his stand on epistemology. A cognition presenting different objects, its content is in reality a unitary entity, indivisible into several individual cognitions (*VP.* II.8-9). We say that a multi-coloured object is one integrated whole, although we can analyse it into parts such as blue etc. Bhartṛhari presents a number of illustrations i.e. *narasiṁha, gayal,* 'fetch a cuckoo from the woods'[32] to make his point clear. These will be discussed in the next section. Everywhere he tries to justify that the meanig is instantaneously grasped without knowing the division of an utterance and its meaning. Its division is aimed to meet the grammatical exigencies. The division is artificial and the sentence is ultimate reality.[33] while establishing the indivisibility of the sentence and its meaning, Bhartṛhari brings the discussion of a vital problem of linguistics, that is the role of the sequence in the process of communication. The sequence is connected with the sound. The sentence is manifested by the sounds and these sounds have sequence. This sequence is perceived in the mind. Because of this sequence the indivisible sentence appears to be divisible.[34] According to Bhartṛhari, the sound of the sentence which is uttered brings about certain sequences into mental comprehension. So the sounds are gradually and separately cognised. But this goes against the doctrine that the sentence has no parts. Bhartṛhari answers this objection. He says that the sounds occurring in the sentence may be divided into parts, but since the comprehension of the sentence is a mental one, it is artificial. The actual reality is an indivisible sentence utterance. In these words, 'the indivisible sentence is understood as having the capacity for sequence at the time of artificial separation. Hence its meaning, though devoid of all divisions is perceived as having division.[35]

Bhartṛhari says that sequence which belongs to the phonological act is imposed upon time. Intellect gets expanded alongwith the sequence of sounds it perceives and so sequence leaves its marking on intellect. Intellect has a dual ability, namely to grasp wholes with and without sequence, and so becomes capable of perceiving one object in 'singleness' and diversity. Finally, since sounds appear in our notion with a sequence, the meaning which comes from sounds also appear to have a sequence in our notion, although it is indivisible. These are pre-suppositions for understanding the character of meaning.

Bhartṛhari further states that which has no division is devoid of any sequence.[36] The sequence involves priority and posterity which are absent in the sentence. The sentence as true form of speech has no sequence in reality; it is one and indivisible.[37] The phonemes and words have no separate existence without the sentence.[38] Bhartṛhari explains it by an example. A single word segregated from a compound has no meaning. The word *'brāhmaṇa'* separated from a compound *'brāhmaṇa-kambala'* is meaningless. Similarly, if a word i.e. Devadatta is separated from a complete sentence, it is without meaning.[39] What is true of the sentence, holds true of the sentence-meaning (*pratibhā*). It is also partless and without any sequence.

***Reality of the words in the sentences according to Bhartṛhari** : Pratibhā,* as a meaning of the sentence rests on the whole sentence. The meanings of indivisible words reveal this unified meaning of the sentence. These words and word-meanings are a language apparatus responsible for the description of the language, but they do not exist in the described events. When something is uttered we understand the meanings. We do not care to analyse it into phonemes, words, stems, suffixes etc. This is the work of grammarians to meet the necessities of grammatical operations. But if we do the analysis of sentence in the course of utterance we fail to understand the meanings of the sentence. So in order to understand or communicate the meanings, the whole sentence is grasped and not the parts.

The *Mīmāṁsakas* utilise the parts of the sentence for their ritualistic end. They regard the parts of the sentence as realily. To them the individual words are real and they are the source of the sentence. They exist before the sentence. The sentence and sentence-meanings are the outcome of the smaller units in the form of words and word-meanings.

Bhartṛhari represents the views of the grammarians. According to him, the words have no reality in the meaningful language which is used for communication. His views on the words and their meanings and their relation with the sentence and sentence-meaning are analysed herewith.

(i) Bhartṛhari holds that for grammatical purposes a sentence is split into words. A word would have been real if it would not be changing. The word *'rājan'* has many inflectional forms. Similarly, the compound word *'rājapuruṣa'* is not exactly equivalent to its corresponding constituents as far as the meaning is concerned. The forms of individual words change from sentence to sentence because they appear differently in different inflections. This change is responsible for difference in the meanings of the said words.[40] So the words cannot be the reality of language.

(ii) We can offer various explanations in deriving a word. If the word has many meanings, any one of them can be used as the basis of derivation. The words such as *vaira, vāsiṣṭha, giriśa, ekāgārika* are explained variously by various people with different analysis. The word *vaira* can be derived in the sense of *tasyedam* (P.4.3.120), *tatra bhavaḥ* (P.4.3.53), *tata āgataḥ* (P.4.3.74), *labdham* (P.4.3.38). The word *vāsiṣṭha* can be derived in the sense of *vasiṣṭhasyāpatyam* (P.4.1.114), *tena proktam* (P.4.3.101), *kṛte granthe* (P.4.3.116). The word *giriśa* can be derived in the sense *giraṅu śete*(P.3.2.15), *girir asya asti* (P.5.2.100).

The word *aikāgārika* can be derived by P.5.1.113 from *ekāgāra* by adding *ṭhañ*. I do not find any other derivation of this word. Thus words can be analysed differently. Therefore, grammatical analysis is artificial. Similarly, abstraction of words from the sentence is also fictitious.

The grammatical elements come into existence only after dividing actual words and sentences into their constituent parts. According to Bhartṛhari, grammatical analysis is superimposed on words in the sentences. The words are abstracted from actual sentences in the same way as grammatical elements are abstracted by grammarians from words. Thus Bhartṛhari denies reality and independence of words in the sentences. The grammatical analysis or explanation handles stems and suffixes in various ways. A word can be analysed and derived variously whether in different systems of grammar or in the same system.[41]

(iii) In a sentence each subsequent word in association with the preceding word conveys the sense. When a sentence is uttered, each preceding word gives its own meaning to the subsequent word. The

> subsequent word denotes its meaning alongwith the relation of the meanings of the preceding word. Since the full meaning of a sentence in this way can be grasped from the last word only, the preceding words and their meanings shall be left without any purpose. Therefore, the theory which maintains that the sentence meaning is the meaning denoted by the last word of the series, must be abandoned. This leads to the conclusion that a sentence and its meaning are single units and they cannot be cut into parts.[42]

A man-lion *(narasiṁha)* is a single entity quite different from a lion and man put together. But a layman thinks that there are partial similarities of a man-lion, viz. with a man and lion. Similarly, a '*gayal*' appears to have some parts which are not quite similar to those of a cow. A layman describes the situation by saying that some parts of a *gayal* are familiar to him and some are not. Following the same line people consider that the meaning of a particular word in a sentence is known to him or not. In reality the whole sentence is unknown to him. The sentence 'fetch a cuckoo from the woods' is not understood first as a sequence of words put together, because the full meaning of 'fetch' in the sentence (i.e. mode of fetching) is only grasped together with the meaning of cuckoo, and someone ignorant of the meaning of the cuckoo is therefore to some extent ignorant of the meaning of the rest of the sentence. The word units in a sentence can be indentified as one-word sentence or as manyword sentences, but for the speaker and hearer they are primarily single sentence entities. The words and word meanings are the creations of grammarians. The grammar being conscious of speakers and listeners analyse and classify sentence meanings in terms of smaller components. In the words of Bhartṛhari, 'just as in the words of a '*gayal*' or 'man-lion' even if they become the object of a single cognition (i.e. even if they are perceived as a single whole), one recognises partial similarities (in such a whole which (whole) belong to a different species together. (In such a situation), a stupid person always thinks that his lack of knowledge is with reference to the part only, which he conceives of as being unfamiliar and as not seen before (But, in fact, according to Bhartṛhari, the whole object is unknown to him).

Similarly, when the sentence, 'fetch a cuckoo from the woods' is totally different from the sentence 'fetch a tree from the woods' owing to (its) conclusion with the word *pika* 'cuckoo' etc. (the stupid person thinks that he has apprehension of meaning as if (coming from) the similar part when it is (actually) not so.[43]

When a person, who has not previously heard the name of a bird 'cuckoo' hears the sentence, 'fetch a cuckoo from the wood', he thinks that he cannot understand the sentence, because he has no knowledge of the word cuckoo'. However, it would be adequate to say that the person concerned cannot assign a meaning to the word 'cuckoo' because he does not understand the sentence as a whole. When the stupid person compares the two sentences : 'fetch a cuckoo' from the wood' and 'fetch a tree from the woods', he thinks that anyone can perceive the same meaning from the identical words. However, according to Bhartṛhari, the substitution of the word, *pika* 'cuckoo' for the word *vṛkṣa* 'tree' renders the sentence entirely different. If the meaning of the one word is not understood then the whole sentence is not understood. Thus Bhartṛhari thinks that isolated words are in fact only grammatical fiction and apparatus of grammatical analysis.

From the above discussion it is clear that the meanings of the words used in the middle of the sentence are unreal. In the course of utterance the words and word meanings no doubt help in the cognition of the sentence and its meanings.They only help in the comprehension of the sentence and the meaning of the sentence until the whole utterance is complete.[44] Keeping this in mind, Bhartṛhari says, (irrespective of the fact) whether (words are) meaningless because they are(fictional) devices, or meaningful because (they denote individual) word meanings, when they are uttered in a sequence, words convey the sentence-meanings which has a different character (from a mere series of individual word meanings).[45] It should not be assumed that words are absolutely useless. In reality the cognition of the word meanings help the cognition of the sentence-meaning.[46] When a sentence is uttered, each word, in course of utterence, contributes to the totality of sentence-meaning. But when the utterance is complete, the situation becomes different and the sentence meaning is understood as a flash which is altogether different from the individual or collective word meanings.[47] The units of meaning cognised from the sentence as a whole is called *pratibhā*. This *pratibhā* is dependant on the individual word meanings which function only as a means to reveal *pratibhā*. The meaning of a sentence is not grasped from the knowledge of the lexical meaning assigned to the words, but from the whole utterance. The sentence meaning is grapsed by *pratibhā* which is the guiding instinct for the understanding of the meaning conveyed by a language.

The sentence meaning (*pratibhā*) is over and above the word meanings

According to Bhartṛhari, the sentence and its meanings are more than a coalescence of words and word meanings respectively. An ordinary collection of word meanings in particualr order cannot build a sentence meaning. When a collection of word meanings is accompanied by a flash of understanding it is called the meaning of the sentence.[48] It is more than the sum total meaning of the words. This meaning is primary meaning or denotative meaning of the sentence. It is believed that the grammarians approve only the primary sense which is based on lexical meaning. They deal with the common speech in the daily use. But there are expressions used in everyday speech activity whose meanings cannot be understood by knowing the meanings of the sentence only. In such cases the primary senses fail to express the import of the sentence. Bhartṛhari has observed in the expressions of worldly use that apart from the ordinary meaning of the sentence there are some extra-lingual meanings which are over and above the ordinary meaning of the sentence.[49] This is a secondary meaning of the expression which is either based on speaker's intention, or on contextual factors. Although a sentence is regared as a basic meaningful unit, sometimes its meaning cannot be fixed apart from the context. Context means what precedes any particular passage of the text. In its wider sense it means the circumstances in which a speech act occurs. Any further factor that helps to determine the meaning of a speech is called context. Bhartṛhari gives a list of such factors.

Factors which determine the meaning of the sentence

Every sentence has external as well as internal force. We do not determine the meaning of utterances only by external words or sentences but also by the manner of the speech, the expression of speechless face, speaker's movements, situation, propriety, place and time. Such contextual factors which determine the special meaning of speech are enumerated by Bhartṛhari. Bhartṛhari's word *prakaraṇa* is to be understood in a wider sense. It means various types of circumstances.[50] Again in the case of obscurity, the primary word meanings are determined by the connection, separation, association, opposition, meaning, context, indication, presence of another word, suitability, propriety, place, time, gender and accent etc.[51] By stating these factors Bhartṛhari has laid down the foundation stone of a type of suggestion, namely *abhidhā-mūlā vyañjanā* (suggestion based on the power of denotation).

From the above discussion it is clear that the concept of *pratibhā* of Bartṛhari frames general conditions for the spoken language. The sentence is the ultimate reality of the speech and its meaning is *pratibhā*. This *pratibhā* is indivisible, self completed and without sequence. As a semantic unit, *pratibhā* cannot be further subdivided into smaller semanitc units. By means of it, one can communicate his ideas. In the course of human communication, the words and word meanings rendered themselves subservient[52] to the sentence and sentence meaning respectively. The sentence meaning appears as a sudden flash of understanding.[53] The individual word meanings function only as a means of revealing *pratibhā* .

Similarly, according to Ānandavardhana, the suggested sense is that in which the primary senses of the expression subordinate themselves to the beauty of the poetic expression.[54] This suggestive meaning brings extraordinary charm to the poetic expression. When this suggestive meaning is comprehended, the primary sense becomes colourless.

Thus it is clear that Ānandavardhana has founded his famous *dhvani* doctrine on the same general conditions on which Bhartṛhari has developed his *pratibhā* doctrine. He has successfully extended the ideas coming from words or from impressions left by words to emotive language which is classified into thousandfold divisions.

This problem will be discussed exhaustively in the fourth chapter.

Pratibhā as an instinct

The instinct is an inner urge which inspires all activities of animals. According to Bhartṛhari, *pratibhā* is an instinct which regulates all activities of the creatures. In spring season, *pratibhā* transforms the voice of a male cuckoo into the sweetest melody. It teaches the spiders to weave their weds. It is of the nature of inner drive that creates the desire for food and shelter, singing and mating, fear and attack amongst wild beasts and birds. This *pratibhā* is the inner urge in birds which creates a desire to build nest before germination. It also acts as an inner urge for perpetual hostility amongst mouse and cat, serpent and mongoose, horse and buffallo etc. It also creates the urge of love and hatred. It generates the idea of swimming among all species.[55] In other words, all mental and physical propensities spring from *pratibhā*. Thus, *pratibhā* is the guiding instinct which by appropriate meaning-whole, leads to proper action. It is not only comprehension or manifestation of an idea, but also the knowledge of how to act. It covers practically the whole domain of acting based on instinct, and, therefore, it is identical in man and animal. The *pratibhā* is a unifying and selecting instinct which organise the isolated parts of a meaning situation into a structural whole of meaning. Without *pratibhā* we cannot grasp the situation. How *pratibhā* unifies and selects can not be explained, but certainly in our acting we are motivated by *pratibhā*.

Acquisition of language by a new-born child

At the time of birth, the human infants do not know how to speak. But they have an inner urge of expression which remains latent in them. This inner urge contains the seed of knowledge residing latent in each human being. The infant tries variously. Suddenly *pratibhā* activates the vocal cords as a flash and the child utters his first speech.[56]

Bhartṛhari has referred to the causes of language acquisition by children.

(i) He states that *pratibhā* is activated by 'tradition' *āgama* accompanied by *bhāvanā*.[57] In Vedic learning where direct reasoning fails, tradition or continuity works.[58] Even sages depend upon the previous tradition to understand religious scriptures.[59]

(ii) Referring to *saṁskāra* as the cause of *pratibhā*

Bhartṛhari argures that the new-born infants learn to acquire language on the basis of the impressions *saṁskāra* accrued from the deeds of previous birth. The *adṛṣṭa*[60] arouses the predisposition the present existence, recollecting the activities of the past in the form of 'remembrance' *smṛti*. This awakened predisposition persuades the child to speak. Bhartṛhari says, 'all knowledge of what is to be done in this world depends upon the word. Even the child, with its residual traces from the previous birth has such knowledge.[61] Not only the *adṛṣṭa* revives the latent speaking ability in human infants, birds and beasts, but also it causes the extra-ordinary perception of *pitṛs*, ghosts etc. with the impressions of the deeds of previous birth.[62]

(iii) Bhartṛhari has stated that, according to some, *pratibhā* is produced by constant 'practice' *abhyāsa*. Some are of the opinion that this practice is inherited from the previous birth, whereas others hold that it is possible in this present birth.[63]

A human child and animals understand certain meanings because of instruction and practice. The horses act in a particular way when they hear the sound of the whip. The sound of the whip flashes *pratibhā* in them which sets them to a particular type of action. Similarly, the elephant knows the command from the use of the hooks. A particular movement of the hook creates *pratibhā* in the elephant which makes it to understand what the master wants. Therefore, among animals *pratibhā* is a non-speaking language which sets them to a particular action.[64] When a particular language is repeatedly used before the children and animals, it creates a particular attitude in a particular situation. Then they learn the implication of the language. Therefore, it is assumed that *pratibhā* has flashed the cognition.

Amongst the three causes of *pratibhā* (i.e. unbroken

tradition, predisposition and practice) it is very difficult to say which view Bhartṛhari favours. He does not favour that convention is the cause of *pratibhā*.[65] Most probably he favours that the predisposition or the residual impressions of the verbal action of the previous existence, help the infant to acquire the language. All our actions and psychological activities remain compressed in subtle form which reappear as innate tendencies in the next birth. This is the central theme of Indian philosophy. Bhartṛhari is a staunch follower of Vedantic system which approves the doctrine of rebirth in which the concept of *saṁskāra* plays a vital role. So it will not be redundant to conclude that Bhartṛhari accepts residual impression as the cause of *pratibhā*.

Modern psychological research[66] claims that every creature is endowed with certain inborn instincts, such as the desire of hunger, shelter, fear etc. These instincts induce one to action. Form this standpoint *pratibhā* can be considerd to be an instinct.

In connection with language, when a word or a sentence is uttered, it produces a particular *pratibhā* in the listener's mind. At this stage, the utterance does not denote any external object. The utterance initially creates *pratibhā* in the listener's mind which later stands for the thing meant. For instance, when the word *vṛkṣa* is uttered, it creates *pratibhā* in the listener's mind without directly standing for the object. Goading on elephant with the hook produces some kind of *pratibhā* in the mind of the elephant.[67] It does not mean that linguistic expressions 'produced directly by words'[68] are the cause of *pratibhā*. In fact, *pratibhā* is a peculiar type of instint or intuition or insight which induces one to action. It is a mystery. Even a person who experiences it does not describe it.[69] It is beyond the description of words in terms of 'such as this'.[70] Its comprehension is absolutely mental.[71] It is always new and real.[72] It is indivisible.[73] Its division into parts, which are fictitious, only help to know its indivisibility.[74] It impels animals to act.[75] Several objects merge their identity into this single entity.[76] Everyone can experience it. But no one can ascertain how it works. It is perceived through a series of errors.[77] The sequences in the uttered sentence are helpful to explain it.[78] The *pratibhā* is a power to grasp a situation and to act. It is very difficult to define *pratibhā*.

Modern psycholinguists have tried to find out the cause of instinct which inspires the child to speak. In this connection Gray[79] holds that the ideas remain in the speaker's mind in a vague form. If an idea flashes suddenly without effort or previous thought, it is due to reason only. This flash of understanding is automatic and quasi-instinctive. Thus he finds that the role of instinct is not so useful in the child's acquisition of language.

Hörmann analyses different views on language acquisition theory. He refers[80] that against Thorndike's Skinner's language acquisition theories, *Tolman* argues that before the child suddenly utters his first word, he has learnt something. The babbling is pre-linguistic sound contact brought to the child by the environment. This is called 'Latent Learning'. Conditions for this 'Latent Learning' may be that the organism does not execute the response to be learned. There is no differential reinforcement, and the learning process can only be identified at a later stage by the effect it has produced.

Though this 'Latent Learning' theory goes nearer to Bhatṛhari's cause of *pratibhā* (i. e. practice in this present birth), it fails to explain the instinctive ability of the child to acquire language.

Hörmann states two more views as to how the child acquires language. Accordingly, Carmichael[81] (1964) holds that the child speaks because his anatomical, psychological conditions and motor mechanisms of speech are ready to function at birth. This biological theory also fails to explain the child's instinctive ability hinted by Bhartṛhari.

Mowrer[82] believes that beyond all actions of the infants lies the instinctive emotional tendency which sets the child to speak.

Bhartṛhari's concept of *pratibhā* as a means of language acquisition for children can be better explained by Chomsky' s cognitive capability'[83] Every newborn child has 'cognitive capability' for language. This power has creative and intuitive ability. The 'cognitive capability' is dependant on the sentence meaning and commonsense understanding. By commonsense understanding, Chomsky means, a cognition by intuition.[84] The cognitive development in babies goes beyond the language. Language is a means to express cognitive intention.[85] According to him, the infants have a vision which helps them to see the objects.[86] They develop a grammar (generative) in themselves by intuition to express themselves.[87]

What Chomsky has emphasised for language acquisition is intuition. Though in treatment he is different from Bhartṛhari, in reality both *pratibhā* and intuition serve the same purpose. Both are instinctive in nature and explain the process by which the newborn infant acquire language.

Pratibhā according to rhetoricians

Bhartṛhari's semantic and psychological study of *pratibhā* becomes a source of inspiration to the rhetoricians. Ānanadavardhana (875-900 AD) has been tremendously influenced by the concept of *pratibhā*, adumbrated by Bhartṛhari. According to him, *pratibhā* encircles all the activities of the universe. It includes mainly the linguistic and psychological activities. On this guideline of Bhartṛhari, Anandavardhana builds his superstructure of *pratibhā*. According to him, *pratibhā* encircles the whole gamut of *rasa*. It includes the emotive language and various psychological strata of human beings in relation to refined poetic activity.

Both these great thinkers are similar on many matters.

They believe that *pratibhā* cannot be explained by words. But it exists and regulates all verbal and non-verbal activity of all creatures. They further agree that *pratibhā* appears as a flash of understanding. No reason can explain its manifestation. It is a creative faculty which governs all activities. It is intuitive in nature. Bhartṛhari has applied the theory of *pratibhā* in connection with the meaning grasped from the ordinary speech. Ānandavadhana applied it to poetic language. Ānandavardhana's assimilation and extension of the concept of *pratibhā* of Bhartṛhari has led to a new wonderland of poetry through the magical touch of suggestion.

Before a thorough discussion on Ānandavardhana's idea on *pratibhā,* a bird's eye view of his predecessors' understanding of it is essential. This attempt will be conducive to a proper evaluation of Ānandavardhana's concept of *pratibhā,* in contrast to his predecessors' thoughts.

In the field of Sanskrit poetics the concept of *pratibhā* emerges as an essential equipment of making poetry. Bharata, the earliest systematic writer of dramaturgy, does not exclusively mention *pratibhā* in the *Nāṭya Śāstra.* But it is apprehended that he has the idea of *pratibhā* or creative genius when he contemplated to stage the '*Amṛtamanthana*' for the first time. Further, Bharata says that Brahmā is the cosmic creator. It therefore suggests that creative power is an essential factor in the poet.[88]

Rhetoricians other than Bharata mention other casual factors of poetry, namely, 'erudition' *vyutpatti* and 'practice' *abhyāsa* alongwith *pratibhā.* Another term for *pratibhā* used by these scholars is *śakti* 'innate power'.

Bhāmaha is the first rhetorician who emphasised that *pratibhā* is the most essential element for composing poetry. One is able to read scriptures with the help of the teacher, but no one can compose poetry without creative ability, known as *pratibhā.*[89] Bhāmaha further states that effort and practice are less essential elements in comparison to *pratibhā*.[90] The factor *yatna* 'effort' mentioned by him is similar to the 'erudition' *vyutpatti* of later rhetoricians.

According to Daṇḍin, *pratibhā* is an inherent facultly of a poet.[91] It comes to the poet as residual traces of an earlier action. Daṇḍin does not refer to the nature of *pūrva vāsanā*. Whether *pūrva vāsanā* implies the impressions gathered in this birth or previous birth, is not clear from Daṇḍin's phrase. The *pratibhā* is a wonderful faculty of natural disposition and inborn gift in the poet. But in lieu of this faculty one can acquire poetic power by virtue of diligent study and sincere practice.[92]

Vāmana proposes that *pratibhānam* or intuition is the germinal cause of poetic faculty.[93] But it is not the sole reason of composing poetry, since it is one amongst other casual factors namely 'erudition' *lakṣyajñāna* or *anuśilanam*, 'practice' *abhiyoga*' 'knowledge from the preceptor' *vṛddha-sevā*, use of proper words *'āvekṣana'* and 'concentration' *avadhāna*.[94] Vāmana's approach to *pratibhā* is peculiar. He emphasises the importance of the knowledge of the three, namely the world, the branches of learning and miscellany. Under miscellany he puts *kāvyāṅgas* as a subsidiary thing which always serves as a help to the main thing *'pradhānas-yopakārakam aṅgam'*. In the *vṛtti* of *sūtra* No. 25 and 29 he states that *aṅgas are* necessary and helpful for poetic production. It is a wonder that though Vāmana has given prime importance to *pratibhā* without which the poetic production is impossible as a sprout without a seed, he has put this *pratibhā* as a *kāvyaṅga* in the miscellany.

According to Rudraṭa, *pratibhā* is a poetic power which awakens in the concentrated mind many novel ideas. Easily and quickly it finds appropriate expressions for appropriate purposes. It is twofold in nature, namely, 'inborn' *sahajā* and 'cultivated' *utpādyā*. In its first aspect, it is natural faculty which causes the erudition and practice.[96] In its second aspect, it is attained through learning and practice.[97]

Rudraṭa's concept of *pratibhā* differs from others. The two terms, *visphuraṇa* 'bursts forth' and *vibhānti* 'revealed' (*KLR*.1.15) imply immediate manifestation of *pratibhā* as spontaneous outburst which can be comparable to Ānandavardhana's spontaneous *pratibhā*.[98] But when Ānandavardhana's concept of *pratibhā* moves with suggestion, *Rudraṭa's* concept of *pratibhā* operates with erudition and practice only.

As an *ālaṁkārika,* Rudraṭa has associated *pratibhā* with the essential elements of poetry. These essential elements of poetry, according to him, are words and sense, figures and styles. In fact, external arrangements and embellishments of expressions are not essential elements of poetry. It is the suggestion with which *pratibhā* should have been associated. Though Rudraṭa has gone a step further in the quest of the real cause of poetry in contrast to his predecessors, he could not dismember *śakti* from other casual factors of poetry. This has brought *pratibhā,* from the highest creative faculty down to the general intelligence to which Hemacandra refers to by the term *prajñā.* But in spite of all discrepancies, Rudraṭa unconsciously comes nearer to the elements of suggestion in the treatment of figures which are perfectly displayed in the *Dhvanyāloka* of Ānandavardhana.

Ānandavardhana's concept of *pratibhā*

Ānandavardhana has edumbrated the concept of *pratibhā* in a unique fashion. Earlier rhetoricians concluded that *pratibhā* is an essential equipment for composing poetry. They connected *pratibhā* with the words and senses only because according to them both these elements constitute the body of poetry. But Ānandavardhana is quite different from others. For the first time in Indian poetics he associated *pratibhā* with suggestion. Though the *dhvanikāvya* can be divided into *vastudhvani, alaṁkāradhvani* and *rasadhvani,* the last one is the best form of peotry. This *rasadhvani* absorbs the entire charm of 'suggestion' *vyañjanā*.[99] Ānandavardhana's *pratibhā* in its novel approach encircles the whole gamut of *rasa*.

Nature of *pratibhā* according to Ānandavardhana

Ānandavardhana in his epoch-making work *Dhvanyāloka* has treated the concept of *pratibhā* differently. His concept of *pratibhā* has been rendered as 'poetic imagination'. Sometimes the concept of *prajñā* comes together with *pratibhā*. In ordinary jargon, both *pratibhā* and *prajñā*, appear to have the same implication. But as a matter of fact both the concepts are diametrically opposite. *Pratibhā* is the creative imagination. It is flashed in the rare great poets of the stature of Vālmiki and Kālidāsa, etc. As a special poetic vision or fancy, it surpasses conventional limitations. Only a few poets have the privilege to possess it. Therefore *pratibhā* is a type of special kind of intelligence.

But *prajñā* is the general intelligence. All minor poets and critics possess this quality. When *pratibhā* offers multitudinal innovations to the poetic speech, *prajñā* provides repetitions. Again when *pratibhā* produces only poetry *'kavikarma'*, *prajñā* leads to the requirements for the study of *śāstras*. *Pratibhā* erupts like the burst of the volcano and poetry emerges from it in thousandfold new forms.

Thus a 'special type of intelligence' *viśiṣṭāprajñā* known as creative imagination is *pratibhā* and the 'general intelligence' *sāmānyāprajñā* is known as ordinary *prajñā*.[100] Ānandavardhana's concept of *pratibhā* has to do with communicating something more than the grammatical or logical meaning of the sentence.

Ānandavardhana in his *Dhvanyāloka* has mentioned the nature of *pratibhā* as an instantaneous flash *parisphurantaṁ pratibhāviśeṣam*. When the great poets compose poetry, they do not engage in a lot of deliberations and contemplation. The poetic speeches, ever pregnant with sweet senses flow form their mind as an instantaneous flash. This abrupt manifestation of beautiful poetic compositions in their mind is by virtue of *pratibhā.* The *pratibhā* is ever bright and unique. The poetic speeches are the touchstones of this rare creative faculty. In the words of Ānandavardhana, "the speech of first rate poets streaming forth that sweet content reveals clearly their extraordinary genius which is as unearthly as it is ever bright"[101] Ānandavardhana's statements, *parisphurantam, abhivyanakti* and *jhaṭiti avabhāsanam* suggest the abrupt manifestation of *pratibhā* on the minds' plane. As its presence is observed like a flash, its absence is felt immediately. The ignorance of the poets may be noticed, but their lack of creative genius *pratibhā* draws immediate attention.[102] Ānandavardhana gives an example. In *Kumārasaṁbhavam* the incident of love play of Śiva and Pārvatī has been delineated. But the impropriety and indecorum caused by the obscenity of love sports of eternal father and mother, have been camoufleged there by Kālidāsa's superb genius. Here poet's powerful genius covers the blemishes of the poetry and enhances the beauty of *śṛṅgārarasa.*[103] In another context Ānandavardhana remarks that the principles of poetry are designed such as to reveal the concealed ideas. While the proponents of the *rīti* school show the vague flashes of poetry, the *dhvani* theorists demonstrate it clearly by suggestive elements.[104] This principle of poetry as a flash reveals the intention of the great poets. This flash is known as *pratibhā.* Ānandavardhana further states that *pratibhā,* as a flash, gives a new dimension to the poetic speech which can absorb the old objects and ideas.[105] While defining poetry Ānandavardhana has pointed out the flashlike nature of *pratibhā.* He says, "like-wise that (suggested)sense bursts forth in a flash in the minds of sensitive readers who (wish to) experience the essential meaning (of poetry) and who (are) really indifferent to the explicit meaning".[106] Not only the speakers (poets) of the poetic expressions comprehend this nature of *pratibhā*, but also the listeners (critics and readers) feel the pulse of *pratibhā* as an unique flash. The connoisseurs form favourable opinion on poetry because of the existence of *pratibhā* in them. Ānandavardhana rightly remarks, "Whatever themes it might be so long as it produces the impression in the minds of peopie : yes, this is a lovely and unique flash".[107] As according to Ānandavardhana *pratibhā* has flash-like nature, according to Bhartṛhari *pratibhā* has some flash-like nature. All verbal activities are the outcome of *pratibhā*.[108] According to Bhartṛhari, *pratibhā* is a unifying and selecting instinct which organises the isolated parts of meaning into a structured whole of meaning. The *pratibhā* makes to understand an utterance. Bhartṛhari's *pratibhā* includes grammatical meanings as well as speakers' intentions. But according to Ānandavardhana, affective and emotional values are conveyed by *pratibhā*. Āanandavardhana's *pratibhā* investigates the facts of expression from the standpoint of their affective and emotional context. Details of this aspect will be discussed in the fourth chapter of this work.

Pratibhā as conditioned by rasa

In relation to the concept of *pratibhā*, Ānandavardhana has tremendous influence on Bhaṭṭa Tauta (950-980 A. D.), the celebrated teacher of Abhinavagupta. According to him *pratibhā* is directly conditioned by *rasāveśa* which produces creativity at once vivid and beautiful. Ānandavardhana has explained this nature of *pratibhā* by the famous story, as to how the first poet Vālmiki was blessed with the creative genius. In a serene sylvan setting a couple of Krauñca birds were dallying. Suddenly one of them was killed by a hunter, the other one wailed being afflicted by the separation form his female counterpart. Vālmīki watched this sanguinary scene and his heart was overpowered by deep sorrow. This sorrow got released as a spontaneous outburst which took the shape of a couplet.[109] This sorrow is the permanent mood of *karuṇarasa*. The cause of Vālmīki's sorrow is the sight of the blood-pool as well as the lamentation of the surviving Krauñca bird. So this sorrow is not poet's personal sorrow. Had it been so, the poet would have wept like ordirany mortals, which would have made him unable to compose any poetry. He is overwhelmed by pathetic sentiment which is extraordinary and manifested spontaneously. In the course of the manifestation, the sentiment takes the shape of unprecedented poetic speech. This incident proves that the creative process of the poet is spurred into activity because of *rasāveśa*.[110]

Ānandavardhana has vividly analysed in the fourth *udyota* of the *Dhvanyāloka* that poet's *pratibhā* is fruitful only in relation to *rasa*. *Pratibhā* gets endlessness by virtue of principal suggestion and subordinate suggestion. In other words, the touch of *dhvani* gives many varieties to *pratibhā*. If a poet has creative imagination, he can bring variety and superb charm to the poetic speech. Only with a single variety of *dhvani*, the stale speech can appear new, if it is handled by a poet having *pratibhā*.[111]

So according to Ānandavardhana, *dhvani* is the touchstone of *pratibhā*. The element of suggestion makes the *dhvanikāvya*. *Rasadhvani* is the finest form of poetry which completly exhausts the suggestion. *Rasa* is an undercurrent in all elements of poetry. It remains in all figures, styles, blemishes, merits and *saṅghaṭanā* etc. All these elements are conditioned by *rasa*.

Rasa belongs to a class of *dhvani* called '*asaṁlakaṣyakrama vyaṅgya*' at once revealed without noticing the order'. Here *rasa* is simultaneously suggested by the denotative sense, but this denotative sense is not asscociated with *rasa* inseparably revealed.[112] The *rasa* is the soul of a poem whose body is constituted of a 'theme' *itivṛtta* and a 'style' *vṛtti*.[113]

In ordinary communication temporal sequence remains. But in the case of *rasa*, the process of realisation is so rapid that the sequence is not closely felt. It is absolutely incorrect to hold that *rasa* is communicated at a time when the denotative function exhausts its operation. Words in music have some temporal sequence between the hearing of the sound and the appreciation of suggested sentiments. But in cases where the suggested *rasa* is in perfect harmony with the expressed sense, the temporal sequence may not be closely marked. It is because various 'agencies' *ghaṭanā* operate too rapidly for the process of realisation of *rasa*.[114] Rasa emanates not only from words and sentences, but also from phonemes, 'modes of arrangements' *saṅghaṭanā* and from entire 'composition' *prabandha*.[115] The entire poetic work can be charged with striking novelty if the poet concentrates on *rasa* and other complimentary accessories of *rasa*.[116] The range of *rasa* is infinite. Its infinitude is due to various stimuli, responses and fleeting moods. Ānandavardhana has rightly remarked that, "the extensive domain of (*dhvani*) such as *rasa*, etc. should be followed according to this method (namely the use of *dhvani*) in all its varied forms, for it is by recourse to this, that the path of poetry, otherwise limited, reaches into infinity".[117] The ancient poets deal with *rasa* in various ways, so it becomes a multitudinous. The poets even handle a subject culled from ordinary life.The subjects tinged with the muse of gifted poets appear to be unknown in common life.[118] The celebrated poets give great importance to *rasa*. *Rasa* attaches poetic beauty to the dry and insignificant things. Even the inanimate objects appear to be animated by the touch of *rasa*.[120] Here he follows Bhartṛhari, according to whom, *pratibhā* as instinctive urge in the cuckoo alters its note in spring. The *pratibhā* teaches the insects etc. to weave their webs. It impels the wild beasts and birds for eating end mating (*VP* II.149-150).

Ānandavardhana further states that *rasa* makes old senses into new one. In a beautiful analogy he describes that just as at the advent of spring season the old trees appear quite new and charming, similarly old meaning and themes become new in poetry in association with *rasa*[1.21] By the touch of *rasa*, the poetic themes acquire manifoldness and novelty.[122] This *rasa* excells every variety of suggestions. So the poets should concentrate on delineating it properly.[123]

Repetition of poetic description does not vanquish novelty if *rasa* prevails there. In the battle scence of the *Rāmāyaṇa* and the *Mahābhārata* there are a number of repetitions of the same theme and technique. But the presence of *rasa* in those descriptions covers blemishes caused by repetitions, and lends wonderful charm to the epic. In both the epics through several varieties of *rasas* are described, only one *rasa* dominates over the other *rasas*. For example, in the *Rāmāyaṇa* the sentiment of 'pathos' *karuṇarasa* prevails over the other *rasas*. Vālmīki preserves this unity of one *rasa* varily from the begining to the end in the eternal loss of Sītā from Rāma.[124]

Similarly, in the *Mahābhārata*, in spite of the existence of various sentiments and heterogeneous elements, the unity of one *rasa* is preserved throughout the epic. The *Mahābhārata* ends with a note of dejection and despair. In its descriptions various kingdoms bubbling with activites, and great heroes even Lord Kṛṣṇa meet the inevitable doom. The whole work is surcharged by the undercurrent of final emancipation *mokṣa*. All types of pleasures and prosperities as well as heroism are temporary and trivial. So there is an inevitable need for tranquility which is the eternal cry of this great epic. Here, from poetic point of view, the *śāntarasa* 'sentiment of quietude' is the principal *rasa*. It is characterised by heightened tranquillity and happiness at the cessation of desire.[125]

In the *Harivaṁśa* also the principle of unity in the relation to chief *rasa* is preserved. Vyāsa suggests that devotion to ultimate Reality (i.e. Lord Vāsudeva) through rigorous spiritual discipline can end the failures and frustrations of mundane existence. The *Gitā* proclaims this idea clearly.[126]

From the critical assessment of Ānandavardhana's analysis, it is clear that poetic speech can attain novelty at everytime, if the principle of unity for a particular *rasa* is preserved throughout the work.[127] According to Ānandavardhana, the idea of *rasa (rasārtha)* is a unity, just as according to Bhartṛhari the idea or meaning of a sentence (*pratibhā*) is a unity. We will discuss it at great length in the last chapter.

The main *rasa* unifies the isolated *rasas* into a structured whole. The suggestion constitutes the soul of *rasa*. In the *rasadhvani* type of poetry the role of suggestion is absolutely essential. In the other two types of poetry (i.e. *vastudhvani* and *alaṁkāradhvani)* suggestion plays the same role although to a lesser degree. Even a little touch of suggestion in any expression makes it emotive (*rasayukta)*. Thus in *vastudhvani* and *alaṁkāradhvani* types of poetry, *rasa* exists, because suggestion is there.

The ideas amongst literary circle are communicated by expressions which bear the touch of *rasa.*[128] *Rasa* brings infinite varieties to poetic speech. The poetic speeches which have suggested elements in it are activated by *pratibhā* in a sudden flash. Only gifted poets present the poetic speeches having suggestive elements and therefore emotive in infinite varieties by virtue of *pratibhā.*[129]

Thus it is clear that Ānandavardhana has associated *pratibhā* with suggestion. By virtue of this suggestion of the poetic speeches being surcharged with rasa delineate various beautiful things. In a way the whole poetic speech is 'emotive' *rasayukta* in character. It is matured by suggestion and flashed by *pratibhā*. In other words, there can be no poetry without *rasa*. There can be no *rasa* without suggestion. The suggestion is expressed by poetic speech. The *pratibhā* flashes the poetic speeches which have suggestive elements in them. The spark of *pratibhā* brings innumerable varieties to poetic expression. Since the poetic expressions are many, *pratibhās* as their causes are also multiple. In this way *pratibhā* triggers the emotive-expressions and encircles the whole gamut of *rasa.*

Pratibhā gives infinite varieties to poetic speech and theme

It has been already stated that *pratibhā* gives infinite varieties to poetic speech with the help of suggestion.[130] It can also provide endless varieties to poetic themes with the help of denotative function (*vācyavācakabhāva*) or words. Ānandavardhana has stated by its nature (*svabhāvataḥ*) (i.e., even without the help of suggested sense), the purely denoted sense is infinite.[131]

The *pratibhā* with the help of denotative power brings varieties to poetic themes on the basis of circumstances, place and time. At every stage it brings freshness and new significance. Illustrating as to how *pratibhā* brings novelty and variety to a poetic theme, Ānanadavardhana refers to a poetic situation in the *Kumārasaṁbhavam*. The poet describes the situation when Śiva sees Pārvatī for the first time as a damsel of supreme and enchanting beauty. Pārvatī is described in several verses. Ordinarily these descriptions appear to be tautology. But in reality each description is striking and charged with invigorating freshness and rich significance. This is due to poet's *pratibhā*[132] Again sometimes a different type of situation occurs where the insentient objects appear to be sentient. In the *Kumārasaṁbhavam,* Himavān and the Gaṅgā are described as persons having the qualities of sentient beings.[133] This situation is also created by *pratibhā*. Among the sentient themes, childhood and among the insentient themes the germination etc. brings variety to poetic descriptions.[134] Further poetic themes may be infinite on the basis of place. The blow of wind, the flow of water, the bloom of flowers in different places bring varieties to poetic theme. Again when the beasts and birds of the forest are brought to cities they can provide infinite varieties for description. Innumerable poetic themes may be possible on the basis of the difference of men and women of different places. Their different ways of speaking and clothing are a source of numerous themes. Again different seasons, atmosphere, sky and water in different times can provide manifold varieties to poetic themes.[135] All these great varieties of poetic themes can be fabricated and utilised by the good poets who possess *pratibhā*.[136]

In this context Ānandavardhana raises an objection and subsequently removes it. The objection is that, *pratibhā* cannot bring varieties to poetic themes. The objects are communicated because they possess universal character, and not because of their specific traits. Following this principle, the poets universalise their personal experience in poetry. The poets have no direct vision into the specific variations of the things of past, present and future. This universalised generic nature of experiences which is common to all men have been fully utilised by great ancient poets. They have left no varieties for modern poets except presenting the old ideas in a new style.[137]

But the above assumption is wrong according to Ānandavardhana. If the ancient poets had exhausted the poetic themes on the basis of generic nature of poetic experience, then there would have been no second poet after Vālmīki. Again, if the varieties have been possible by *uktivaicitrya,* then there would be varieties of matter any way to be presented. Ānandavardhana suggests that endless varieties can be achieved in many ways. It can be possible by 'manner of presentation', *bhaṇitivaicitrya* twisting the popular figures of speeches, bringing the ideas of one language to another language and so on.[138] All these varieties are due to *pratibhā*. Ānandavardhana sarcastically remarks, "if we admit *pratibhā* with regard to the subject matter (of poetry) even in the case of a single poet apart from Vālmīki, (then we must perforce admit that) the creative imagination is inexhaustible".[139]

Futher Ānandavardhana argues that primary sense (*DL.* IV.7) can bring endless variety to poetic themes. But it will be more striking only if they are associated with *rasa.* [140] He states that though endless varieties and novelty are possible through the denotative sense, still it is the suggestive sense which brings everfreshness and charm to the varieties. *Rasa* is the finest manifestation of this suggestive sense, which is sparked by *pratibhā.*

The fields of poetic themes are so vast that the divine preceptor Vācaspati with all his might cannot exhaust this field.[141] The vast varieties of poetic themes, *rasa, bhāva* etc. are balanced by the sense of propriety of the poet. Thus all the poetic activities are based on *pratibhā.*

In order to establish the vital role of *pratibhā* in poetic activities, Ānandavardhana brings out the context of plagiarism which in its turn can make *pratibhā* unproductive. According to him, plagiarism is not an offensive mistake. It does not stop the activities of *pratibhā.* The poets can utilise the old letters, old themes and old ideas.[142] There are plenty of coincidences among great poets. But it is not a crime.[143]

According to Ānandavardhana, one can escape plagiarism or tautology, if he utilises suggestion in the poetry properly. This suggestion appears as a unique flash of understanding and enhances charm and strikingness to the similar poetic theme. It is due to suggestion, the connoisseurs appreciate old poetic theme.

In his words, "any theme whatsoever will be beautiful even though it resembles a previously existing one as long as the thought arises in the mind of the people that this is ineffably quivering(with beauty). It can be used by a good poet without his incurring any blame".[144]

Ānandavardhana in the begining of the *Dhvanyāloka*

clearly mention the nature of *pratibhā*. *Pratibhā* like a sudden flash of understanding, overshadows the suggested sense of poetry. It remains in the speech of great poets (DL. I. 6). The suggested content which is comparable to the grace of a lady (*DL*. 1. 4) is manifested by the spark of *pratibhā*. *Pratibhā* conceals the blemishes out of repitions and lends delightful charm to poetic diction. The expressions, i.e. *sphurati* (*DL*. IV.15) and *sphurita* (DL. IV. 16) suggest the sparklike nature of *pratibhā* which can metamorphose the trodden field of poetry with over-whelming freshness and charm in association with the elements of suggestion. Thus *pratibhā* is the guiding principle of all poetic activities.

Cause of *pratibhā* according to Ānandavardhana

Ānandavardhana has only given a passing remark on the cause of *pratibhā*. According to him, it is an outcome of fruition of excessive merit amassed by the poets in their past births.[145] Thus the great poets inherit their poetic genius '*pratibhā* ' from their previous birth. In this respect he follows Bhartṛhari who says that *pratibhā* is directly caused by words in this life or in previous life (*VP*. II. 151).

The impressions of the past birth as the cause of *pratibhā* which flashes the *rasa* 'aesthetic experience' may be compared with Hegel's 'recognitive nature of aesthetic experience' as referred by K.C. Pandey.[146] Hegel does not believe in the existence of the previous birth. But according to him, mind is very powerful and capable of knowing itself and all that originates from it. Mind not only absorbs its products it also recoginses itself in the medium of various propensities, i.e. impulses, inclinations and interests. In a word of art the sensous materials are transformed into thought and expressions. The art experience as a ' recognitive experience' cognises something that was known before in circumstances and form. It is different from those in which it is presented. Mind cognises itself again in the work of art, under the garbs of external form. In the present context the reality of impression can be interpreted without taking rebirth into account.

The impressions in the poets are relics of the past experiences. In this birth those poetic experiences are absorbed in the mind. This experience may be gathered by practice, or education, or association with learned circles. These poetic impressions get out of the mind in favourable situations and take the form of poetic speech. As the retaining capacity varies from person to person, so also the releasing capacity varies. On this ground some poets are good, because they release the impressions perfectly, and others are not so good, because they fail to bring out the impressions completely. That is why, *pratibhā* varies from person to person and poet to poet.

That which is true in case of *pratibhā* is also true in the case of general intelligence *'prajñā'*. The general intelligences differ among the students who are taught in the same class. Some of them whose intelligence is powerful ratain more, and they are regarded as good students, and those who retain less are bad students.[147]

On the basis of the preceding discussion it appears that Ānandavardhana's *pratibhā* as a flash of understanding of the past experiences may be close to 'recognitive experience' of Hegel. But its causes are more than the absorbed propensities of the mind. Its manifestation does not follow any rule whereas the cognition of 'recognitive experience' follows certain principles. The revelation of *pratibhā* is absolutely unexpected and spontaneous like flash of lightning, or the eruption of a volcano. Vālmīki's famous outburst of the poetic experience is not due to any previous similar experience which was dormant in him in this birth. At least there is no proof in this regard. Probably that is why Ānandavardhana has assumed that the cause of *pratibhā* is mysterious and lies in merit earned in previous births. It is manifested in the present birth in the form of impression (*saṁskāra* or *bhāvanā*). The cycle of life and death is a well honoured concept in the Indian philosophy. Ānandavardhana has accepted it in order to explore the causes of *pratibhā* or poetic genius.

Concept of *pratibhā* according to later rhetoricians

BhaṭṭaNāyaka and Bhaṭṭa Tauta

Besides Ānandavardhana, Bhaṭṭa Nāyaka (900-1000 AD) and Bhaṭṭ a Tauta (950-980 A.D.) have also given exposition to their ideas on *pratibhā*. But these are available only in fragments. Bhaṭṭa Nāyaka, though an opponent of the *dhvani* school, appears to have linked *pratibhā* or creative genius with suggestion in the following expression : "The cow, in the form of speech, gives a unique drink (*rasa*) out of love for her young calf. That (*rasa*, i.e. bliss) which is milked by the *yogins* cannot be compared to it. Without being possessed by *rasa*, the *yogins* laboriously milk-out (bliss)"[148] Following the trends of Ānandavardhana, Bhaṭṭa Tauta, the celebrated teacher of Abhinavagupta, has analysed *pratibhā* in relation to rasa.[149]

Hemacandra has quoted a similar passage of Tauta which may be translated as follows : "*pratibhā* is an intelligence (*prajñā*) whose nature is to create new things. One can be a poet, if he is influenced by *pratibhā* to describe things in a graphic way. Then only, the creation of the poet can be called *kāvya*".[150] Further Hemacandra's three verses quoted in different places reveal the nature of *pratibhā*. They run as follows : "One who has vision, is called a sage. A poet is not without the vision of a sage. Poetic vision is the visualisation of the essences of poetry which are marked by peculiar feelings. In the scriptures, one is called poet who realises these essence. A poet is he, who visualises and delineates the poetic essence in this world. This happened, in the case of the first poet (*Vālmīki*) eternally clear vision. Unless there is description, there can be no poetry in this world".[151]

From the above extracts, BhaṭṭaTauta's concept of *pratibhā* becomes clear. According to him, *pratibhā* is the poetic vision, which is responsible for all creative works, especially poetry. A poet, possessing *pratibhā,* can always bring newness and fresh charm to the poetic diction. It is not generated, but it is flashed. It delineates the essence of poetry which is no other than *rasa.* It is sometimes mystic, because as a special type of intelligence in contrast to the general intelligence (*prajñā*), it can visualise the events of the past, the present and the future. These ideas are described in another extract of Tauta, quoted by Rājacūdāmaṇi Dīkṣita in *Kāvya Darpaṇa* : "Memory deals with the past events, farsight with the future, and talent with the present one. But *prajñā* deals with the three events. When *prajñā* as a flash, creates novel things, it is called *pratibhā.* The goddess of speech reveals herself in two ways, namely through scriptures and through poetic work. One, who has *prajñā* (general intelligence) can write scriptures, and the other who has *pratibhā* (special type of intelligence) can compose poetry".[152] Thus Bhaṭṭ Tauta is a true representative of Ānandavardhana in connection with *pratibhā.* According to him, *pratibhā* in its creative capability pervades the whole entity of *rasa* in particualar and *dhavanikāvya* in general. In this respect also he has tremendously influenced his famous student Abhinavagupta.

Pratibhā according to Abhinavagupta

Abhinavagupta is a critic in the line of Ānandavardhana. He deals with *pratibhā* from monistic Śaivaite standpoint as well as from literary view points. In the Locana and the Abhinava Bhāratī he analysed *pratibhā* as the poetic faculty. According to him, *pratibhā* is a most essential element to compose poetry. This power is an ability by which novel things are delineated in poetic speech.[153] It is a power of the mind by which all poetic activities shine objectively.[154] It works in association with *rasa*. It is not perceived as an inference. Only great poets possess this faculty.[155]

Like Ānandavardhana, Abhinavagupta states that *pratibhā* is manifested as an instantaneous flash. He has suggested this nature of *pratibhā* in the words jhaṭiti, *sphuraṇa*, *parisphurantam* and *abhivyanakti* etc.[156] Abhinavagupta mentioned that *pratibhā* flashes the poetic speech which conveys the *rasa*. The *rasa* is again brought about by suggestion. In this perspective that which arouses the suggested meaning in *dhvanikāvya* is called *pratibhā*.[157] But in order to understand the suggested meaning, one has to know the denotative, indicative and contextual meanings.[158] The suggested meaning is directly experienced.[159] So the *pratibhā* in relation to suggestion is a direct exeperience. A person having aesthetic sense experiences it through identification. This *pratibhā* manifests itself in aesthetic configuration.

Pratibhā as a power of imagination builds up new imaginative fabric to present beautiful ideas leading to rasas. All blemishes and improprieties can be avoided by virtue of *pratibhā* The aesthetic experience is brought forth by *pratibhā*. It is due to this faculty that no one observes the sequences at the time of realisation of *rasa*. Abhinavagupta states that just as at the time of fight which brings praise to the warrior, no sequence is observed, similarly while realising *rasa*, which is caused by *pratibhā* and which puts one in perfect bliss, no sequence is observed.[160]

With regard to the other natures of *pratibhā*, Abhinavagupta only elucidates the idea of Ānandavardhana. *Pratibhā* can bring various perculiarities to poetic creation.[161] It can bestow novelty on poetic speech in relation to *rasa*.[162] From time to time, it gives new meanings to poetic dictions.[163] Plagiarism is not a demerit if *pratibhā* is there. It is the harbinger of poetic senses.[164] It attains beauty and superb peculiarities through suggestion.[165] It is immeasurable because it presents numberless suggested contents. Though varieties are brought into poetic works by denotative power on the basis of circumstances, time and place, etc. yet the real endlessness of poetic speech, is achieved by suggestion in association with *pratibhā*[166] Abhinavagupta says that the result of cognition of *dhvani* is endlessness of *pratibhā*, and the result of endlessness of *pratibhā* is novelty in poetic speech.[167] This novelty in poetic speech can be brought about by the endlessness of poetic senses.[168] Abhinavagupta further states that *dhvani* is related to poetry and *pratibhā* is connected with the poet. Sometimes he uses the term *pratibhāna* instead of *pratibhā* to express the same sense. It is, according to him, a special type of intelligence which remains in the poetic words and senses.[169] In the context of dramaturgy, Abhinavagupta states that *pratibhā* gives a clear idea of the characters to the actors.[170]

Thus in the treatment of *pratibhā* from literary point of view, Abhinavagupta intimately followed Ānandavardhana. According to him, this faculty of *pratibhā* is a power of the mind. It appears as a flash of understanding in the mind. In its creative capability, it is responsible for all poetic creations including music. According to him, *pratibhā* encircles the whole poetic speech. It is a wonder that as a versatile writer on Kashmir Śaiva philosophy, Abhinavagupta has not imposed the philosophical aspect of *pratibhā* on its literary counter-part. He has brought clarity to the brief exposition of *pratibhā* of Ānandavardhana, and put it on solid foundation for the assessment of later rhetoricians.

Pratibhā according to Rājaśekhara

Rājaśekhara has given his independent views on *pratibhā*. According to him, *pratibhā* is the mother of poetry. It originates from *śakti* which is the original source of poetry. Concentration and effort produce this *śakti*.[171] This *śakti* appears in the form of *pratibhā* and *vyutpatti* 'erudition'. The *pratibhā* manifests the expressions and accessories for poetic composition in the mind's eye. One can visualise the objects which are not present, by virtue of *pratibhā.* It can inspire to those who are born blind to compose poetry.[172] According to him, *pratibhā* may be *kārayitrī* and *bhāvayitrī*. It is *kārayitrī* because it is essential for the poets. It is of three types. When *pratibhā* is inherited from the previous birth it is *sahajā* ; and when it is acquired by practice or erudition it is *āhāryā;* and when it is produced by preceptors, gods and tantric methods it is *aupadeśikī.* The *bhāvayitrī pratibhā* belongs to the connoisseurs achieved through careful perusal of contemplation on the poetic production.

According to Ānandavardhana, *pratibhā* excels erudition. But Rājaśekhara holds that just as good figure and grace are required for a beautiful women, so also erudition and *pratibhā* are required for a good poetry.[173] While Ānandavardhana's concept of *pratibhā* is an inborn faculty which appears like a flash and concretises in endless dimensions in the form of suggestive poetry, Rājaśekhara's doctrine of *pratibhā* stands for inborn, or acquired, or advisable features. He gives to *pratibhā* a secondary position. Its position comes beneath the *śakti.*

Mammaṭa (1050-1100 AD) in the same line has identified *śakti* with *pratibhā*. According to him, the *śakti*, 'intellectual backgroud and practice' constitute the cause of poetry.[174] Thus in his opinion *pratibhā* has no special role to play. It stands on par with *abhyāsa* and *vyutpatti.*

Hemacandra, the author of *Kāvyānuśāsana*, has been greatly influenced by Ānandavardhana and Bhaṭṭa Tauta in his analysis of *pratibhā*. He states that *pratibhā* is the only essential faculty for any creative work.[175] Erudition and practice are only means to polish the *pratibhā.* It can either be natural or conditional. Explaining the revelation of *pratibhā* he states that when obstacles of knowledge are totally removed and when there is no further apprehension of obstruction, *pratibhā* in its *sahajā* form manifests itself in full lustre. Its revelation is compared to the bright appearance of the Sun when the clouds which cover it, are removed.[176] This is similar to the Rājaśekhara's *sahajā pratibhā*

Again *pratibhā* may be *aupādhikī* 'conditional' if it is acquired by mystic practice. In both cases total 'removal' *kṣaya* and 'checking' *upaśama* are necessary for manifestation. But in *sahajā* type these elements appear naturally, where as in *aupādhikī* they occur artificially.

Though Hemacandra follows Rājaśekhara in the classification of *pratibhā,* he follows Ānandavardhana so far as the working of *pratibhā* is concerned. The *vyutpatti* and *abhyāsa* are only means to polish *pratibhā.* But these two elements are absolutely useless without the existence of *pratibhā.*[177] Thus Hemacandra considers *pratibhā* as an essential cause of poetic composition.

Kuntaka is a true successor of Ānandavardhana in various ways. He has given new orientation to the literary theories of Ānandavardhana in his idea of *vakrokti.* If *pratibhā* of Ānandavardhana covers the whole gamut of *rasa,* then *pratibhā* of Kuntaka encircles the entire range of *vakratā* 'charming expression'. While according to Ānandavardhana, the suggestion provides endless varieties of *pratibhā,* according to Kuntaka, *vakratā* offers innumerable outlets to poetic imagination. Just as Ānandavardhana models his concept of *pratibhā* after the philosophy of *dhvani,* so also Kuntaka has fashioned his *pratibhā* on the basis of *vakratā.* The method of approach by both the great thinkers are alike.

Kuntaka has defined *vakrokti* on the basis of creative imagination which is nothing but *pratibhā.* In contrast to Ānandavardhana, Kuntaka (also Bhaṭṭanāyaka) holds that the soul of poetry cannot be the meaning of poetry at all.

Only the *kavivyāpāra* 'creative power' of the poet is the meaning of the poetry. According to him, poetry is that by which something is made or created by the poet (*kaveḥ karma kāvyaṁ*). So the soul of poetry should be the poets creative art (*kāvya-vyāpāra*). Kuntaka has built the super structure of *vakrokti* on this basis.

The poets' creative art is marked by the striking mode of speech which deviates from denotative use of language. The three functions of words, i.e. referential, secondary and suggestive[178] which remain in poetry and non-poetry, are rendered uncommon by virtue of poet's creative imagination. *Vakrokti* may be of endless varieties by virtue of *pratibhā* .

Kuntaka further states that *pratibhā* brings out inner charm, *saubhāgya* to poetic diction which elates the heart of the connoisseurs.[180]

Poetic lapses are due to inadequacy of *pratibhā* If in a poetic composition the verbal acrobatics supersede, and the beauty of the matter is neglected, then poets' poverty of *pratibhā* is obvious there.[181]

Like Ānandavardhana, Kuntake holds that *pratibhā* appears as a flash. It operates in two stages. In the first stage it is a bare flash of some original ideas. At this time it is as good as unpolished gem without much lustre. In the second stage it is an artistic embodiment. Here it is absolutely a perfect gem polished by the grind stone with full lustre.[182] All figures of speech emerge from *pratibhā*.[183]

According to Kuntaka, *pratibhā* is also the cause of all poetic styles. Both *sukumāra mārga* and *vicirtra mārga* are the outcome of *pratibhā*.[184] In *sukumāra mārga* fresh words and meanings blossom forth, lovely ornaments appear effortlessly (*VJ*.I.25) because of poet's *pratibhā*. In this style, *pratibhā* manifests the beauty of the composition as a flash (*VJ*.1.29).

Pratibhā as creative imagination operates with suggestion

Following the footsteps of Ānandavardhana, Kuntaka states that by the touch of suggestion *pratibhā* brings about a new shape to the poetic expression.[185]

Thus *pratibhā* is a power among the poets.[186] It inspires to select suitable images and crystallises the single ideas.[187] Reiterating the ideas of Ānandavardhana on *pratibhā* Kuntaka says, "in the world of poet's creative imagination, things come to life with a touch of original invention or their real nature gets veiled by *arich afflatus* calculated to present the subject in a most attractive light, as such, the process of communication is a slave to the poetic intention.".[188]

According to Kuntaka, *pratibhā* is due to residual impressions of the previous birth which is polished by education in this birth. So he believes the *saṁskāra* and teachings as the causes of *pratibhā*.[189]

From the above discussions it is clear that Kuntaka follows Ānandavardhana in the treatment of *pratibhā*. All the traits of *pratibhā* as set out by Ānandavardhana have been extended and adjusted to the poetic situations of *vakrokti*. Further Kuntaka's debt can be proved from the fact that in poetic speech *pratibhā* works with suggestion. In brief, Ānandavardhana's concept of *pratibhā* has been accepted and approved indirectly by his formidable opponent Kuntaka.

Concept of *pratibhā* according to Jagannātha

Jagannātha is the last creative writer of *dhvani* school of Sanskrit poetics. He does not follow slavishly the doctrine of *pratibhā* of Ānandavardhana. He connects *pratibhā* as a creative faculty with his peculiar definition of poetry. He states that suitable words and senses conducive to composition of poetry is *pratibhā*.[190] This power remains latent in the poet. It can be cognised from poetic works. It is the only cause of poetry.[191]

In connection with the causes of *pratibhā*, Jagannātha argues hotly. That *pratibhā* is not inherited from the previous birth. It can be accrued in this birth. *Pratibhā* can be produced by *adṛṣṭa* 'merit', acquired from the benedictions or blessings of gods or teachers. In this respect it is similar to the *'aupadeśikī'* type of *pratibhā* of Rājaśekhara and Hemacandra.[192]

Again *pratibhā* can be produced by 'erudition' *vyutpatti* and 'practice' *abhyāsa*. Rājaśekhara and Hemacandra call it *āhāryā* 'acquired type' of *pratibhā*.[193]

In brief, Jagannātha holds that *pratibhā* may be produced either by *adṛṣṭa* or by erudition and practice together. But *pratibhā* is not different owing to its different causes. It is one as a power for poetic composition.

It appears that Jagannātha has analysed *pratibhā* from a broader perspective. His *pratibhā* is a faculty which is responsible for creating great poets, i.e. Vālmīki, Kālidāsa as well as minor poets i.e., Bhāravi, Māgha, Bhavabhūti etc. Though Bhāravi, Māgha, Śrīharṣa and Bāṇa etc. possessed *pratibhā*, their scholastic attitude and poetic acrobatics subdue the true poetic flavour. In the true sense of the term Vāmīki and Kālidāsa possess *pratibhā*. It is a rare gift. In the judgement of Ānadavardhana, the poets namely Bhāravi, Māgha etc. have *prajñā* or general intelligence. They have no *pratibhā* which is an inborn creative power that can never be acquired or taught. Thus Jagannātha has brought *pratibhā* from its highest glory of rare creative power, down to the general ability for composition.

A survey of *pratibhā* from Bhartṛhari to Jagnnātha reveals many things. Bhartṛhari, as a grammarian has made the infrastructure for the concept. He considers this concept from linguistic and psychological points of view. From linguistic point of view, *pratibhā* represents the semantic unity which cannot be further divisible into smaller fragments. According to Bhartṛhari, there are two types of meanings, natural and artificial. An utterance used for communication has natural meaning. A sentence in the context has its natural meanings. The parts of the sentence have artificial meaning. The sentence which is out of context has its artificial meaning because it cannot be fixed by itself in most cases. The natural meaning is called *pratibhā* which is indivisible. The abstraction of *varṇa* and the abstraction of *pada* is artificial. He prefers unity to diversity. Preference for unity is characteristic not only of Bhartṛhari but also of Ānandavardhana. Dividing the indivisible form and meaning into their parts is considered to be lower reality. While grammar is famous for the study of words, *Mīmāṁsā* investigates the study of sentence.

Both Bhartṛhari and Ānandavardhana claim that the meaning of sentences and words are not only based on words and sentences but on the manner of speech, speaker's attitude and contextual factors. It is not difficult to say when the functions of *pratibhā* and *dhvani* begin. *Dhvani* and *pratibhā* are based on words. If *dhvani* is an element of communication beyond the use of language then there will be no relation, between *sphoṭa*, grammar, *pratibhā* and *dhvani*. Bhartṛhari says that *pratibhā* is based on words and Ānandavardhana says that *dhvani* is related to primary meaning and secondary meanings. The speaker may communicate something more than lexical meaning or sentence meaning. What is additionally communicated is through the operation of *pratibhā* or *dhvani*.Bhartṛhari and Ānandavardhana both tried to show that additional contents of expression understood through the function of *pratibhā* and *dhvani* have definite relation to linguistic form. *Dhvani* and *pratibhā* can be traced back to the words and expressions used by speakers. *Dhvan*i and *pratibhā* take all the aspects of literary form into account in order to study emotional overtone or instantaneous grasp of the sentence meaning. Paralinguistic features like stress, accent, or sentence intonation play a crucial role in the interpre-tation of the intention of the speaker (P.8.1.8). Thus the affective and attitudinal meanings have definite relation with the linguistic form of an expression. Many times the meaning of the sentence changes according to the presuppositon of the speaker. When Bhīma pronounces *guruḥ khedaṁ khinne mayi bhajati nādyāpi kuruṣu (Veṇisaṁhāra,* I. 11) with emotional intonation (*kāku*), it indicates a sign of dissent with Yudhiṣṭhira. There are many examples which show that emotional or affective contents of expressions have definite relation to linguistic form. We also know that the sentence *sūryaḥ astaṁ gacchati* has many implications because we know the intention of the speaker which is to be transmutted to a listener. But this sentence would not have emotional value if it is taken out of the context. The traditional study of rhetoric mainly recommends the use of *guṇa* and *alaṁkāras and* avoidance of *doṣas*. The works of the rhetoricians did not attain the status of science in the days earlier to Ānandavardhana. Ānandavardhana tried to give a systematic status to the theory of *dhvani. Dhvanikāra* takes into account all the aspects of linguistic expressions in order to study their emotional features. The expressions not only convey literal meanings but sometimes the attitudes of speaker, meaning revealed through the contexts and natural association of words and expressions. According to Bhartṛhari and Ānandavardhana, the function of *dhvani* and *pratibhā* cannot be divorced from the scope of linguistic expression. The study of linguistic features is considered to be an important aid to understand emotional and affective meaning. Therefore the communicative aspect of *dhvani* and *pratibhā* is not beyond the use of language. The *sphoṭa* theory makes a distinction between the gross physical performance of talking and the sound received by listener without reference to meaning. Since *dhvani* and *pratibhā* are not elements of communications beyond the use of language, there is definite relation between *sphoṭa, abhihitānvayavāda, anvitābhidhānavāda, pratibhā* and *dhvani.*

Therefore the working of *dhvani* is an extended branch of the linguistic science, and it deserves a place on par with the other branches of linguistic science, namely phonetics, grammar, *sphoṭa*, morphology, syntax *(anvitānvayavāda, abhihitānva-yavāda)* etc. It is the main intention of the work to point out a connection between the several branches of linguistics.

Bhartṛhari's concept of *pratibhā* has many faces. Its linguistic features are discussed above. Psychologically it is similar as basic instinct which is the guiding principle of all sorts of activities on this earth. This instinctive type of *pratibhā* has further been utilised, adjusted, and extended by rhetoricians mainly as an instrument of poetic work. The basic theory remains the same. But the writers of *alaṁkāra* school attach it to figures Ānandavardhana with suggestion and Kuntaka with *vakrokti*. On the basis of the above discussion, we will connect the different concepts of grammar with rhetoric in the fourth chapter of this book.

References

1. *VP*. I. ed. K.A.S. Iyer, Deccan College, 1966, 1-2.
2. *Ibid*., I.123.
3. *Ibid*., I.113(121) :
   itikartavyatā loke sarvā śabdavyapāśrayā ı yāṁ pūrvāhitasaṁskāro bālo'pi pratipadyte
4. *Vṛtti* on *VP*. 1.114 (122) :
   tathā hy anupadeśasādhyāḥ pratibhāgamyāḥ evā karaṇavinyāsāda-yaḥ
5. *Vṛtti* on *VP*.1.134 (142):
   paraiḥ saṁvedyaṁ yasyāḥ śrotraviṣayatvena pratiniyataṁ śruti-rūpaṁ śā vaikharī ı śliṣṭā vyaktavarṇasamuccāraṇā prasiddhasādhu-bhāvā bhraṣṭasaṁskārā ca tathā yā 'kṣe yā dundubhau yā veṇauvīṇāyām ity aparimāṇabhedā ı
6. *Ibid*., p.114 : *madhyamā tv antaḥsaṁniveśinī parigṛhītakrameva buddhimātropādānā ı sā tu sūkṣmaprāṇavṛttyanugatā kramasaṁhāra-bhāve'pi vyktaprāṇaparigrahaiva keṣāñcit ı ı*
7. *Ibid*., pp.214-215 : *pratisaṁhṛtakramā saty apy abhede samāviṣṭa-kramaśaktiḥ paśyantī ı śā calācalā pratilabdhasamādhānā cāvṛtā ca*

viśuddhā ca, sanniviṣṭajñeyākārā pratilīnākārā nirākārā ca paricchinnārtha pratyavabāsā saṁsṛṣṭārtha pratyavabhāsā praśāntasarvārtha pratyavabhāsā cety aparimāṇabhedā ।

8. *Ibid.*, p.116 : *paraṁ tu paśyantīrūpam anapabhraṁśam asaṁkīrṇaṁ lokavyavahārātītam* ।
9. *Ibid.*, p.119 : *avibhāgā tu paśyantī sarvataḥ saṁhṛtakramā* । *svarūpajyotir evāntaḥ sūkṣmā vāg anapāyinī* ।।
10. For details see K.A.S. Iyer, Bhartṛhari, pp.139-141.
11. *Vṛtti* on *VP* I.123(131) p.202 : *tad abhyāsāc ca śabdapūrvakaṁ yogam adhigamya pratibhāṁ tattvaprabhavāṁ bhāvavikāraprakṛtiṁ sattāṁ sādhyasādhanaśaktiyuktāṁ samyag avabudhya niyatā kṣemaprāptir iti* ।
12. *Vṛtti* on *VP*. I. 14, p.48 : *so'vyatikīrṇāṁ vāg avasthām adhigamya vāgvikārāṇāṁ prakṛtiṁ pratibhām anuparaiti tasmāc ca sattānuguṇyamātrāt pratibhākhyāc śabdapūrvayogabhāvanābhyāsākṣepāt pratyastamitasarvavikārollekhamātrāṁ paraṁ prakṛtiṁ pratipadyate* ।
13. H.G. Coward, *The Sphoṭa theory of language*, Delhi, 1980, pp.14-15.
14. See footnote No. 12, Ch. II.
15. K.A.S.Iyer, "*pratibhā*, as the meaning of a sentence". *POC* Tirupati, 1940, p.327.
16. *VP*. II, ed. Raghunath Sharma, Varanasi, 1980, 1 : *buddhy anu sharma-saṁhṛtiḥ*
17. See p. 17 of this book.
18. K.A.S. Iyer, *Bhartṛhari*, pp.158-159.
19. *Ibid.*, "Bhartṛhari on the sentence", *ALB*, Vol.44-45, 1980-81, p.46
20. S.D. Joshi, *Sphoṭa Nirṇaya*, p.37.
21. *VP*. II.1
22. *VP*. II. 8-9 : *citrasyaikasya rūpasya yathā bhedanidarśanaiḥ* । *nīlādibhiḥ samākhyānaṁ kriyate bhinnalakṣaṇaiḥ* ।। *tathaivaikasya vākyasya nirākāṅkṣasya sarvataḥ* । *śabdāntaraiḥ samākhyānaṁ sākāṅkṣair anugamyate* ।।
23. *VP* II.7 : *yathaika eva sarvārtha pratyayaḥ pravibhajyate* । *dṛśyabhedā nukāreṇa vākyārthānugams tathā* ।।
24. See discussion in *VP*. II. 327.
25. *Ibid.*, *VP*. II. 41-46.
26. *Ibid.*, *VP*.II. 7-16, 56.
27. *Ibid.*, *VP*.II. 56.

28. *Ibid.*, *VP*.II. 49- 53.
29. *Ibid.*, *VP*.II.30-33,
30. *Ibid.*, *VP*.II.47-48.
31. *Ibid.*,
32. *VP*.II.90-92.
33. *Ibid.*, II. 10 : *yathā pade vibhajyante prakṛtipratyayādayaḥ* ı *apoddhāras tathā vākye padānām upavarṇyate* ıı "Just as in a finished word we make a division of a stem and a suffix, etc. so also in a sentence we show isolation (separation of words)."
34. *Ibid.*, II.19 : *avyaktaḥ kramavān chabdaḥ upāṁśu yam adhīyate* ı *akramas tu vitaty eva buddhir yatrāvatiṣṭhate* ıı
"The unrevealed word (i.e. a word in the process of transmission) is grasped indistinctly and successively. However, (the word), on which the intellect as if expanding (with the successive sound of words) settles, is want of any sequence".
35. *Ibid.*, II.27: *bhāvanāsamaye tv etat kramasāmarthyam akramam* ı *vyāvṛthabhedo yenārtho bhedavān upalabhyate* ıı
36. *Ibid.*, I. 48.
37. *Ibid.*, II. 22 : *nityeṣu tu kutaḥ pūrvaṁ paraṁ vā paramārthataḥ* ı *ekasyaiva tu sā śaktir yad evam avabhāsate* ıı
"In the case of eternal (things) how can there be before or after in the true sense of the term. What makes it senses so (before or after) is the innate efficiency of what is only one."
38. *Ibid.*, I. 73 : *pade na varṇā vidyante varṇesv avayavā na ca* ı *vākyāt padānaṁ atyantaṁ praviveko na kaścana* ı
"There are on phonemes in the words, and there are no parts in the phoneme. There is no absolute and clearcut separation of words from a sentence."
39. *Ibid.*, II. 14 : *brāhmaṇārtho yathā nāsti kaś cid brāhmaṇakambale* ı *devadattādayovākye tathaiva syur anarthakāḥ* ıı "The meaning of the word brāhmaṇa does not exist in the compound brāhmaṇakambala 'a wollen blanket for a brahmin so also the words devadatta, etc. have no separate meaning in the sentence."
40. *Ibid.*, II. 35 :
We apprehend the meaning of king from the word *rājan* which appears in different forms (in a phrase). In a compound we use it in a different form (like *rāja*(*n*) which resembles a verb (i.e. the imperative form of the verb *rājā*).

41. *Ibid.*, II. 170-171 :
anvākhyānāni bhidyante śabdavyutpattikarmasu ı bahūnāṁ sambhave' rthānāṁ nimittaṁ kiṁ cid iṣyate ıı vairavāsiṣṭhagiriśās tathaikāgārikādayaḥ ı kaiś cit kathaṁ cid ākhyātā nimittāvadhi-saṅkaraiḥ ıı
"In the derivation of words, one resorts to many way of explaining them where many meanings are possible, a particular one is taken as the basis of derivation.
Words like *vaira, vāsiṣṭha, girīśa* and *ekāgārika* have been explained by some on the basis of a variety of meanings".
42. *Ibid.*, II. 34 :
"If one assumes that the meaning of an individual word exists on the authority of its apprehension, it follows that (each preceding word) would be meaningless, as abandons the meaning of (each preceding) word, once it has collected together with the meaning of (the following word)."
43. *Ibid.*, II. 91-92 :
aprasiddhaṁ tu yaṁ bhāgam adṛṣtam anupaśyati ı tāvatya asaṁvidam mūḍhaḥ sarvatra pratipadyate ıı tathā pikādiyogena vākye' tyanta vilakṣaṇe ı sadṛśasyaiva saṁjñānam asato'rthasya manyate ıı
44. *Ibid.*, II. 30 :
also H.R. Robins in his *A history of Linguistics*, London, 1967, p.139, finds echo of Bhartṛhari's idea in that of Malinowskin's which states that 'the isolated words are in face only linguistic figments, the products of advanced linguistic analysis'.
45. *Ibid.*, II. 55 :
anarthakāny apāyatvāt padārthenārthavanti vā ı krameṇoccāritāny āhur vākyārthaṁ bhinnalakṣaṇam ıı
46. *Ibid.*, II. 437-438.
47. *Ibid.*, II. 143 :
vicchedagrahaṇe'rthānāṁ pratibhā'nyaiva jāyate ı vākyārtha iti tām āhuḥ padārthair upapāditām. ıı
"After the meanings of (the individual words) have been separately grasped, an intuition (*pratibhā*) is produced which is altogether different (from the cognition arisen from the individual word-meanings). This is what is called the meaning of the sentence, which is brought (to our mind) by the meaning of words."
48. *Ibid.*

49. *VP*. II. 310-313.
50. *VP*. II. 314 :
vākyāt prakaraṇād arthād aucityād deśakālataḥ । *śabdārthāḥ pravibhajyante na rūpād eva kevalāt* ॥
"The meanings of words are determined according to the sentence, situation, meaning, propriety, place and time and not according to mere external form."
51. *VP*. II. 315-16 :
saṁsargo viprayogaś ca sāhacaryaṁ virodhitā । *arthaḥ prakaraṇaṁ liṅgaṁ śabdasyānyasya sannidhiḥ* ॥ *sāmarthyam aucitī deśaḥ kālo vyaktiḥ svarādayaḥ* । *śabdārthasyānavacchede viśeṣa smṛtihetavaḥ* ॥
52. Cf. *DL*. I. 13 :
upasarjanīkṛta svārthau.
53. See footnote No.47. ch. II
54. *DL*. I. 13
55. *VP*. II. 149-50 :
svaravṛttiṁ vikurute madhau puṁskokilasya kaḥ । *jantvādayaḥ kulāyādikaraṇe kena śikṣitāḥ* ॥ *āhāraprītyapadveṣaplavanādikriyāsu kaḥ* । *jātyānvayaprasiddhāsu prayoktā mṛgapakṣiṇām* ॥
"Who alters the note of the cuckoo in spring who teaches the insects etc. to weave their webs etc.? Who impels the wild beasts and birds in the acts like eating, mating, hating or swimming (and in all other actions) well-known (determined by) heredity."
56. *Vṛtti* of *VP*. I. 114 (122) :
anādiś caiṣā śabdabhāvanā pratipuruṣam avasthitajñānabījaparigrahā na hy etasyāḥ kathañcit pauruṣeyatvaṁ saṁbhavati । *tathā hy anupadeśasādhyāḥ pratibhāgamyāḥ eva karaṇavinyāsādayaḥ*.
"This residual trace of speech has no beginning and it exists in everyone as a seed in the mind. It is not possible that it should be the result of the effort of any person. Movements of the articulatory organs by children are not due to instruction by others but are known through intuition."
57. *VP*. II. 151 : *bhāvanānugatād etad āgamād eva jāyate*
58. *VP*. I. 28-30 : *vyavasthā nityatā*.
59. *Ibid*., I. 31, 41, 43.
60. *Ibid*., I. 28-30
61. *Ibid*., I. 113, also footnote No.3, Ch. II.
62. *Ibid*., I. 36
63. *VP*. II. 118 :

anāgamaś ca so'bhyāsaḥ samayaḥ kaiś cid iṣyate ı anataram idaṁ kāryam asmād ity upadarśnam ıı
"The repeated usage (of words leading to activity) is itself regarded as (established) convention, which cannot be said to have started at a definite time. This convention points out that 'after this' (i.e. two particular utterances) this is to be done."

64. *Ibid.*, II 117 :
abhyāsāt pratibhāhetuḥ śabdaḥ sarvo'paraiḥ smṛtaḥ ı bālānāṁ ca tiraścāṁ ca yathārtha pratipādane ıı
"The others regard that every (kind) of word (i.e. articulated or inarticulate, actual or in the form of impression) causes *pratibhā* (intuitive cognitive flash) on account of constant observation (of usage leading to activity) for (the purpose of) making the children as well as the animals apprehend appropriate meaning."

65. *Ibid.*, II. 118 : *samayaḥ kaiś cid iṣyate*
" Some look upon it as convention".

66. Richard Muller Freienfels composed the history of the study of psychology of instinct in America in his *The Evolution of Modern Psychology* (1948), pp. 255 ff. In this field of instincts first zoologists show interest. Loloyd Morgan and William James are famous among them. Afterwards McDougall concentrates and contributes immensly to this field. He has developed this theory of instinct in *An outline of Psychology* (1923) which was published much earlier in *Introduction to Social Psychology* (1908).
Apart from him, Thorndike in *The Original Nature of Man* (1913), and R.S. Woodworth in his *Dynamic Psychology* has also exhaustively dealt this problem of instinct in mamals. However, McDougall is most fundamental and important among them. He defines instinct by distinguishing it from emotion. In his words, emotion was regarded as a mode of experience which accompanies the working within us of instinctive impulses. It was assumed that human nature (our inherited inborn constitution) comprises instincts that the operation of each instinct, no matter how brought into play, is accompanied by its own peculiar quality of experience which may be called a primary emotion; and that, when two or more instincts are simultaneously at work in us, we

experience a confused emotional excitement, in which we can detect something of the qualities of the corresponding primary emotions. The human emotions were then regarded as clues to the instinctive impulses, or indicators of the motives at work in us."

An outline of Psychology, p. 128.

For instincts see the above book, pp. 121-176.

Freienfels presents McDougall's concept of instict elegantly: "according to McDougall, these instincts are either singly or collectively the motivators of all human activity. Even the faintest and calmest thought is ultimately rooted in instinct. The most complicated intellectual functions serve the gratification of instincts, and the pleasure pain principle serves only in a minor capacity. Without instincts the organism would be an inert lifeless mass. Instincts are the motivators and shapers of all individual and social life; in them dwells the central mystery of life, of mind and of will". *op. cit.* pp. 257-258. McDougall gives a list of instincts *in Outline of Psychology.* pp. 121-176:

(i) Parental or protective instinct.
(ii) Instinct of combat.
(iii) Instinct of curiosity.
(iv) Food seeking instincts.
(v) Instinct of repulsion.
(vi) Instinct of escape.
(vii) Gregarious instinct.
(viii) Instinct of self assertion and submission.
(ix) Mating instinct.
(x) Acquisitive instinct.
(xi) Constructive instinct.
(xii) Instinct of appeal.
(xiii) Minor instincts;

P.V. Kane has attempted to fit these instincts to permanent modes of various *rasas* :

See *History of Sanskrit poetics*, 4th edition Delhi, 1971, p. 358; also see George A.Miller, Language and Communication, Chapter II, Words, sets and thoughts; also see *The Collected works of* C.G. Jung,Vol. 8, The Structure and Dynamics of Psyche, translated by R.F.C. Hull, Routledge & Kegan Paul, London, 1960, p. 135 :

"instincts are typical modes of action, and wherever we met

with uniform and regularly recurring modes of action and reaction we are dealing with instinct, no matter whether it is associated with a conscious motive or not"
For details see *Ibid*. p. 129-138.

67. Commentary of *Tatvasaṁgraha* by Kamalaśila, V.892 and *pañjīkā* there on.
68. *VP*. II.146:
sākṣāt śabdena janitām
69. *Ibid.*,
kartrāpi na nirūpyate
70. *Ibid.*, II. 144:
"This *pratibhā* cannot be described by others in terms such as 'it is this', its functioning is established in every individual, but even the person who experiences it cannot describe it".
71. *Ibid.*, II. 441.
72. *Ibid.*, II. 437.
73. *Ibid.*, II. 413
74. *Ibid.*, II. 439.
75. *Ibid.*, II. 148.
76. *Ibid.*, II. 7.
77. *Ibid.*, II. 410.
78. *Ibid.*, II. 415-420.
79. L.H. Gray, *Foundations of language*, pp. 93-95.
80. Hans Hörmann, *Psycholinguistics*, pp. 258-60.
81. *Ibid.*, p. 265.
82. *Ibid.*, p. 285.
83. Noam Chomsky, *Reflections on Language*, p. 36.
84. *Ibid.*
85. D.I. Solbin, *Developmental Psycholinguistics*, p. 312.
86. Chomsky,op, cit., p. 8.
87. *Ibid.*, pp. 49-50.
88. Abh. on *NS*. Vol.I, GOS, 15-6.
evaṁ pitāmaha sadṛśena sarvadā nāṭyaveda śarīra-rūpaka nirmāṇe kavinā bhāvyam iti
cf. *DL*.III p. 250 : *apāre kavisaṁsāre* etc.
89. *KA*.1.5 : *gurūpadeśād adhyetuṁ śāstraṁ jaḍadhiyo'pyalaṁ kāvyaṁ tu jāyate jātu kasyacit pratibhāvataḥ* ।
90. *Ibid.*, 1.8 : *yatno viditavedyena vidheyaḥ kāvya lakṣaṇaḥ* ॥
91. *KD*. 1.103 : *naisargikī ca pratibhā*
92. *KD*.1.104 : *na vidyate yadyati pūrvavāsanāguṇanubandhi pratibhānam adabhūtam* । *śrutena yatnena ca vāgupāsitā dhruvaṁ karoty eva kam apyanugraham*, also *Ibid.*, 1.105.

93. *KSV* 1.3.16 : *kavitāvījaṁ pratibhānam*
94. *Ibid.*, 1.3.1, 1.3.11
95. *KLR.* ed. Satyadev Choudhri, Delhi, 1965, 1.15 : *manasi sadā susamādhini visphuraṇam anekadhābhidheyasya akliṣṭāni padāni ca vibhānti yasyām asau śaktiḥ*
96. *Ibid.*, 1.16 : *puṁsā saha jātatvād*
    anayostu jyāyasī sahajā
97. *Ibid.*, 1.17 : *utpādyā tu kathaṁcid vyutpatyā janyate parayā*
98. *DL.* 1.5 : *parisphurantaṁ pratibhā viśeṣam*
99. K. KrishnaMoorthy, *Essays in Literary Criticism*, p. 187 : *Dhvanyāloka and its Critics*, 1968, p. 198.
100. *Bhāmahālaṁkāra*, ed. Sankarram Śāstrī, p.6 :
    smṛtir vyatītaviṣayā
    matir āgāmigocarā ı
    buddhis tātkālikī proktā
    prajñā traikālikī matā ıı
    The above verse is also quoted in Vidyācakravartin's *Saṁpradāyaprakāśinī*.
    cf. *KM* of Rājaśekhara, ed. Patna, ch.4, p. 25 :
    tridhā ca sā (buddhi) smṛtir matiḥ prajñeti atikrāntasyārthasya smartrī smṛtiḥ vartamānasya mantrī matiḥ anāgatasya prajñātrī prajñeti
    cf. Mahimabhaṭṭā holds that *prajñā* and *pratibhā* are identical which have access to three spheres of the time. See *Vyaktiviveka*, ed. R. Dvivedi, Varanasi, 1964, 2, pp. 117-118 :
    rasānuguṇaśabdārtha
    cintāstimita cetasaḥ ı
    kṣaṇaṁ svarūpasparśotthā
    prajñeva pratibhā kaveḥ ı
    sā hi cakṣur bhagavata ı
    stṛtīyam iti gīyate ı
    yena sākṣāt karotyeṣa
    bhāvaṁ straikālyavartinaḥ ı
    cf. V. Raghavan, "writers quoted in *Abhinava Bhāratī*" *JOR*, Vol. VI, 1932, Madras, p. 154 :
    dve vartmani girāṁ devyāḥ
    śāstraṁ ca kavikarma ca ı
    prajñopajñaṁ tayor ādyaṁ
    pratibhodbhavam antimam ıı
    "The goddess of speech has two paths, academic work and poetry. The first of them is understood by the intellect, and

the second is realised by the imagination".
cf, C.K. Ogden and I.A. Richards,
The meaning of meanings, London, 1960, p. 155.

101. *DL*, ed. K.Krishnamoorthy, p.14. 1.6 :
sarasvatī svādu tad artha vastu
niḥṣyandamānā mahatāṁ kavīnām ।
aloka sāmānyam abhivyanakti
parisphurantaṁ pratibhā viśeṣem ॥

102. *DL*. III p. 124, 9-10 :
avyutpattikṛto doṣaḥ
śaktyā saṁbriyate kaveḥ ।
yastv aśaktikṛtas tasya
jhaṭityevāvabhāsate ॥

103. *DL. Vṛtti*, p. 124, 11-16 :
tathā hi mahākavīnām avyutpatti kṛtam apy uttama etc.
"That is why there are times when great poets will write about love making among the highest gods along the lines of love making common to mortals. Though this is improper *anaucityam* because it is overshadowed by imaginative genius, it does not strike us as vulgar *'grāmya'*. An example is the description of (Siva's) love making with Pārvatī in the *Kumārasaṁbhava*. In another similar situations it has been explained later how impropriety can be avoided *aucityātyāga* by means of positive and negative examples, *anvaya vyatireka*. The power of imaginative genius to overshadow (other faults) in a poem is apparent. That is why, if a poet devoid of this imaginative genius were to describe love making in such a case, his work would clearly appear faulty.

104. *DL*. III.46, p. 260; 9-10:
asphuṭasphuritam kāvyatatvam
etad yathoditam
aśaknuvadbhir vyākartuṁ
rītayaḥ saṁpravartitāḥ
rītilaksaṇa vidhāyināṁ hi
kāvyatatvam etad sphuṭatayā
manāk sphuritam āsīd iti lakṣyate
"The (doctrine of) *rīti* was invented by those unable to explain this truth of poetry, as we have explained it, as it was only vaguely perceived by them"
For it is observed that rhetoricians who dealt with *rīti* had

a dim perception of this truth of poetry, that is, they had only a slight perception of the truth of poetry.

105. *DL.* IV. 15 :
nūtane sphurati kāvyavastuni
vyaktam eva khalu sā na duṣyati
There is absolutely nothing wrong with writing about an older subject (*vastu)* as long us there is the arousal of a new poetic *(kāvyavastu* in the form of suggested sense *dhvani).*
106. *DL.* I. 12.
107. *DL.* IV. 16
108. *VP.* II. 146.
109. *DL.* I.5 : *krauñca dvanda viyogotthaḥ*
śokaḥ ślokatvam āgataḥ
"The sorrow (of the first poet) that sprang from the permanent disruption of the sandpipers' *(Krauñca)* love-making was transformed into verse".
cf. *Raghuvaṁśam,* XIV. 70 :
niṣāda viddhāṇḍajadarśanotthaḥ
ślokatvam āpadyata yasya śokaḥ
cf. J.L. Masson, "Who killed cock Krauñca" JOI. Baroda, Vol. XVIII, No.3, March, 1969
110. *Locana* on *Dhvanyāloka,* ed. Jagannath Pathak, Varanasi, 1965, p. 93-94 :
'pratibhā apūrvavastunirmāṇakṣamā prajñā tasyā viśeṣo rasāveśaviśadyasaundaryaṁ kāvyanirmāṇakṣamatvam ।
"*Pratibhā* (imagination) is the mental faculty which is able to fashion new things. A 'particular kind' (of imaginative faculty) refers to the power to fashion poetry (which contains) beauty and clarity because of the fusion (into it) of *rasa.*"
111. *DL.* IV. 1-2
dhvaner yaḥ saguṇībhūta vyaṅgyasyādhvā pradarśitaḥ ।
anenānantyam āyāti kavīnāṁ pratibhāgunaḥ ॥
ato hy anyatamenāpi prakāreṇa vibhūṣitā ।
vāṇī navatvam āyāti pūrvārthānvayavatyapi ॥
112. *DL.* III p. 190, 3-6 :
atrocyate yadi rasādimayam eva vācyam etc.
113. *DL.* III. *Vṛtti,* p.188, 18-20 :
vṛttayo hi rasāditātparyeṇa saṁniveśitāḥ
kām api nātyasya kāvyasya ca cchāyām āvahanti ।
rasādayo hi dvayor api tayoor jīvabhūtāḥ

itivṛttādi tu śarīrabhūtam eva.
"For the *vṛttis,* if they are introduced with *rasas* as their major object, will impart a most wondorous beauty to poetry. For *rasas* etc. are the life-breath of both of them. The plot, etc. is merely the body".

114. *DL.* III. *Vṛtti,* p.192, 13-15 :
niyamabhāvī kramaḥ । *tat tu śabdasya kriyāpaurvāparyam ananyasādhya tat phalaghaṭanāsvāśubhāvinīṣu vācye-nāvirodhinyabhidheyāntara vilakṣaṇe rasādau na pratīyate* ।
"There is necessarily a sequence between the perception of their phonetic form and that of the suggested sense. But this sequence betweeen the perception of the literal meaning and perception of the suggested meaning of words is not noticed in the case of *rasa,* etc., which are altogether different from the literal meaning and where the suggested meaning is not opposed to the literal meaning, where the various accessories convey the *rasa* etc. with lightning quickness, since these accessories have only one aim, and result only in one thing (namely the perception of the *rasa*, etc.)"

115. *DL.* III. 3-4.

116. *DL.* IV. p. 272, 15-16 :
rasabhāvatadābhāsarūpe hi vyaṅgye tad vyañjakeṣu ca yathā nirdiṣṭeṣu varṇapadavākyaracanāprabandheṣv avavahitamanasaḥ kaveḥ sarvam apūrvaṁ kāvyaṁ sampadyate ।
"All the poems of the poet who concentrates on the suggested sense in the form of *rasa, bhāva, rasābhāsa* and *bhāvābhāsa,* and on their suggesters which are mentioned earlier, namely letters, words, sentences, sentence structure (*saṅghaṭanāracanā)* and whole words, turn out original".

117. *DL.* IV. 3

118. *DL.* IV. p. 268, 13-14 :
yasya rasāder āśrayādayaṁ kāvyamārgaḥ purātanaiḥ kavibhiḥ sahasrasaṁkhyair asaṁkhyair vā bahuprakāraṁ kṣuṇṇatvan mito'py anantatām etc.
"By having recourse to the use of *dhvani* consisting of *rasa,* etc. this path of poetry which is otherwise limited in the

sense that it has been trodden in many ways by thousands or even a countless number of older poets, achieves endlessness."

119. *DL.* III. p. 188, 9-11 :
ayam eva hi mahākaver mukhyo vyāpāro
yad rasādīn eva mukhyatayā kāvyārthīkṛtya
tad vyaktyanuguṇatvena śabdānām
arthānām copanibandhanam
"for the major activity of a great poet is that he should use words and meanings in a manner suited to the revelation of *rasa*, etc. as the principal subject matter of his poetry."
120. *DL.* III p. 248, 11-15; p. 250, 1-8 : IV p,268, 20-21.
121. *DL.* IV. 4.
122. *DL.* IV. p. 270, 1.
123. *Ibid.*, p. 272, 12.
124. *Ibid.*, p. 274, 3-4.
125. *Ibid.*, p. 278, 10-12.
126. *Ibid.*, pp. 276-278, 15-18, 1-7.
127. *Ibid.*, p. 280, 3-4.
128. *Ibid.*, p.280, 1-2.
129. *Ibid.*, *kā*. 1-2.
130. *Ibid.*
131. *Ibid.*, *kā*. 7.
ānantyam eva vācyasya
śuddhasyāpi svabhāvataḥ
132. *Ibid.*, p.284, 10-11 :
na ca te tasya kaver ekatrai vā sakṛt kṛtā
varṇanaprakārā apunar uktatvena vā
navanavārthanirbharatvena vā na pratibhāsante
"And all these descriptions, repeated several times by the poet in a single poem, do not seem either repetitive or lacking in completely fresh ideas".
133. *Ibid.*, p. 284, 17-18 :
yad acetanānāṁ sarveṣām cetanaṁ dvitīyaṁ rūpam
abhimānitvaprasiddhaṁ himavad gaṅgādīnām
134. *Ibid.*, p. 286, 2-3, 5-6 :
cetanānāṁ ca bālyādyavasthābhir anyatvam ।
acetanānāṁ ca bhāvānām ārambhādy avasthābheda-
bhinnānām ekaikaśaḥ svarūpam
upanibadhyamānam ānantyam evopayāti

"The novelty (achieved) through the (description) of different conditions of sentient beings such as childhood etc. (is well known).... Endlessness is also achieved when one describes, one by one, the individual peculiarities of insentient objects which have a variety of different conditions, such as the 'early stage' and so forth."

135. *Ibid.*, p. 286, 11-17 : *deśabhedānnānātva* etc.
136. *Ibid.*, p. 286, 17 :
upanibadhyate ca tat sarvam eva
sukavibhir yathā pratibham
137. *Ibid.*, p. 288, 5-12.
138. *Ibid.*, p. 290, 4, 9-14.
139. *Ibid.*, p. 290, 7-8.
140. *Ibid.*, p. 292, 5, 7:
bhūmnaiva dṛśyate lakṣye
tat tu bhāti rasāśrayāt
141. *Ibid.*, *kā.* 9-10.
142. *Ibid.*, *kā.* 15.
143. *Ibid.*, *kā.* 11 :
saṁvādās tu bhavanty eva bāhulyena sumedhasām ।
naikarūpatayā sarve te mantavyā vipaścitā
"Among great minds, similarities are frequent. The wise man must not consider them all to be the same".
also K.A.S. Iyer, "originality and Sanskrit poetics", *JGJRI*, Nov. 1943;
V.M. Kulkarni, "Sanskrit writers on plagiarism", JOI, Baroda, III, 1954;
C.R. Devadhar, "Plagiarism - its varieties and limits", ABORI, XXXV, 1954, 210-218.
144. *DL.* IV. 16
145. *DL.* IV. p. 298, 9:
sukavīnāṁ prāktanapuṇyābhyāsaparipākavaśena
pravṛttā vāk
The creative activity of good poets is indeed an outcome of the ripening *'paripāka'* of excessive merit and assidous practice".
146. K.C. Pandey, *Comparative Aesthetics*, Vol. II. 1959, pp. 462-64.
147. cf. *Uttararāmacaritam* of Bhavabhūti, Viśvavidyālaya Prakāśana, Varanasi, 1977, 11.4 :

vitarati guruḥ prājñe
vidyāṁ yathaiva tathā jaḍe ।
na khalu tayor jñāne
śaktiṁ karoty apahanti vā ।।
bhavati ca tayor bhūyān
bhedaḥ phalaṁ prati tad yathā ।
prabhavati śucir bimbagrāhe
maṇir na mṛdādayaḥ ।।

"The teacher imparts knowledge to the clever as well as to dullard; but he doesnot, indeed give them the talent for learning nor does he take it away; and there is a great difference between them with respect to results; it happens thus: a pure jewel is able to take in a reflection; not so a lump of clay and other things".

148. Quoted in *Locana, DL.* 93 :
vāg dhenur dugdha etaṁ hi
rasaṁ yad bālatṛṣṇyā ।
tena nāsya samaḥ sa syād
duhyate yogibhir hi yaḥ ।।
tad āveśena vināpyākrāntyā hi
yo yogibhir duhyate ।
cf. P.V. Kane, *History of Sanskrit poetics,* 1971, p.223:
K. Krishnamoorthy, *DL,* 1974, p. 316

149. See footnote No. 110, ch.II.

150. *Kāvyānuśāsanam* of Hemacandra,
Mahavir Jaina Mahavidyālaya, Bombay 1938, Vol. I, p.3:
prajñā navanavonmeṣaśālinī pratibhā matā
tad anuprāṇanājivad varṇanā nipuṇah kaviḥ
tasya karma smṛtaṁ kāvyam;
cf. *Kāvyaprakāśa saṁketa* of Māṇikyacandra, Poona, 1921, p. 5

151. Hemacandra quoted by K.Krishnamoorthy, *DL,* p. 316; also V.Raghvan, "Writers quoted in *AbhinavaBhāratī*" also *Kāvyānuśāsanam* of Hemacandra, Nirṇayasāgar a Press, Bombay, 1934, p. 379.
nānṛṣiḥ kavir ity uktam ṛṣiś ca kila
darśanāt । vicitrabhāvadharmāśśa tatva
prakhyā ca darśanam ।। sa tatvadarśanād
eva śāstreṣu paṭhitaḥ kaviḥ । darśanād
varṇanāccātha rūḍhā loke kaviśrutiḥ ।।

tathā hi darśane svacche nitye'pyādikaver
muneḥ । noditā kavitā loke yāvaj
jātā na varṇanā ॥

152. V. Rāghvan, *op. cit.*, p. 154 : also 2.5.2.1; also foot Note No. 100, ch. II :
smṛtir vyatītaviṣayā
matir āgāmi gocarā ।
buddhis tātkālikī proktā
prajñā traikalikī matā ॥
prajñā navanavonmeṣaśālinīm
pratibhāṁ viduḥ ।
dve vartmani girām devyāḥ
śāstraṁ ca kavikarma ca ॥
prajñopājñaṁ tayor ādyaṁ
pratibhod bhavam antimam ॥

153. *Locana, DL.* ed. Jagannath Pathak, 1965, p. 346 :
śaktiḥ pratibhānaṁ varṇanīyavastu
viṣayanūtanollekhaśālitvam

154. *Abh.* Vol. II,GOS, p. 298 :
vyāpāro'pi ca tadvidāṁ tu tadābhyāsaparāṇāṁ
ca tathābhūta kāvyātmaka viṣayāvalokane
jhaṭity eva pratibhāti
"When connoisseurs and persons of literary activities see the description of good poetry, it (*pratibhā*) flashes in them".
cf. *Locana*, p. 94 :
yad āha muniḥ-'kaver antargatam bhāvam' iti
"As sage (Bharata) has said (it reveals) the emotional state (*bhāva*) of the poet's mind."

155. *Locana*, pp. 93, 94 :
abhivyanakti parisphurantam iti pratipatṛn
prati sā pratibhā nānumīyamānā । api tu tad
āveśena bhāsamānety arthaḥ
abhivyaktena sphuratā pratibhāviśeṣeṇa nimittena
mahākavitvagaṇaneti yāvat.
"Reveals a certain kind of shimmering. This imaginative faculty in the poet is not to be merely inferred by the senstitive readers as existing in the poet, rather it is directly experienced (*bhāsamāna*) because the spectator himself is overcome with *rasa.* Because of this brilliantly shining

imaginative faculty that is bestowed upon the poet by Sarasvatī, the expression, 'great poetry' is used."

156. *Locana*, p. 62
   (i) *sa eva jhaṭiti vākyenābhidhiyate, Ibid.*, p. 257
   (ii) *ākṣipto'pyākṣiptatayā jhaṭiti sambhāvayitum ārabdho'pītyarthaḥ, cf. DL.* 1.12
157. *Locana*, pp. 60-61 :
   tac chakti trayopajanitārthāvagamamūlajāta-tatpratibhāsapavitrītapratipatṛpratibhā-sahāyārthadyotanaśaktir dhvananavyāpāraḥ
   "The function of suggestion is that power to convey a sense, assisted by the imagination of the listener, that is refined by the understanding (*pratibhāsa*) of the suggested meaning that arises from (and after) the perception of the meanings conveyed by the three powers (already mentioned):
   Ibid., p. 68:
   pratipatṛpratibhāsahakāritvaṁ hy asmābhirdyotanasya prāṇatvenoktam
   "For we have rather said that suggestion is essentially helped by the imagination of the reader".
   Ibid., pp. 68.69 :
   tarhi vaktṛpratipattṛ-pratibhāpraṇito dhvananavyāpāraḥ kiṁ na sahyate.
158. *Abh.* on *NŚ.* Vol. II, GOS, p. 337. 12-15 : *yasyārthasya* etc.
159. See Foot Note No.148, ch. II.
160. *Locana*, p. 346 :
   saṁbhogo'pi hy asau varṇitas tathā pratibhānavatā kavinā yathā tatraiva viśrāntaṁ hṛdayaṁ paurvāparyaparāmarśaṁ kartuṁ na dadāti yathā nirvyāja-parākramasya puruṣasyāviṣaye'pi yudhyamānasya tāvat tasmin navasare sādhuvādo vitīryate na tu paurvāparya-parāmarśo tathā trāpīti bhāvaḥ
   "Even this actual love-making has been described by the poet (vis. kālidāsa(gifted with imaginative genius, in such a fashion that our hearts come to rest in the description itself, with no scope for reflection on propriety. The case is similar to one in which there is described a genuinely courageous man who is fighting for a wrong cause (*aviṣaye*).

For the moment, we say "Bravo". But not upon later reflection. The same is true in the case of the description of love-making among the gods".

161. *Locana*, p. 586 :
kṣaṇe kṣaṇe yan navatām upaiti tad eva rūpaṁ ramaṇīyatāyā
"That which at every moment attains novelty,
that alone is the form (and essence) of loveliness".
cf. *Śiśupālavadham* of Māgha, IV. 17.

162. *Locana*, p. 582 :
nanu yady api varṇyam apūrvan nāsti tathāpy uktiparipākagumphaghaṭanādy aparaparyāyabandhacchāyā navanavā bhaviṣyati
"It may be that there is nothing new left to describe; still, the beauty of composition (style) for which the words *ukti*, *parīpākagumpha*, *ghaṭana* etc. are all synonymous, can be ever new."
NB. The expressions *paripāka* refers to the fact that words in a poem are not interchangeable and that to substitute synonyms for the words actually used is to destroy the poem. However, neither Ānandavardhana nor Abhinavagupta has not discussed this important aspect. Rājaśekhara, Vāmana (*KSV*. 1.2.21, 1.3.15, 3.2.15) and Vidyānātha elaborate this aspect. Their *'drākṣāpāka'* and *nārikelapāka* are famous. cf. S.K.*De. History of Sanskrit poetics*, 11 p. 240-242.

163. *Locana*, p. 583 :
apūrvabandhacchāyāyuktānām api paropanibaddhārthanibandhane parakṛta kāvyatvavyavahāra eva syād ity arthasyāpūrvatvam āśrayaṇīyam kavanīyaṁ kāvyaṁ tasya bhāvaḥ kāvyatvam
"Even though a poem composed by a writer on a theme already used by an earlier poet is marked by a new style, it will have (according to the view of opponents) to be regarded as poetry compared by the later poets. Therefore, it must be accepted that (for a composition to be regarded as poetry) there must be novelty of ideas (arising from the use of one or other variety of *dhvani*. The word *kāvyatva* means 'the state of being poetry' and the word *kāvya* means 'fit to be recited' *kavanīya* (being derived from the root *ku*

to utter or recite by adding the potential participle suffix *ya*)".

N.B. This above passage is also a part of definition of *pratibhā* according to Bhaṭṭa Tauta. See FN No. 150, ch. II.

164. *Locana*, p. 587

tad vat parakīyaśikṣānapekṣanijapratibhāguṇa-niṣyandabhūtaḥ kāvyārtha iti

"The essence of poetry is that which flashes from (poet's) own *pratibhā*, without waiting for the teachings of others".

165. *Ibid.* :

uttarakālantu vyaṅgyasparśanena
vicitratāṁ parāṁ bhajatān nāma

"Later on with the touch of suggestion it (poetic speech) attains peculiarities."

166. *Ibid.*, pp. 583-84 :

yadi vā vācyān tāvad dvividhavyaṅgyopayogi
tad eva ced anantaṁ tad valād eva vyaṅgyānantyaṁ
bhavatīty abhiprāyeṇedaṁ prakṛtam evocyate
vyaṅgyaviṣayo yo vyāpāraḥ tat śparśaṁ vināpy
ānantyaṁ svarūpamātreṇaiva paścāt tu tathā
svarūpeṇānantaṁ sad vyaṅgyaṁ vyanaktīti bhāvaḥ
na tu sarvathā tatra vyayaṁ nāstīti mantavyam
ātmabhūtatadrūpābhāve kāvyavyavahārahāneḥ

"Or else one can explain (this digression) as follows : The literal sense is itself useful to the different kinds of suggested sense. If this literal sense is endless, then through the force ot this, the suggested sense is also endless. From this point of view it (*kā*. 7) is contextual and not incidental. When he says : 'the purely denoted sense' the meaning is that even without the benefit of that function (namely suggestiveness) that takes for its province the suggested sense, there is endlessness, quite on its own, and that the literal sense, endless on its own, later reveals the endlessly diverse suggested sense. One should not think that in such cases there is no suggested sense at all, because one could not even call a work a poem at all if it did not have (some connection) with a suggested sense, which is (after all) the very soul (of poetry)."

167. *Locana*, p. 559 :

uktavaicitryeṇa tu ta evārthā niravadhayo

bhavantīti tad viṣayāṇāṁ pratibhānām ānantyam upapannam iti । *nanu pratibhānantyasya kiṁ phalam iti nirṇetuṁ vāṇī navatvam āyātīty uktam tena vāṇ-īnāṁ kāvyavākyānāṁ tāvan navatvam āyāti* ।

"But because of the variety of striking ways of expressing things, those same topics (*artha*) become inexhaustible, and thus it is only reasonable to say that the faculty of *pratibhā* with respect to them is also endless. objection : what is the purpose of the endlessness of *pratibhā.* In order to explain this he said : literature appears afresh'. By this (employment of different varieties of *dhvani*, speech, that is, poetic sentences, (ultimately) become novel."

168. *Ibid.*:

tac ca pratibhānantye saty upapadyate ।
tac cārthānantye tac ca dhvaniprabhedād iti

"This (i.e. novelty of poetic sentences) takes place when there is an endlessness of *pratibhā.* And this takes place when there is an endlessness of themes. And this takes place through varieties of *dhvani.*"

N.B. The causal chain is therefore as follows :
dhvanibhedāśrayaṇa gives rise to *arthānantya,*
which gives rise to *kavipratibhānantya,* which
gives finally rise to *kāvyavākyānāṁ navatam.*

The only convincing link is *kavipratibhā* which one would expect to precede *arthānantya.* The *pratibhānantya* need not precede *arthānantya.* Rather it should follow *arthānantya.* Employment of one or another kind of *dhvani* gives rise to *arthānantya; arthānantya* gives rise to *pratibhā-nantya* (for unless there is diversion of topics, the poet cannot have an imaginative fusion of them, the poets imagination cannot visualise them). Finally *pratibhānantya* gives rise to novelty of poetic utterance.

169. *Locana*, p. 559 :

varṇanīyavastuniṣṭhaḥ prajñāviśeṣaḥ pratibhānam

" The *pratibhāna* is the special intelligence that remains in the objects described."

cf. Vasugupta, *Spandakārikā,* IV. 7; L. Silburn, *Vātulanāth sūtra,* p. 14. 38; Masaki Hattori, *"Apoha and pratibhā" Sanskrit and Indian Studies,* Essays in Honour of Daniel H.H. Ingalls, D.Reidel publishing company, Dordrecht, Holland, p. 61-

73, Introduction to S.K. De's ed. of *Vakrokti jīvita*, pp. XXIV ff. T.N. Sreekantiya, "Imagination in Indian poetics", IHQ. 13, p. 59, 1937; Haricand Sastri, "Kālidāsa et L Art Poetique de 1' Inde., p. 64: D.D. Ruegg, *Contributions*, p. 57: Gauriñath Śāstri, *Philosophy of word and meaning*, p. 89, Somānanada's *Śivadṛṣti* 11. 64 (p. 78); *YogaŚūtra*, 111. 36: *sivapurāṇa* XXIX. 78; *Mahābhārata* XII. 236.20, XII.260.1, XII. 274.7, XII. 316.14, XIII 239.24; *Saṁyutta Nikāya* 1.187 (8.3); *Aṅguttara Nikāya* 111. 239; *Abhisamayālaṁkāra* 1.68 (p.27, ConZe's ed. ISMEO, 1954); *Mahāvastu*, 1.134. 7: Śuresvara's *Vārttika* on the *Taittirīya Upaniṣad* 9.V.160; *Uttararāmacaritam* of Bhavabhūti, 11.45; K.C. Pandey, *Abhinavagupta*, 1963, pp. 692-732.

170. *Abh.* III. GOS. p. 306 :
paramārthas tu parakīyaprotsāhanatāratamyodita-prakṛtibhānapratyayabalena vā svataḥ pratibhānamāhātmyena vā tatra pūrvā manuṣyaniṣpāditatvān mānuṣīty ucyate

171. *Kāvya Mīmāṁsā* of Rājaśekahra, ed. Kedarnath Sharma, Patna, 1965, ch. IV. p. 27:
samādhir ānatarah prayatno bāhyas tv abhyāsaḥ ı tāvubhāvapi śaktim udbhāsayataḥ śā kevalaṁ kāvye hetuḥ iti yāyāvarīyaḥ

172. *Ibid.*:
yā śabdagrāmam arthasārtham alaṁkāratantramuktimārgam anyad api tathāvidham adhihṛdayaṁ pratibhāsayati sā pratibhā. apratibhasya padārthasārthaḥ parokṣha iva, pratibhāvataḥ puna apaśyato'pi pratyakṣa iva

173. *Ibid.*, V. p. 40 :
pratibhāvyutpattīmithaḥ samavete śreyasyav iti yāyāvarīyaḥ na khalu lāvaṇya lābhād ṛte rūpasampad ṛte rūpasampado vā lāvaṇya-labdhir mahate saundaryāya

174. *KP.* 1.3

175. *KS.* p.6
pratibhānavanavollekhaśāliniprajñā asya kāvyasyedaṁ pradhānakāraṇaṁ vyutpattyābhyāsau tu pratibhāyā eva saṁskāraka

176. *Ibid.*

savitur iva prakāśasvabhāvasya
ātmano 'bhrapaṭalam iva jñānāvaraṇīyādyā
varaṇam tasyoditasya kṣaye 'nuditasya
upaśame ca yah prakāśāvirbhāvaḥ sā
sahajā pratibhā

177. *Ibid.*: *vyutpatyābhyāsābhyāṁ saṁskāryā*
178. VJ. ed. K.Krishnamoorthy, 1977, 1.40
179. *VJ*. p. 36, 16-17, 18-19 :
sa ca vakrabhāvas tathāvidho yaḥ
sahasradhā bhidyate bahuprakāraṁ
bhedam āsādayati yasmāt kavipratibhānām
ānantyān niyatatvaṁ na sambhavati
"The artistic beauty which is under consideration now is thousandfold in its manifestations. That is to say it is analysable into numerous varieties since the ways of poetic imagination are endless, no specific number of varieties can be laid down."
180. *Ibid.* , p. 39, 2-3.
181. *Ibid.*, p. 7, 10-11; p. 8, 3-4.
182. *Ibid.*, p. 9, 1-4:
sphuritam eva kavicetasi prathamaṁ ca
pratibhāpratibhāsamānam
aghaṭitapāṣāṇaśakalakalpamaṇiprakhyam eva
vastu vidagdhakaviviracitavakravākyopārūḍhaṁ
śāṇollīḍhmaṇimanoharatayā
tadvidāhlādakārikāvyatvam adhirohati
".... a subject when it first flashes across the poetic imagination will be no better than a very rough stone; it comes to be finally polished by the poet in the course of being embodied in beautiful language, and strikes the man of taste as a precious diamond fully polished".
cf. *VP*. I.82-84; *SS*. p.43.
183. *VJ*. p. 44, 4-5 :
tat sarvam alaṁkārādipratibhodbhavaṁ
kaviśakti samullasitam eva
184. *Ibid.*, I. 34.
185. *Ibid.*, pp. 58-59, 21-23, 1:
yat pratīyamānatvenodāracaritasya etc.
186. *Ibid.*, p. 54, 1-2,

pratibhāyāḥ kaviśakter caramollekhāvasare

187. *Ibid.*, p. 11, 21-23.
188. *Ibid.*, p. 16.
189. *Ibid.*, p. 45, 3-5: also see K.Krishnamoorthy, "The nature of creative *pratibhā* according to Kuntaka". Indologica Taurinensia, Vol. VIII-IX, 1980-81, Tonno
190. *RG.* Vol. I, BHU, 1963, p. 48
    sā ca kāvyaghaṭanānukūlaśabdārthopasthitiḥ
191. *Ibid.*, p. 46.
    tasya ca kāranaṁ kavigatā kevalā pratibhā
192. *Ibid.*, pp. 49-51:
    tasyās ca hetuḥ kvacid devatāmahāpuruṣa-prasādādijanyam adṛṣṭam
193. *Ibid.*, pp. 51-51.
    kvacic ca vilakṣaṇavyutpatti kāvyakaraṇābhyāsau...

3

Dhvani

Dhvani theory of Ānandavardhana

The *dhvani* theory of Ānandavardhana has been discussed profusely by ancient and modern scholars from different angles. The aim of the present book is to trace the origin of this theory in the *Vākyapadīya* of Bhartṛhari. It also aims to analyse the suggestive semantics of Ānandavardhana. Therefore in previous chapters an account of the theories of *sphoṭa* and *pratibhā* of Bhartṛhari has been given with special reference to the prominent traits which would have been the source of the *dhvani* theory. In this chapter the *dhvani* theory is analysed from linguistic point of view as seen by Ānandavardhana.

The *dhvani* concept is a new device in Sanskrit poetics. It deals with a secret language formula, other than conventional denotation which is generally practised by poets. Long before Ānandavardhana there were traditions of Sanskrit literary criticism. Bhāmaha, Daṇḍin, Vāmana and Rudraṭa are the great critics whose contributions to Sanskrit poetics are quite considerable. They handle poetic speech differently. Bhāmaha, the most fundamental thinker of *alaṁkāra* school, subsumes poetic speech under two heads, namely *svabhāvokti* and *vakrokti*. The *svabhāvokti* is a special type of speech which describes the object as it is and its use is approved for *vārtābhidhāna* and *varṇanā*[1].

But *vakrokti* is a striking mode of expression which is the mother of all figures of speech[2]. It is a type of speech which is liked by the poets.[3] According to them, a poet should express the poetic situations either in natural language or in artificial language. This treatment of poetic language appears to be hazy. No evidence is available as to the fact that the great predecessors of Ānanadavardhana chalked out a language to describe emotive situations. They only analyse the external decorations and organs of poetry without having an insight into the inner agitation. Ānanadavardhana's discovery of *dhvani* reveals many aspects about the understanding of poetry. His concept of *dhvani* is a frozen language formula which manifests the 'poetic relish' *rasa*. The *rasa*, according to him, remains in all elements of poetry without which the poetic speech is reduced to ordinary talk.

When an imaginative link between the poet and the reader is created, poetic communication becomes possible. The function of speech is to link what the poet speaks and what the reader or listener comprehends. This is of two typess, i.e. primary and secondary. This law of dichotomy is the undercurrent of Ānandavardhana's *dhvani* language. He has divided speech into two halves, i.e. 'denotative' *vācya* and 'suggestive' *pratīyamāna*. Both are essential for poetry. The suggestive elements of language are more essential in poetry than the denotative elements. But the suggestive elements of language have no physical existence although they are indirectly connected with the elements of speech. They are manifested through denotative elements.

In this perspective, Ānanadavardhana's view resembles with the views of modern linguists and psychologists. According to them, language may be divided into two classes, i.e. symbolic language and emotive language. This symbolic language is similar to the denotative elements of speech. It expresses general ideas pertaining to history and religious works. The emotive language is similar to *dhvani* language. It describes the poetic ideas and creates aesthetic delight in the poet and connoisseurs. The difference between symbolic and emotive language has been analysed by Ogden and Richards in *The Meaning of Meaning*, 1960, p. 149. According to them, "the symbolic use of words is statement, the recording, the support, the organisation and the communication of reference. The emotive use of works is a more simple matter, it is the use of words to express or excite feelings and attitudes....Each of these contrasted functions has, it will be seen, two sides, that of the speaker and that of the listener. Under the symbolic function are included both the symbolisation of reference and its communication to the listener, i.e. the causing in the listener of a similar reference. Under the emotive function are included both the expression of emotions, attitudes, moods etc. in the speaker, and their communication, i.e. their evocation in the listener."

Like Ogden and Richards, Ānandavardhana holds that 'denotative word' *vācaka śabda* and 'denoted sense' *vācya artha* are necessary for ordinary descriptions, whereas 'suggestive word' *vyañjaka śabda* and suggested sense' *vyaṅgya artha* are to be used for poetic delineations. In poetic speech, the denotative elements are subordinate to suggestive elements. But the latter depends on the former for manifestation. Ānandavardhana compares the denotative elements of speech (*DL* 1.9) with a candle on which the suggestive elements, as light, remain.

Ogden and Richards state exactly the same thing :

'It is true that some element of reference probably enters, for all civilised adults at least, into almost all use of words, and it is always possible to import a reference, if it be only a reference to things in general. The two functions under consideration usually occur together but none the less they are in principle distinct....provided that the attitude or feeling is evoked the most important function of such language (i.e. poetic language) is fulfilled, and any symbolic function that the words may have is instrumental only and subsidiary to the evocative function' (*The Meaning of Meaning*, 1960, p. 150).

Thus the truth behind the philosophy of poetic language described by Ogden and Richards and Ānandavardhana appears to be the same. A detailed accounts of Ānandavardhana's linguistic philosophy is made in the forth coming sections.

Dhvani language and suggestion

The *dhvani* theory has a long tradition which came down through the preceptors and pupils. Probably at the time of Ānandavardhana it came to a saturation and he propounded the theory. This *dhvani* language is a special type of poetic speech which is marked by the existence of suggestion. It has a very wide field. The phonemes, roots, prefixes, suffixes, words, part of words, sentences, essays and complete works are the varied fields of *dhvani* language. By the touch of suggestion all these above elements transform their common properties of speech to poetic diction. Ancient Indian philosophers admit that language has four functions to cognise meanings, namely denotative, indicative, suggestive and purport. When a listener hears an utterance he understands the surface meaning of the expressions. The meaning is the relation between words and objects meant by them. The surface meaning is known by the denotative or primary function of language. Eight methods[4] and contextual factors[5] help to determine this primary meaning. But when this primary meaning of an expression fails to reveal the actual intention of the speaker, another function known as indicative is invoked. This is called *amukhyā vṛtti* or *gauṇī vṛtti*. Incompatibility of the primary sense is an essential condition for accepting the secondary sense. But when this function also fails, we have the suggestion which is based on denotation and indication.

According to Ānandavardhana, speech is of two types, i.e. primary and suggestive. The poetic senses are expressed by both these speeches. The poetic speech is marked by the existence of figures, merits and different types of charming expressions. But these are external decorations which do not enhance the beauty of the soul. These are surface properties of the poetic expression which are known through the denotative function. The true spirit of poetry is something else. It is suggestion which reveals the beautiful meaning of the poetry. Connoisseurs admit its existence (*DL* 1.3). It pervades the whole poetic composition giving novel charm and meaning to it. The *dhvani* language is marked by the suggestive elements. It includes the suggestive word, suggestive sense, suggested sense, the function of suggestion, and the work as a whole. The suggestive elements are different from the denotative elements in poetry. He gives a beautiful analogy to explain it. As the glamour of a beautiful woman is different from her physical frame, similarly, the real beauty of poetic diction is different from the structures of poetic expression. The real beauty of poetry is the suggestive element which is as good as the glamour of a beautiful enchantress. The denotative elements are comparable to the various limbs of the body of the lady[6]. The suggestive elements may be traceable in different forms of speech-manifestations i.e., in facts, figures and aesthetic delights. This is the idea of *dhvani* language in a nutshell. Before making a critical analysis, its existence should be traced back in the works of earlier rhetorics. It will help to evaluate the concept of *dhvani* properly and its real contribution can be measured successfully.

Latent hints of *dhvani* in earlier works on rhetorics

The term *dhvani* is used many times in the poetic works before Ānandavardhana. The great poets, namely Kālidāsa, Bhāravi and Māgha etc. use the term *dhvani* in the sense of sound. Kālidāsa used it either for the murmur in the forest, or for the sound of a drum; again it is found to connote the sound of the sea, or sounds of the instrumental or vocal music.[7] Bhāravi and Māgha use the term in the same sense as Kālidāsa.[8] Bhavabhūti uses the term to denote *svara.*[9]

It has been stated that, according to Ānandavardhana, *dhvani* stands for a language formula of poetry. It arises when the surface meaning of the expression loses its significance to some other meaning. This idea of *dhvani* was in vogue long before Ānandavardhana.

In the *Nāṭya Śāstra* of Bharata latent existence of *dhvani* can be traced. Abhinavagupte claims that the existence of *dhvani* in earlier works of rhetorics is indirect. Bharata was aware of *dhvani* meaning of the poetic expression. *Rasa,* according to him is suggested. Though he analyses *rasa* in relation to drama, his *rasa* can be applicable to poetry also. His references to suggested sense may be found out in the *Nāṭya Śāstra.* He says, "how is *rasa* tasted? (In reply) it is said that just as well disposed persons while eating food cooked with many kinds of spice, enjoy *(āsvādayanti)* its tastes, and attain pleasure and satisfaction, so the cultured people taste the durable psychological states while they see them represented by an expression of the various psychological states with words, gestures, and the *sattva* and derive pleasure and satisfaction. Just as a connoisseur of cooked food (*bhakta*) while eating food which has been prepared from various spices and other articles tastes it, so the learned people taste in their heart (*manas*) the durable psychological states (such as love, sorrow etc.) when they are represented by an expression of psychological states with gestures. Hence these durable psychological states in a drama are called sentiments.[10]

In the above passage Bharata has consciously used two terms, namely *vāgaṅga sattvopetān* 'with words, gestures, and the *sattva,* and *bhāvābhinayavyañjitān* 'represented by an expression of the various psychological states' to imply that *rasa* is suggested. He could have used the term *saṁbandhān* instead of *vyañjitān* which would have given the same literal sense. But he has the idea of suggestion in his mind. So he consciously uses these terms.

Again in the verses VI. 32-33 quoted above, Bharata has consciously uses the terms, *vudhāḥ* 'learned' and *manasā* 'in the mind'. The literal sense of these two words could have been denoted by *paṇḍitāḥ* and *cetasā* respctively. By these particular terms Bharata intends that the relish of *rasa* is dependant on suggestion. The relisher is a connoisseur and not an intellectual. The relish is felt in the mind and not in the intellect.

(ii) Bharata was aware of the *abhivyaktivāda* which Abhinavagupta has expounded in connection with *rasa*. This theory implies that *rasa* is manifested by the power of suggestion. It can neither be created nor informed nor enjoyed. It is a state of the mind. It is brought by various propensities which are inherited from previous birth of a human being. Bharata suggests this idea in the following passages : "Now the durable psychological states are eight in number. The complementary psychological states are thirty three and the *sāttvika* states are eight in number. These are the three varieties of psychological states. Hence we are to understand that there are fortynine psychological states capable of drawing out the sentiment from the play. These sentiments arise from them when they are imbued with the quality of universality. The psychological states proceeding from the thing which is congenial to the heart, is the source of sentiment and it pervades the body just as fire spreads over dry wood".[11]

Further, Bharata's idea on *abhivyaktivāda* is prominent in the following passage : It is said in this connection, if the fortynine psychological states being represented by determinants and consequents coming into contact with one another become sentiments when they are imbued with the quality of universality, how is it that durable psychological states only are changed into sentiments (and not others) ? (In reply to this) it is said : "just as among persons having the same characteristics and similar hands, feet and belly and celebrity, some due to their birth manners, learning, skill in arts and crafts, attain kingship, while others endowed with an inferior intellect become their attendant, in a similar manner, determinants, consequents and complementary psychological states become dependent on the durable psychological states. Being the shelter (of others) the durable psychological states are masters. Similarly, other psychological states (lit. feelings) reduced to subordination take shelter with them (i.e. the durable psychological states) due to superior merit (of the latter). Those becoming their retinue are the complementary psychological states. Is there any parallel instances? (Answer) Just as only a king surrounded by numerous attendants receives this epithet and not any other man, be he ever so great, so the durable psychological states only followed by determinants, consequents and complementary psychological states, receive the name of sentiment".[12]

Unless one has no idea of suggestion, how can he claims that the 'psychological states' *bhāvas* are suggested. Bharata was certainly aware of the poetic meaning of language other than the surface meaning.

(iii) In the seventh chapter of the *Nāṭyaśāstra* (GOS, Verse.4-5), it is stated that *bhāvas* are the causes of the manifestation of *rasa*. It has been stated there that *rasas* are *vyaṅgya* 'suggested' and *bhāvas* are 'suggesters' *vyañjakas.*

(iv) Abhinavagupta in his commentary on the *NŚ. VI.*33, analyses the terms *vyañjita* and *vyaṅgya* etc. In the word *āsvādayanti* 'relished' used by Bharata, he notes

the traces of suggestion in the prefix *ā*.[13] Abhinavagupta is a true successor of Ānandavardhana. He has analysed Bharata's concept of *rasa* and *bhāva* from the standpoint of suggestion. There are ample evidences with regard to the fact that where Bharata would have uttered the word *rasa*, Abhinavagupta would say that suggestion must be there[14].

(v) There are parallel ideas in the passages of the *Dhvanyāloka* and the *Nāṭya Śāstra* :

DL. 1-2 :

kāvyasyātmā dhvanir iti

'the soul of poetry is *dhvani* suggestion.'

NŚ. VI. 38. GOS, p. 294 :

yathā bījād bhaved vṛkṣo
vṛkṣāt puṣpaṁ phalaṁ yathā ।
tathā mūlaṁ rasāḥ sarve
tebhyo bhāvā vyavasthitā ॥

NŚ. VII.7, GOS, p. 348 :

yo'rtho hṛdayasaṁvādī
tasya bhāvo rasodbhavaḥ ।
śarīraṁ vyāpyate yena
śuṣkakāṣṭham ivāgninā ॥

"Just as a tree grows from a seed, and flowers and fruits from a tree, so the sentiments are the source (lit. root) of all the psychological states, and likewise the psychological states exist (as the source) of all the sentiments."

"The psychological states proceeding from the thing which is congenial to the heart, is the source of the sentiment and it pervades the body just as fire spreads over dry-wood."

Following the foot-steps of Bharata, Ānandavardhana says that *rasa* is the life of poetry and drama[15]. What Bharata implies by the term *rasa,* Ānandavardhana suggests it by *rasadhvani*[16]. Both agree on the point that there can be no poetry without the existence of *rasa.* This concept of *rasa* is as old as the work of Bharata[17].

(vi) Bharata has described thirty six *nāṭya lakṣaṇas.* Abhinavagupta has discussed all these *lakṣaṇas* exhaustively and concludes that each of them is a peculiar type of 'denotative function' *abhidhāvyāpāra*[18]. But in reality all these *lakṣaṇas* are not normal denotative functions obtained by various methods namely *śaktigraha* etc.[19]. They gradually, quickly and quietly prepared the ground for 'denotation, merged in other meanings. *arthāntarasaṁkramitavācya* 'denotation completely lost', *atyantatiraskṛta vācya,* 'suggestion whose sequence is visible', *saṁlakṣyakramavyaṅgyadhvani,* suggestion based on 'idea', *vastu,* 'figures of speech', *alaṁkāra* and 'sentiment' *rasa*[20]. In all thirty six *lakṣaṇa* the reverberation of another meaning other than surface meaning is noticed. Though in each *lakṣaṇas* the element of suggestion based on figures of speech remains, it is more prominent in the list mentioned below :

śobhā	*Nāṭyaśāstra*	*XVI. 7*
udāharaṇa	do	XVI.9, 11 (*anubandha*)
manoraths	do	XVI.20, 36 *(anubandha)*
ākhyāna	do	XVI.21
leśa	do	XVI. 39
arthāpatti	do	XVI.39
bhraṁśa	do	XVI.27

It is clear from these above evidences that Bharata was aware of the intrinsic meaning of the poetic expression other than the surface meaning which Ānandavardhana calls *dhvani* meaning.

Traces of suggestion in the *Kāvyālaṁkāra* of Bhāmaha

Bhāmaha is not the founder of the *alaṁkāra* school. There was a long tradition of the use of figures of speech as decorations to the poetic expression, probably before Bharata. In the *Ṛgveda*, figurative uses are very common[21]. According to Bhāmaha, poetry is built of words and senses which are embellished by figures of speech. By this act he seems to emphasise on the contextual sense of the expression. But his awareness of non-contextual sense is prominent from the use of certain figures of speech. He uses certain terms, namely, *guṇasāmyapratītiḥ, KL.* II. 34, 'cognition on the basis of resemblance', *gamyate'nyo'rthaḥ, KL.* II.79, 'another meaning being implied', *avagamayati, KL.* VII. 40, 'suggested' which are abundantly found in the *Dhvanyāloka.* Bhāmaha's idea of suggestion may be noticed in the following figures of speech :

(i) In *prativastūpamā* 'typical comparison', the common attributes are implied[22].

(ii) In *samāsokti* 'condensed metaphor' some non-contextual meanings are suggested *gamyate*[23].

(iii) In *paryāyokta* 'periphrasis' the actual import is different from the surface meaning of the expression. Bhāmha's example is noteworthy here. When Śiśupāla requests to take food in his house, Lord Kṛṣṇa refused. He says that whether in the house or outside, he does not take food unless brahmins have taken it first. He fears Śiśupāla may mix poison with his food. Kṛṣṇa's hesitation suggests that Śiśupāla will not mix poison in the food for the fear of killing brahmins which is a sin[24]. According to Bhāmaha, this indirect beautiful meaning of the expreasion is implied. In this case Ānandavardhana would have said that this is due to suggestion.

(iv) In *arthāntaranyāsa*. *KL*.II.71, 'transition' *ākṣepa*, *KL*.11.68, 'paraleipsis', *apahnuti* *KL*.III.21, 'fancied denial' *rasavat*, *KL*.III.6, 'impassioned', *vyājastuti*. *KL* III.31, 'artful praise' the beauty lies in the non-contextual sense.

Ānandavardhana is also aware of the fact that the figures of speech as defined by Bhāmaha are touched by the suggestive elements. In his words : "that the group of expressed figures of speech, when it is accompanied by a suggested element, be it either a figure of speech or a situation as the case may be, endows them with great beauty, has been partially shown by elder rhetoricians. Most of the figures of speech when they are closely examined are found to be like this (i.e. accompanied by a suggested element). And thus generally *dīpaka*, *samāsokti* and other similar figures of speech are found to involve some suggested figure of speech or other, or some suggested situation or other. For in the first place, all figures of speech contain some exaggeration (hyperbole). When great poets use it, it endows with a quite special poetic beauty. For how can a judicious use of 'hyperbole' *atiśaya* fail to impart to poetry a high degree of excellence? As has been said by Bhāmaha when dealing with hyperbole : All the figures of speech are just this *(atiśayokti)*. Through this, (ordinary) ideas are beautiful. A poet should make efforts with regard to that. What figures of speech can there be without hyperbole? In this matter, whatever figures of speech possesses hyperbole through the force of poetic imagination, that figure of speech becomes exceptionally beautiful, whereas if hyperbole is not there it will be merely a plain figure of speech. And so, since hyperbole is able to incarnate itself into all figures of speech, one says, through 'metaphor based on identification' *abhedopacāra*, that hyperbole alone is the form of all figures of speech. 'This is the only meaning that one should understand (from the stanza of Bhāmaha).[25] Thus, according to Bhāmaha, the existence of hyperbole is an essential element in all figures of speech. Ānandavardhana in this case adds that this element of hyperbole in poetic figures is a stepping stone to the hierarchy of suggestion. In this connection, S.K. De says that Bhāmaha cannot be included among *dhvanyābhāvavādins* 'those who deny the existence of *dhvani'*, rather he is an *antarbhāvavādin* who has merged *dhvani* in the figures of speech[26].

From the above discussion it is clear that though Bhāmaha did not define the suggestive element categorically be knew its existence through non-contextual meanings and hyperboles. Ānandavardhana has utilised this finding of Bhāmaha in this work.

Suggestion in the kāvyādarśa of Daṇḍin

Daṇḍin knew the suggested sense. He has used the terms *pratīyate* 'suggested' in the context of *udāraguṇa* *KD*.I.76, and *vyañjitam* 'suggested' in the context of *udāttālaṁkāra, KD*.II.303. He also uses the term *guṇavṛtti* to imply the secondary meaning other than the primary meaning, *KD*.I.95. According to him, the 'quality of excellence' *udāraguṇa* is suggested. In the example of *udāttālaṁkāra,* he has shown that the greatness of Rāma and prospertiy of Rāvaṇa are suggested[28]. Further, he has said that the behaviour of the non-contextual is superimposed upon the contextual in *samādhiguṇa* and condensed metaphor[29]. Daṇḍin's *upamālaṁkāra* 'simile' is marked by the primary and secondary meanings, *KD*.II.14. In his *tulyayogitā* 'equal pairing' and *prativastūpamā* 'typical comparison', the similitude is obtained by implication[30]. Other important figures of speech, namely *atiśayokti,* 'hyperbole'[31] *paryāyokti* 'periphrasis'[32] and *aprastutaprasaṁśā* 'vicarious reference' convey the beautiful meaning through implication only.

Daṇḍin has started an objective inquiry into the soul of poetry[34]. Ānandavardhana succeeded in this attempt. Vāmana also investigates the causes and nature of poetry before Ānandavardhana. But when Bhāmaha emphasises on the surface structure of the poetry, Daṇḍin and Vāmana attempt to find out internal essence that is soul of poetry. According to Vāmana, the soul of poetry is 'style' *rīti*[35], whereas, according to Ānandavardhana, it is *dhvani* 'suggestion' which deals with the value of speech form beyond the expressive level of language.

Elements of suggestion in the *Kāvyālaṁkārasārasaṁgraha* of Udbhaṭa

Udbhaṭa alongwith Bhāmaha and Daṇḍin discovers a peculiar type of meaning in the figure *paryāyokta* 'periphrasis', other than the denotative meaning. He says that in this figure something is indirectly stated. This indirect meaning is suggested by *avagamana*. Though he does not state that *avagamana* is a function, yet from his treatment one can infer it so. According to Udbhaṭa, the periphrasis[36] is a mode of speech which is known by a peculiar way of expression other than the denotative one. This *avagamana* is nothing but suggestion. Ānandavardhana believes that Udbhaṭa knows the nature of suggestion.[37] Thus what Udbhaṭa wants to say by *avagamana,* Hemacandra and Kaniṣṭha Vāgbhaṭa after hundreds of years say by suggestion.[38]

Udbhaṭa's idea of *guṇavṛtti*[39] is later on developed into indicative function. He uses certain technical terms which are very essential for *rasa*. They are *bhāva, anubhāva* etc.[40] He has mentioned several *rasas* also[41]. From all these facts it can be assumed that he had hazy notion of suggestion which helps to relish the *rasa.*

Ruyyaka, one of the leading rhetoricians of the post *dhvani* period, thinks that Udbhaṭa and others subsume suggested sense under the figures of speech as an embellishment of denotative sense. Instead of taking this suggested sense independently, they consider it as an accessory of denotative sense. They also think that *rasa* is an accessory element[42]. In this connection S.K. De's remark is noteworthy. He says, "Udbhaṭa can be taken as we have seen, to have been cognisant of a suggested sense, though he never speaks of *dhvani* or deals with it directly; but Pratihārendurāja refers to it in clearest terms and attempts by forced interpretation to make out that Udbhaṭa deliberately included it in the treatment of poetic figures."[43]

Udbhaṭa unconsciously proceeded on the road which led to suggestion. He got inspiration from his predecessors in this regard and developed his ideas which are not actually beyond the events of language. His attempt to do so is a search for the real beauty of poetry and poetic speech which is further clarified by Rudraṭa in his *Kāvyālaṁkāra.*

Suggestive elements in the *Kāvyālaṁkāra* of Rudraṭa

Rudraṭa has a better and clear idea on *pratīyamānārtha* 'secondary signification' than his predecessors. For the first time in Sanskrit poetics he admits ten *rasas* adding two more namely *śānta* and *preyān* (*KLR.* XII.3) to Bharata's eight (*NS.* VI.15). According to him, every poetic expression should have the elements of *rasa*[44]. Earlier to him Daṇḍin had confirmed the existence of *rasa* in poetic speech[45]. But it was not clearly brought out. Rudraṭa does not speak of *dhvani* directly. He feels that poetic emotions and feelings cannot be brought to consciousness by literal expression. It can be made an object of direct experience only indirectly. He has pointed out a kind of meaning in some figures to which the suggestionists may call *dhvani* meaning. His figure of speech, *bhāva*, can be analysed as follows : In this figure, the actual import is a meaning other than the expressed sense that connotes the speaker's attitude. Before actual communication, the speaker has some metabolic changes in his inner being that are manifested through various actions. The causes of those metabolic transformations are not regular causes. They are somehow different and they communicate the actual import to the listener in an unusual way[46]. A beautiful illustration is given by

Rudraṭa, later quoted by Mammaṭa (*KP*.I.5.3) to show what *bhāva* is. This figure *bhāva* is same as suggestion. A young woman has an appointment with a young man in an *aśoka* bower which was a secluded place. But she could not meet him at the appointed hour. The disappointed young man returns with a bunch of *bañjula*. His fiancie saw it and her face became dark. Here the cause of the dark countenance is that she is deprived of the pleasure of love. This beautiful meaning is suggested and not expressed. In the absence of the *bañjula* stalk she could not have understood that she missed the pleasure[47].

Referring to the secondary meaning, Rudraṭa states that a sentence connotes its actual import after expressing its external senses. The actual import can either be comprehended through negation or affirmation. This actual import is *bhāva*. Rudraṭa also gives illustration for it. A rustic woman invites a traveller to her bed through negation by stating that her mother-in-law is deaf and suffers from night-blindness. She is alone and her husband is away. Taking this opportunity the traveller may not creep to her bed[48]. Here the *bhāva* 'feeling' is the invitation for the traveller to the woman's bed. This is suggested by 'intonatioh' *kāku*.

Again Rudraṭa's 'periphrasis' *paryāyokta* is nothing but suggestion. When the literal meaning implies another meaning which is neither producer nor produced, then the figure periphrasis comes into being[49].

Whether Rudraṭa was aware of the function of suggestion, has been analysed by Ruyyaka and his commentator Jayaratha. They mainly argue on the two types of *bhāvālaṁkāra* of Rudraṭa. Sometimes the secondary sense in *bhāvālaṁkāra* is indicative by nature and sometimes it is suggestive by nature[50]. Jayaratha mentions that *rasa* 'sentiment', *preya* 'lovely' and *urjasvin* 'impetuous' of Rudraṭa are conditioned by suggestion[51]. Ruyyaka says that all the three types of *dhvanis* of Ānandavardhana can be merged in the figures of Rudraṭa. Thus the *vastudhvani* can be found in the figure *bhāva, alaṁkāradhvani* can be found in 'metaphor' *rūpaks,* and *rasadhvani* in *rasavat* 'impassioned', *preyes* 'lovely' etc[52]. Inspite of the severe criticism lodged against Ruyyaka's interpretation of Rudraṭa by S.K.De,[53], it is evident that Rudraṭa has gone much closer to the *dhvani* theory than his predecessors. His *bhāvālaṁkāra* and *rasa* are really an advancement to the objective inquiry of actual poetic beauty. The suggestive meaning which occurs in the form of seed in Rudraṭa, becomes a full grown tree in Ānandavardhana.

An inquiry into the secondary meaning from Bharata to Rudraṭa is not absolutely frustrating. A new concept in the field of literary criticism is not an immediate product. It takes centuries for crystallisation, and ultimately it gets concretised at the hands of a talented man. This supposition is true in the case of *dhvani* concept which is somehow connected with the elements of language. It is revealed through primary meaning of the words. This secondary meaning is considered to be the soul according to Ānandavardhana, whereas, according to Bhāmaha, Udbhaṭa and Rudraṭa, it is more or less attached to the external structure of language. That is why they assume it in different figures of speech. Their observation is not deep. They are contented at the external features of language. But they could not see that beyond they physical structure of language, there is something called soul. It is invisible indeed, but not undeniable. It is to be felt and not to be seen. Ānandavardhana is not satisfied at the symphony of sight. He searches into the symphony of sense (feeling). But nevertheless Bhāmaha and his followers had felt the pulse of secondary meaning, though faintly, like the sight of a distant star. They think that this secondary meaning is an instrument of beautification of the body. They did not introspect properly on the nature of poetic language and beauty.

Ānandavardhana proceeds with introspection and retrospection. Before him there is a long tradition of grammar, *Vedānta* and literary criticism. He utilises their findings whenever necessary. He also contemplated the verbal tradition of *dhvani*. Ultimately the famous theory of *dhvani* emerges with wonderful insight, engulfing all the best contributions of different theories of different centuries.

The *Dhvani* theory of Ānandavardhana

In Sanskrit poetics a new era is dawned at the discovery of the *dhvani* theory by Ānandavardhana. He shifts from subjective to absolute objective inquiry into the nature of poetry. When earlier rhetoricians hotly discussed on the external elements of poetry and poetic language, Ānandavardhana contempleted on the inner element of poetic language. The poetic language has certain characteristics which separate it from ordinary speech. The early rhetoricians like Bhāmaha and others, think that these characteristics are mainly figures of speech and poetic merits. Any ordinary speech can be turned into poetic speech by virtue of figures of speech and poetic merits. But Ānandavardhana has gone further. According to him, figures and merits are only external decorations. The spirit or element which transforms the common speech to poetic speech is *dhvani*. This element is sparked by *pratibhā* 'poetic genius' and remains in all poetic speech of great poets. This *dhvani* element in language is brought about by suggestion. When the literal meaning of an expression loses its significance to some external meaning, the *dhvani* language comes into existence. In reality, it has no concrete shape in the form of the words or sentences. Still it is considered to be the characteristic of language. That is to say it rests on the denotative structure of language. This secondary meaning or *dhvani* meaning is considered to be *pratīyamānārtha* in the *Dhvanyāloka*.

Nature of *pratīyamānārtha*

Ānandavardhana has claimed that *dhvani* is the soul of poetry (*DL*.I.1.) It is not necessarily manifested in the speech of a layman which is often without emotion. It is revealed in the speech of great poets (*DL*. I.8). The soul of poetry is linked with the aesthetic enjoyment *'rasa'* when a person reads the work of a great poet he enjoys the descriptions of the composition. At that time, he is forgetful of the adjoining situations, and his personal failures and foibles. He delves deep into the poetic fathom of feelings. This is a peculiar and unprecedented type of enjoyment in contrast to the worldly enjoyments. This is called the relish of *rasa*. In worldly use, different *rasas* create different feelings, for instance, pathos brings sadness, but in poetic descriptions it brings enjoyment. But this is not a sadistic pleasure. The person who can delineate and communicate *rasa* perfectly and successfully, is a great poet. The judgement of poetic genius depends on appropriate display of *rasa*. In this respect Vālmīki is a great poet. He has metamorphosed the worldly sorrow generated from the lamentation of a curlew whose counterpart was slain by a hunter, to the universalised pathos through a poetic composition. (*DL*.I.5). The poetic language which has the potency to communicate the abovesaid *rasa* to the people of literary taste is called *dhvani* language. The power which brings the *dhvani* language into existance is known as suggestive element.

Ānandavardhana's linguistic philosophy can be brought under two levels. The first level consists of the words and senses. These words are built by the rules of the grammar, and they convey the meaning by the potency of denotation. The second level is completely different from the first level. Meaning in this level has variations. It is not fixed in nature. It is based on the denotative function of language. The prefix, suffix, stem, particle, word, sentence and the whole work can convey this meaning of second level. The comprehension of meaning in the first level depends on grammatical knowledge etc., but the comprehension of meaning in the second level depends on the taste of the connoisseurs (*DL*.I.7)[54]. To understand the language of music also comes under the second level. In this case the experts and appreciators realise the language of music. Suggestion as a power of language which Ānandavardhana has discovered is the spirit of life at the second level. According to Ānandavardhana, the first level is the denotative *vācya* level of language and the second level is the 'suggestive' *pratīyamāna* level of language. Both are essential for poetry. But poetry becomes most beautiful and charming only with the second level of language. This is the *dhvani* language of Ānandavardhana. When the words and senses subordinate their primary signification to evoke some other meaning, namely, suggested meaning, the *dhvani* language emerges[55]. This *dhvani* language is based on suggestive function of words. The definition of *dhvani* contains three elements :

(i) There must be suggestive element.
(ii) The suggestive element must be predominant[56].
(iii) It should shine 'prominently' *sphuṭatva*[57].

In a number of place Ānandavardhana insists on *dhvani* as a soul of poetry whose condition is the primacy of the suggested content[58]. *Rasa* is an essential element in the *dhvanikāvya*. Ānandavardhana says that the *dhvanikāvya* is that type of poetry in which *rasa* is predominantly displayed[59]. This aspect will be discussed in proper place of this work (3.5).

Suggestion is dependent on denotation

The suggested meaning does not operate independently. The 'denotative meaning' *vācyārtha* is directly conveyed by the word, but the suggested meaning is not directly conveyed by the words. It is expressed only by denotative elements of speech. Without the help of denotation, the existence of suggestion cannot be determined. Ānandavardhana explains it by an analogy. Somebody desirous of light brings a candle. Though the light is different from the candle, it is based on the latter. The candle is the receptacle. It is essential before the light is lit. But once it is lit, the light is more important than the candle. Similarly, the denotative elements help the suggestive elements to come to light. They are important until the suggestive elements are comprehended. Once the suggestive elements are realised, the charm of denotative elements are suppressed by the glowing brilliance of the beautiful meaning of suggestion[60].

Ānandavardhana has produced another example which is directly taken from Bhartṛhari. Just as, according to Bhartṛhari, the meanings of smaller units help to comprehend the meaning of the whole sentence, similarly, according to Ānandavardhana, the denotative elements help to arouse the suggestive elements which appear as a flash of lightning. The reality of *dhvani* language is marked by suggestion. Its comprehension is an integrated and unified whole. The denotative elements lose their significance as soon as the suggestive elements are revealed[61]. Suggestion is a separate function of the word which can never be subsumed under other functions, namely, 'denotation' *abhidhā* 'indication' *gauṇīvṛtti* or *lakṣaṇā*, 'purport' *tātparya* and 'inference' *anumāna*[62]. Abhinavagupta says that suggestion can operate through word, sense and function separately and collectively.[63] Thus *dhvani* language is linguistic by nature. It is not extra linguistic as sometimes it is thought of. It is expressed through various media which will be discussed in the subsequent sections.

Process of manifestation of suggestion

The suggestive elements of the *dhvani* language appear suddenly in the unstained mind of the people of literary taste. They appear both in the poets and in the connoisseurs by virtue of '*pratibhā*. In this connection Ānandavardhana says, 'like-wise that' suggested sense bursts forth in a flash in the minds of sensitive readers who (wish to) experience the essential meaning (of poetry) and who are (really) indifferent to the explicit meaning[64]. The suggested meaning flashes in the speech of great poets and lends unearthly delicacy to language. It is the harbinger of poetic speech. Ānandavardhana fancies that Goddess of speech provides in abundance the essential suggested element to the great poets that reveals a shimmering type of poetic imagination[65]. Thus the process of manifestation of suggestion is spontaneous in nature.

Necessity of suggestion for poetic speech

Suggestion is the touch stone of poetic language. No poetry is possible without suggestion. In the words of Ānandavardhana, 'there is by no means any form of poetry which will entrance the sensitive critic where the beauty is not caused by association with a suggested sense. This is the highest secret of poetry which should be meditated on by the wise'[66]. Emphasising the role of suggestion, Ānandavardhana brings about an analogy. The real decoration of women is blush even though they wear ornaments. Similarly, different shades of suggestive meanings are most beautiful embellishments of poetic speech, though they are adorned with poetic figures[67].

The suggestive elements of language are known to connoisseurs (*DL*.I.12). Since the finest sentiments are brought forth by the suggestion, only the refined persons can realise it. They are like goldsmiths who examine the chastity of gold. The excellence of poetry is known by the existence of suggestion in it[68].

Are *pratīyamāna* and *vyaṅgya* different?

A. Amala Dass in his Ph.D. dissertation has stated a very objectionable view in connection with *pratīyamāna*. He says that *pratīyamāna* and *vyaṅgya* are different. Defining *vyaṅgya*, he says, 'it is not an intellectual idea, but an emotionally experienced content, a poetic mood, a situational and social spiritual atmosphere in which it is produced'. According to him, *pratīyamāna* is the way or process by which *vyaṅgya* is known or revealed[69]. But this is not so. The *vyaṅgya* is not a poetic mood; it has nothing to do with social and spiritual atmosphere. Ānandavardhana has never uttered even once about its spiritual nature. He never says that it is produced either in religious places or spiritual gatherings. Again, he never says that the *vyaṅgya* is revealed by *pratīyamāna*. The *pratīyāmāna* is never a way or process by which *vyaṅgya* is manifested.

According to Ānandavardhana, the *pratīyamāna* is an undescribable potencey which remains in poetic work. It is over and above the words and sense. It is similar to the grace of a lady which is different from the limbs (*DL.* I.4). Its presence in one place, beautify the whole composition. If the face of a lady is graceful, and her other parts of the body are not so, even then it is said that the lady is beautiful. Ānandavardhana clearly states *pratīyamāna* as a type of meaning. It is based on 'denotation' *vācya,* and both constitute the body of *dhvani* language (*DL*.I.2). Its synonyms are *avagamana, vyañjanā, dyotanā* etc. It is nothing but suggestion, a function and not a process as Dass thinks. It is not beyond the elements of language which is generally used in poetry. Thus *vyaṅgyārtha* is not connected with social and spiritual atmosphere. It is rather restricated to poetic atmosphere. It is comprehended by connoisseurs and people of literary taste. Thus A.Dass's speculations are not based on the facts of the text.

Genesis of the *dhvani* theory of Ānandavardhana

Ānandavardhan has unequivocally stated that he has adopted the concept of *dhvani* from the grammarians[70]. It seems that he has assimilated the grammatical philosophy of Bhartṛhari. He has built the superstructure of the *dhvani* theory on the nomenclatures of *sphoṭa* and *pratibhā* theory of Bhartṛhari. The whole fourth chapter of this book is devoted to investigate and establish the source of the *dhvani* theory of Ānandavardhana in the *sphoṭa* and the *pratibhā* theory of Bhartṛhari.

Medium of the dhvani language

The *dhvani* language propounded by Ānandavardhana deals with meaning which is over and above the denoted meaning. This language cannot be considered beyond the elements of the ordinary language. But the functions of words namely denotative, indicative, import and inference cannot explain this language. It brings out the true spirit of poetry delineating the most delicate and beautiful ideas and emotions in most delicious manner. But it has no concrete shape. The denotative elements of speech work merely as substratums, nothing more.

The *vastu* 'matter', *alaṁkāra* 'figures of speech' and *rasa* 'poetic relish' may act as mediums of the *dhvani* language. These are ' suggested contents' *vyaṅgyas*. The *dhvani* language is best manifested through *rasa* alone. In case of *vastu* and *alaṁkāra* also, even the little presence of *rasa* expresses *dhvani*.

The smallest units of speech, namely, roots, stems, prefixes, suffixes, particles and phonemes which build the word can act as a medium of the *dhvani* language. The words and parts of words which form the sentence are also mediums of *dhvani* language. The sentences which are collectively responsible for complete work are also mediums of the *dhvani* language[71].

Phonemes as medium of the *dhvani* language.

The grammarians hotly discuss whether the phonemes are meaningful or meaningless. Patañjali analyses this problem in the *pratyāhārāhnika* of the *Mahābhāṣya* and concludes that the phonemes may be meaningful or meaningless[72].

According to Ānandavardhana, also the phonemes are sometimes meaningful and sometimes meaningless. The phonemes which appear to be meaningless suggest *rasa* by virtue of their own capability only in some special contexts, but they fail to evoke *rasa* when the speaker uses casually. Ānandavardhana says that profuse use of *ṣ, ś* and conjunct consonants with *r* and *ḍh* are abusive to *Śṛṅgāra rasa* 'erotic sentiment'. But when these letters are used profusely, they suggest *bībhatsa rasa*[73].

In this connection Abhinavagupta raises the objection that the phonemes cannot play any role in revealing *rasa* when it is evoked by excitants, ensuants and accessories. He removes this objection by stating that the evocative spirit of *rasa* emerges from typical type of mellifluous sounds of articulated phonemes. The audible phonemes become tender or harsh in an impartial way. In this respect the phonemes are conducive to the evocation of *rasa*[74].

Ānandavardhana has stated that not only phonemes but subtlest form of speech, namely, 'case-terminations' *sup*, 'conjugational terminations' *tiṅ*, 'number' *vacana*, 'power of case endings' *kāraka śakti*, 'primary affixes' *kṛt*, 'secondary affixes' *taddhita*, 'compounds' *samāsa*, 'particles' *upasarga*, prefixes and tenses act as mediums of *dhvani* language of 'undiscerned sequentiality' *alakṣyakrama-vyaṅgya*[75]. Each of these smallest units of speech evokes *rasa* in association with suggestion.

Abhinavagupta develops the findings of Ānanda-vardhana. Though a linguistic unit is an indivisible whole which cannot be further broken into smaller significant units, yet for the learning of the connoisseurs and poets, the higher linguistic units can be divisible into smallest parts. In the words of Abhinavagupta, "in this way when the suggestion of sentiment of undiscerned sequentiality *alakṣyakramarasadhvani* has been shown to arise from the whole class of suggesters consisting of letters all the way upto passages, nothing else remains to be described, and yet, in order to instruct poets and sensitive readers, by having recourse to negative and positive statements, he mentions the whole collection of suggesters minutely *suptiṅ* etc."[76]

Ānandavardhana has hinted that particular phonemes are responsible for particular 'poetic merit' *guṇas* which are the properties of *rasas*[77]. The sentiments, namely, love in separation and pathos cannot further be used for the 'poetic merit of forcefulness' *ojaguṇa* which is used in the furious sentiment. In the verses of Bhaṭṭanārāyaṇa's *Veṇisaṁhāra,* i.e. *cañcadbhuja* etc.[78] and *yo yaḥ śastram* etc.[79] particular high sounding phonemes bring out tremendous effect which ultimately generates *raudra rasa*[80].

In the later days, Mammaṭa[81] has developed this idea of Ānandavardhana on the role of phonemes with regard to the evocation of *rasa.* He says, "just as bravery and such qualities belong to the soul, not to the body, so sweetness and other excellences belong to the passion, not to the letter. In some cases it so happens that people find bravery co-existing with the large sized body, and come to speak of the body itself as 'brave' and hence in another case also, on seeing a large body, they are led to believe, from the analogy of the former case, that this other man also must be brave, and thus, even a really braveman comes to be belived to be not brave on the ground of the smallness of his body; and such beliefs are very common; in the same manner people (like Vāmana and others) have come to speak (a) of the soft sounding letters as 'sweet', though in reality they are only suggestive of sweetness; and they come to speak of such passion and its accessories as are not really 'sweet', as 'sweet', simply by reason of the softness of the letters (expressing them); in the same manner, they also speak of the really 'sweet' passions and accessories as 'not sweet', when they are expressed in such words as are not soft sounding; and in all this, they do not take into account the passion at all (attributing as they do, the sweetness to the letters). It is in view of all this divergent usage that it has been asserted (in the text) that sweetness and other excellences are properties really belonging to the passion, and what the properly selected letters do is only to render such qualities perceptible; and those qualities do not subsist in the letters entirely."[82]

In this connection Ānandavardhana's objection and answer may be stated. When *rasa* is usually evoked by the power of meaning, how it can be evoked by the minute parts, i.e. phonemes, case terminations, etc.?

Ānandavardhana answers that it is true that *rasa* is evoked by the senses. Yet the denotative function plays a major role in the case of evocation of *rasa* cannot be denied. This denotative function has no power of conveying suggestivity. Sometimes, the music evokes *rasa* without depending on words. But in poetry the meanings which are to be suggested should depend on the words. In order to know the suggestion properly, one has to split the parts of the denotative word or words through which the suggestive elements are often expressed. By this act of spliting, one is able to know the suggestive elements in each part of the crude word.

Ānandavardhana has further stated that the realisation of *rasa* is one and integrated experience of the mind. It is expressed by the meanings which are suggested. The words of the language structure give concrete form to it. The language which expresses the meaning leading to the realisation of *rasa* cannot be divisible into smaller units. If it would be divisible, then *rasa* cannot be an indivisible experience. For the realisation of *rasa* one cannot divide the integrated linguistic unit whose smaller units may have the elements of suggestion. But for the sake of analysis, one can split the larger units of language into smaller units. This division helps to know which part conveys what type of suggestion, and how many suggestive elements it contain[83].

This idea is exactly an echo of Bhartṛhari's linguistic philosophy. According to him, a semantic unit cannot be broken into further fragments. The grammarians for the sake of analysis break an indivisible speech unit into parts. This division is fictitious. The reality of language is an indivisible experience[84]. This will be discussed further as we proceed.

Words as medium of the *dhvani* language

Ānandavardhana always keeps in his mind that the semantic units cannot be further divisible into smaller units. In case of the analysis of words, he follows the same principles. It has been told that the whole poetry is to be regarded as a *dhvani kāvya*[85]. A poetry is a collection of sentences built of meaningful words. In this light a sentence as a whole can be the medium of suggestive sense. As to the question what should be the role of words in the communication of suggested sense, Ānandavardhana answers that the words may act as agents for 'remembrance' *smṛti*, but they cannot denote meanings[86]. It would be a mistake, if one takes words, in its meaning conveying capacity as *prayojaka* of *dhvani* language. But there is an instance where words act as medium of *dhvani* languaage which runs like this : 'Merchant, how could we possibly have elephant-tusks or tiger skins as long as this daughter-in-law of mine roams about in this house with her face covered in dangling curls'[87]. Here the word *lulitālakamukhī* 'her face covered in dangling curls' suggest that the hunter is now interested exclusively in making love and so has become weak and unable to hunt. For the woman to have her hair laying about on her face is a sign of flirtatiousness and of frivolity. Perhaps there is a further suggestion, namely, that the woman has no time to braid and oil her hair properly, so engrossed is she in lovemaking, or perhaps since hair is likely to come undone during love-making and to fall over one's face, the woman is reminding her husband of love by leaving her hair in this state all the time. These suggestive meanings are achieved by the force of the idea denoted by these words in a situation that exists outside of the poet's imagination. Ānandavardhana says that the wholeness of the *dhvani* language is not affected, if the implicit meaning of a part is analysed. To explain this, he gives an analogy. In worldly use, if the face of some person is beautiful we say that his whole body is beautiful. We do not say that only his face is beautiful and other parts of his body are not so. The beauty of one part contributes to the total beauty of the body. Similarly, with regard to *dhvani* language the wholeness is taken into account. That is why, the connoisseurs remark that the poetry is touched by *dhvani,* and therefore, it is beautiful eventhough in reality a word or a part of word may add charm to it. In the abovesaid example *vaṇijaka* etc. the beauty of one word lends charm to the whole poetry. The division of the *dhvani*-sentence into *dhvani* element is done for the sake of 'analysis' *bhedabuddhi.* In fact, the sentence is the conveyer of suggestive meaning, but it does not mean that the constituents of sentence have no role in conveying suggestive meaning[88].

Ānandavardhana in another context has explained the same idea[89]. The words are the parts of the sentence. Each word contributes to the totality of the sentence. When the sentence is constructed and the meaning is conveyed, the individual words and their meanings become redundant. They become fictitious and the reality in the form of the sentence and its meaning emerges. The individual words in a sentence are *smārakas* 'agents of remembrance'. The suggestive words recollect the beautiful suggested sense which brings charm to the whole expression. This idea is hinted at in case of the verse *vaṇijaka* etc.[90] The reality of *dhvani* language is an undivided unity. Separate parts contribute their imports to the whole. The division of *dhvani* sentences into *dhvani* elements is unreal. The unified *dhvani* sentence is reality of the *dhvani* language. In the words of Ānandavardhana, "therefore there is beauty in all the varieties of *dhvani,* which is revealed by mere words, even though words do in fact serve only as reminders. Just as a woman appears lovely through a single ornament beautifully arranged, so also the speech of a good poet appears lovely through *dhvani* revealed in a single word.[91]

The role that words play may be two fold, i.e. in their individual capacity, and in their collective capacity. The words in their individual capacity retain semantic value. But when different words are syntactically connected with each other in a particular order to form a sentence, they surrender their semantic attributes to the semantic upsurge of the sentence. For the sake of the communication of meaning, syntactically connected words cannot be broken. In case they are broken, the meaning cannot be conveyed. But for analysis the words can be separated and can be split into their elements. Meanings cannot be communicated through them. What is true in an ordinary speech is also true in poetic speech. In case of *dhvani* language, each suggested word contributes to the suggested meaning of the whole expression. In the *vaṇijaka* etc.[92] as it is seen, a particular word beautifies the whole expression with its suggested meaning like a graceful face of a woman. Thus a single word as medium of conveying suggested sense is established.

Indivisible sentence as medium of the *dhvani* language

According to Ānandavardhana, the *dhvani* language of *alakṣyakramavyaṅgya* type in the form of sentence is a most important one. The grammarians hold that actual communication is performed by the sentence. It is taken as one linguistic unit which cannot be further subdivided into smaller units if the meaning is to be conveyed.

Following the trends of the grammarians Ānandavardhana holds that the sentence which has suggested elements in it, is an integral *dhvani* language. In the *alakṣyakramavyaṅgya dhvani* of sentence, the sentence and *dhvani* are inseparable from each other. It means the sentence has absorbed the suggested elements. It is taken as a whole. The phonemes, words and parts of the words in the sentence are suggesters of *dhvani.* These phonemes etc. are further accessories of excitants etc. which in turn are suggester of *rasa.* The meaning of the sentence is *rasa.* In support of this Ānandavardhana may be quoted : "because it is admitted that *rasas* are the ultimate sense of a sentence. If the subject and the predicate are found in the literal sentence-meaning, why should they not be found in *rasas,* which are suggested by the force of the literal sentence meaning as a whole?"[93]

The sentence operates naturally in connection with *rasa.* As a whole it acquires excitants etc. and becomes inseparable with *rasa.* The sentence is not an instrument for the manifestation of *rasa* like the phonemes and words. It cognises *vibhāvādi* and manifests itself as *rasa.* So the relation between the sentence and *dhvani* is inseparable. Ānandavardhana maintains that the term *sarvataḥ* in the verse *kṛtaka kupitaiḥ* etc. of the *Rāmābhyudaya* denotes that a particular word does not manifest *rasa.* The *rasa* is manifested as a whole from all angles of the sentence. Here neither a word nor a part of word is the suggester of *rasa.* The sentence as a whole is its suggester. On the one hand, the sentence suggests the respective depth of love between Rāma and Sītā, and on the other hand it (the sentence) absolutely manifests the sentiment of love in separation as a whole[94]. Ānandavardhana in a number of illustrations has shown how the whole sentence acts as a suggester of *dhvani*-meaning[95].

Ānandavardhana has compressed his philosophy of sentence and its meaning in a paragraph which is stated below : "the analogy of the meanings of (individual) words and the meaning of a sentence (as a whole) is not appropriate to the case of literal meaning and suggested meaning. For the apprehension of the literal meaning of a word is unreal according to certain learned men (e.g. the grammarians like Bhartṛhari). Those who do not accept its unreality (e.g. the *Mīmāṁsakas)* will have to accept the analogy of the pot and its material cause (*upādāna,* i.e. clay) to apply to the meaning of the sentence as a whole and the meanings of the individual words. Just as when the pot is completed we cannot perceive separately its material cause (here thought of as particles or small bits of clay); in the same way, when a sentence and its meanings are perceived, we cannot perceive separately the words and their meanings. If (at that time) the meanings of words are separately cognised, then the apprehension of the meaning of a sentence as a whole would recede (from our minds). But this analogy will not hold true in the case of literal meaning and the suggested meaning, because when we apprehend the suggested sense, the literal sense is not discarded (at least in the case of *rasadhvani*), because its revelation is never dissociated from the consciousness of the literal meaning. Therefore the proper analogy between the two is that of the pot and the lamp (which reveals the pot in the dark). For just as when the pot is perceived by means of the lamp, the light of the lamp does not disappear, so also when the suggested sense is understood, the consciousness of the literal meaning does not disappear. What however was said in the first *udyota,* namely 'just as through the meaning of words' etc. was only said in order to show the general similarity, that (the meaning of words and the literal sense) were (both) helpful (to the understanding of the meaning of the whole sentence, just as literal sense is helpful to the understanding of the suggested meaning).[96]

This above passage is the direct echo of Bhartṛhari's philosophy of language[97]. Ānandavardhana has taken it from him and fitted it to the *dhvani* language.

Thus suggestion is the heart of the *dhvani* language. It is an instrument to communicate the poetic ideas. It describes the beautiful ideas of poetry. The saturation of the description in poetry is achieved by the delineation of *rasa. Rasa* is an integral experience of the consciousness. As an experience it should be one and whole. It is manifested by the sentence which has suggestive elements. So the meaning of the sentence is the meaning of the *rasa.* It is sparked by the denotative function of the word. The indivisible sentence which describes *rasa* as an unified experience can be divided into smaller units for the sake of analysis. Parts are no reality in the *dhvani* languages. For the sake of realisation of the beautiful meaning of poetry one should not split the whole sentence into parts. The sentence is indivisible and the reality of language. This is the philosophy of language of Ānandavardhana.

Monistic concept of *rasa*

Bharata is the founder of *rasa* school. Sometimes it appears that *rasa* school of Bharata and *dhvani* school of Ānandavardhana are different. But in reality the *dhvani* school is complementary to *rasa* school. The *dhvani* theory is an extension of *rasa* theory[98]. According to Ānandavardhana, *rasa* is the running thread in the entire *dhvani* language. More or less all the elements of poetry are touched by *rasa.* The *dhvani, pratibhā, guṇa, rīti, vṛtti* and *saṁghaṭanā* etc. are treated from the standpoint of *rasa* in the *Dhvanyāloka.* All the varieties of *dhvani* have different degrees of *rasa.* Ānandavardhana has mentioned that the body of poetry is built of theme and style. Its soul is *rasa*[99]. The excitants etc. bring *rasa* into cognition. The suggestive power manifests *rasa* through the denotative elements of speech. In case of music, sounds are denotative elements which manifest *rasa*[100]. A poet should give foremost importance to *rasa*[101]. Bharata shows on awareness of this fact in the classifications of *vṛttis.*[102]

Monistic concept of *rasa* refers to the state when one *rasa* predominates over the other *rasas.* It may also mean the state when from one *rasa* other *rasas* emerge. Bharata has classified *rasa* into eight types on the basis of eight permanent moods[103]. Abhinavagupta adds *śānta rasa* to them[104]. The monistic concept of *rasa* of the Sanskrit poetics seems to come from the grammatical philosophy of Bharatṛhari. Taking a cue from the *Vedas*[105] Bhartṛhari has developed his grammatical philosophy. According to him, the 'word principle' *śabdabrahman*[106] is one, without beginning and indestructible. It is the ultimate reality which manifests itself into many because of its many powers. It does so without losing its oneness. Although it is not different from its powers, of it appears to be different. Among its many powers, the time is most important. It is one but its divisions are superimposed on it. On it depends all the different kinds of changes which bring about multiplicity in being. The ultimate which is one contains the seeds of all multiplicity. It manifests itself as the experiencer, the experienced and the experience itself.[107]

It appears that Ānandavardhana has taken a cue of his oneness of *rasa* and oneness of its relish, from the concept of *śabdabrahman* of Bhartṛhari. His realisation of *rasa* is similar to the realisation of supreme-brahman. As *Brahman* in *Vedānta* manifests into manyforms but retains its oneness, so also *rasa* manifests into many varieties, but it retains its oneness. In the same way from one *rasa* other *rasas* emerge. This is the central idea of mono-sentimentalism.[108] Those who believe that there is one *rasa* and other *rasas* are different manifestations of it, their views can be brought under mono-rasa cult. There are few streams of mono-rasa cult. Bhoja in the *Śṛṅgāraprakāśa* states that only erotic is the one *rasa* and other *rasas* emanate from it. They are as good as ghosts in the banian tree[109]. It seems that according to Ānandavardhana erotic is the only *rasa*[110], though he has nowhere mentioned about it. He has only mentioned that it is the most delicate and beautiful of all *rasas* and slightest impropriety can cause severe damage to it[111]. It is believed that the *Śṛṅgārarasa* has been camouflaged under the name of *bhakti* by *Viṣṇava* rhetoricians.

S.N. Ghosal states, "the neo-*rasa* (*vaiṣṇsva)* school appreciates the 'devotion' *bhakti* as to be the only relish. The concept of *bhakti* is psychologically nothing but an extension of *rati,* the feeling of the erotic. The unconditional, self-bequest and sublime love is the other name of *bhakti.* Love is either an instinct, or a feeling. Its expression is the erotic emotion, or sex, what a modern school of psychology counts as to be the inertia of all actions and expressions of behaviourism. Philosophy of Indian erotics that attained full maturity in Bhoja's *Śṛṅgāraprakāśa* enjoyed perfection in the works of *Vaiṣṇava* saint aestheticians like Rūpa Gosvāmin, Sanātana Gosvānin, Jīva Gosvāmin, Madhusūdana Sarasvatī and others[112]. This speculation of *bhaktirasa* as an extension of *Śṛṅgārarasa* is doubtful. Psychologically both are the same as *rati.* This *rati* is the permanent mood in both *śṛṅgāra* and *bhakti rasa*. But *bhaktirasa* is metaphysical and religious in character whereas the *śṛṅgāraasa* is worldly and poetic in nature.[113]

Bhavabhūti believes in one *rasa* that is *karuṇarasa*[114]. Nārāyaṇa, the great grand father of Viśvaṇātha Kavirāja holds that *adbhuta* is the only one *rasa*[115]. Abhinavagupta holds that *śānta* is only *rasa.* Apart from these above propounders Śaktibhadra (āścarya arasa) Viśveśvara *(camatkāra rasa),* Dharmadaṭta *(adbhūta rasa)* hold that there is one *rasa*[116].

S. Kuppuswami Sastri presents the development of mono *rasa* cult nicely. He states that in the course of the development of the philosophy of *rasa,* several attempts were made in the direction of synthesising the various *rasas.* The more important results of such attempts were summed up in four kinds of synthesis. Firstly, there is *karuṇa* synthesis which originated from Vālmīki and found its culmination in Bhavabhūti's *eko rasaḥ karuṇa eva* on the practical side, and in Ānandavardhana's *śokaḥ ślokatvam āgataḥ* on the theoretical side.

Secondly, there is *śānta* synthesis which started

perhaps from the *Mahābhārata,* found its fulfilment in works like Aśvaghoṣa's *Sāriputtaprakaraṇa,* Śriharṣa's *Nāgānanda* and Kṛṣṇa Miśra's *Prabodha candrodaya,* and received able advocacy on the theoretical side at the hands of the two greatest *ālaṁkārikas* namely Ānandavardhana and Abhinavagupta.

Thirdly, there is *śṛṅgāra* synthesis which is firmly rooted in human nature itself since the beginning of creation, reached its acme of spiritual refinement, on the practical side, in the self effacing ideal of love delineated in an inimitable manner by the creative genius of great poets like Kālidāsa and Bāṇa, and on the theoretical side, in the wellknown dictum of the royal polymoth Bhoja, *rasā'bhimāno'haṁkāraḥ śṛṅgāra iti gīyate.*

And fourthly, there is *adbhūta* synthesis which on the theoretical side became crystallised in the views of Nārāyaṇa and Dharmadatta referred to by Viśvanātha in his *Sāhitya Darpaṇa* and in the views of Bhānudatta as expressed in his *Rasataraṅgiṇī,* and which on the practical side, led to the production of the wonder dominated dramatic type represented by the older *Āścaryacūḍāmaṇī* and the later *Adbhùtadarpaṇa* of Mahādeva at the end of the seventeenth century.

Thus Kuppuswami Sastri does not establish the pure monistic concept of *rasa.* He attempts to show the development of pure monism of *rasa* which appears to be similar to the Vedic henotheism or pantheism.

Bharata's idea of monism of *rasa*

Bharata has not told anywhere that from one *rasa* other *rasas* emerge. Abhinavagupta interprets the oneness of *rasa* as described in the *Nāṭya Śāstra.* Though *rasa* is divided into eight varieties, it is one from the standpoint of relish. The relish of *rasas* brings pleasure. It is a peculiar type of enjoyment which is different from other worldly enjoyments. It is a common trait in all *rasas.* So in reality the *rasa* is one, and it is many because of its different manifestations. The multiplicity of *rasa* is *vikṛtis* of one *mahārasa*.

The ablative singular use of the term *rasa* in the *NŚ* suggests the monistic concept of *rasa*[118]. Abhinavagupta syas, "earlier the term *rasa* is used in plural number (in *NŚ*) but here it is used in singular number. The purpose behind it is to suggest that *rasa* is one. In this sense it is used in the drama. *Rasa* is many because of 'difference in vision' *bheda dṛṣṭi*[119]." He further says that the drama represents *rasa*. The study of drama brings the realisation of *rasa*. *Rasa* is one from the standpoint of this realisation. All other *rasas* originate from the principal *mahārasa*[120].

Thus Bharata was aware of the fact that inspite of external differences, *rasa* is one and indivisible. The original *rasa* is one *(mahārasa)* from which other *rasas* evolve, just as, according to Bhartṛhari, from the one word-principle, the entire speech with multiple varieties evolve[121]. Thus *rasatattva* 'principle of *rasa*' is just like the Vedic deity who though one manifests into many.

From the philosophical point of view, the concept of *rasa* passes through three different stages, viz. henotheism, pantheism and monotheism.

In the first stage, all *rasas* and their permanent moods are considered separately and independently. In the next stage, a particular *rasa* is taken as predominant one, for instance, *śṛṅgāra* or *karuṇa*. In the third stage attempts are made to discover a common under current in all *rasas*, for instance, someone finds *rati*, others *sama*, still others *abhimāna* as common trend in all *rasas*. Ultimately the concept of *rasa* rises to the height of pure monism, and it is identified with the concept of the soul of the *Upaniṣads*. Here the concept of *rasa* receives the spiritual status[122].

Ānandavardhana's monistic idea of rasa

It has been stated earlier that Ānandavardhana shows

weakness for *śṛṅgārarasa*. He says that it is most delicate of all *rasas*[123]. While discussing the sentiments of the *Rāmāyaṇa* and the *Mahābhārata,* he argues in favour of one *rasa.* The *karuṇarasa* overpowers the descriptions of the whole *Rāmāyaṇa* from the beginning to the end. The *śāntarasa* is the ultimate desired *rasa* in the *Mahābhārata.* Amidst the war and strifes and material prosperity, *śāntarasa* remains as the undercurrent in all descriptions in the *Mahābhārata.* Here *mokṣa* is the ultimate goal of living beings. In *Harivaṁśa* also *śānta* is the only *rasa.* It is suggested by the devotion of Vāsudeva, the renunciation of material possession, the final emancipation and the attainment of Supreme Reality. Even pāṇḍava's exploitations are means of attaining the supreme Reality. So *śānta* is the only *rasa* in the *Mahābhārata* whose nature is tranquillity and happiness at the cessation of desire[124].

Ānandavardhana has dealt with the monistic concept of *rasa* in a different way. The poet may desire many *rasas* in his poetry. But he should stick to one *rasa* as 'principal' *aṅgī* and others should be subordinate to it. He should carefully display other *rasas* which are minor in between the description of the chief *rasa,* so that the importance of chief *rasa* is not lost and its effect on the reader is preserved[125].

Ānandavardhana has admitted nine *rasas* including *śānta rasa*[126]. In the second *uddyota*[127] and third *uddyota*[128] of the *Dhvanyāloka,* he has discussed the theories regarding many *rasas.* But in the fourth *uddyota* he has synthesised all the *rasas* into one. The principle of oneness of *rasa* is followed in the *Rāmāyaṇa (karuṇarasa)* and in the *Mahābhārata (śāntarasa).* He does not say like Bhoja, Bhavabhūti and Rūpa Gosvāmin that there is particular one *rasa,* i.e. *śṛṅgāra, karuṇa, bhakti* respectively, and other *rasas* are the manifestations of that particular *rasa.* His intention is that any *rasa* can be taken as the principal one under which other *rasas* may be portrayed. One *rasa* should discharge tremendous influences over other *rasas* even indirectly in diverse poetic situations. He has shown weakness for *śṛṅgāra* and *śāntarasa*.

In reality, Ānandavardhana's philosophy of *rasa* is monistic in nature. The poet should maintain propriety in their display. There may be many *rasas*, but all of them work for one particular *rasa* in a particular poetic work. One *rasa* ultimately overpowers all and emerges as a principal one. After manifesting one *rasa*, the minor *rasas* mingle themselves with the chief manifested *rasa*. Thus the reality of *rasa* is one and multiplicity in it is a fiction. The minor *rasas* lose significance when the principal *rasa* emerges. This concept is elaborately discussed in the context of the judgement of *karuṇa* and *śāntarasa* in the *Rāmāyaṇa* and the *Mahābhārata* respectively[129]. Ānandavardhana's leaning to the oneness of *rasa* can be further justified from the great number of singular usage of the term *rasa*.[130]

Thus the reality of *rasa* stated above resembles to the reality of sentence meaning of Bhartṛhari. The smaller units of speech help to manifest the larger unit of speech which is one and indivisible. When the larger unit is comprehended, the smaller units have no specific function[131]. This will be discussed in detail as we proceed.

Abhinavagupta's monistic idea of *rasa*

Abhinavagupta is a great Śaivite philosopher as well as rhetorician of repute. So it is possible that his aesthetic doctrines might have been influenced by his philosophical dictates. It happens in his work. As a true medicant of Śaiva-monistic order, he brought the concept of oneness into *rasa*. He claims that *śānta* is the only *rasa* from which other *rasas* originate. When the functions of other *rasas* are over they mingle in that *śāntarasa*. It is the *mahārasa*. In this regard Abhinavagupta has taken the monistic *rasa* philosophy of Ānandavardhana. In the list of 'accessories' *saṁcārī bhāvas*, Bharata has placed *nirveda* in the beginning.

Abhinavagupta considers this *nirveda* as the permanent-mood of *śāntarasa*. Thus it seems that he supports the primacy of *śānta rasa*. This *śāntarasa* is based on serious philosophical thought. The consciousness of this *rasa* and its relish flow amidst the realisation of all *rasas*[132].

Indian rhetoricians always tried to discover a binding thread amongst all *rasas*, externally and internally. External common link is fabricated by Ānandavardhana which is further corroborated by the later rhetoricians, viz. Abhinavagupta, Mammaṭa, Viśvanātha and Jagannātha etc. It is established by the fact that one *rasa* should be principal in a poetic work and other *rasas* are manifestations of that particular *rasa*. The internal common link is established by the two common features which remain in all *rasas* Firstly, the relish of *rasa* is a special type of cognition. Secondly, all *rasas* bring absolute happiness. In vindication to this Ānandavardhana believes that *śānta* is that *rasa* in which all desires are put to rest. It is the ultimate human goal. It is a pleasure comparable to the happiness of attaining supreme *brahman*. In other *rasas* also happiness is the common quality. It is brought forth on the wake of the destruction of all desires. The erotic and other *rasas* sprout from the *śāntarasa* with the appropriate excitants etc. and when the excitants are gone, the *rasas* revealed are again submerged in the *śāntarasa*[133].

The features responsible to establish a common undercurrent among all *rasas* can be linked with the pleasures of realising *brahman* as stated in the *Upaniṣads*[134] The *brahman* is characterised by absolute happiness. It is attainable only by the *yogin* through strenuous austerities. When they realise it they enjoy absolute happiness. This is the highest level of joyful experience which cannot be comparable to ordinary worldly pleasure. Ignorance is an obstacle to attain such happiness. When it is removed by knowledge, the supreme *brahman* characterised by absolute happiness appears in full effulgence. This is the ultimate reality. The *Upaniṣads* identify this stage with *rasa* which is the supreme bliss.

The connoisseurs who read or listen a standard poetic work enjoy absolute pleasure at a certain stage. This is an uncommon experience different from joyous experiences of the world. It is unshaking and singular type of consciousness. First Bhaṭṭa Nāyaka[135], then Abhinavagupta and later on Paṇḍitrāja Jagannātha elaborated this stage of realisation of *rasa* which seems to be similar to the realisation of the Supreme *Brahman*. Bhaṭṭa Nāyaka for the first time in Indian poetics proclaimed that the relish of *rasa* is *hlādaniṣyanda* and *brahmāsvādasahodara*. Abhinavagupta has established this monistic philosophy of *rasa* on firm philosophical ground[136].

Difference between *Brahmānubhūti* and *rasānubhūti*

The realisation of *rasa* and the realisation of supreme *brahman* appear similar. Both the cognitions have similarities and differences. Bhaṭṭa Nāyaka and Abhinavagupta were aware of them. The cognition of the Supreme *Brahman* is one and without differentiation. On the other hand, the cognition of *rasa* is a pleasure of consciousness which is brought about by the diveresified elements, namely, excitants etc[137]. In spite of this fact, both Bhaṭṭa Nāyaka and Abhinavagupta give higher status to the poets than to the *yogins*[138]. However, contrary to it, Abhinavagupta states elsewhere that all types of pleasures are parts of the absolute pleasure of the Supreme *Brahman*[139]. This idea has been further elaborated by Kumārasvāmin, the son of famous Mallināth in his commentary of *Pratāparudrīya yaśobhūṣaṇa*. According to him, all pleasures are similar to the pleasure of attaining Supreme *Brahman*. The yogic pleasure and the pleasure of the realisation of *rasa* are parts of this great pleasure of *brahman*. The pleasure of attaining the ultimate reality remains at the higher stratum than the ordinary pleasures[140].

The *Pañcadaśī* states that *Vāsanānanda* 'pleasures

derived from the instincts' and *viṣayānanda* 'pleasures derived from material possession' are the products of *brahmānanda*. The *vāsanānanda* is the residual impression of *brahmānanda* and the *viṣayānanda* is the reflection of *brahmānanda* in psychoses which cognise object of sense. But both of them lean towards the *brahmānanda*[141].

M. Hiriyanna's observations between aesthetic experience and religion is noteworthy here. He says, "since *rasa* or aesthetic experience also, link like this final one of *jīvanmukti*, is characterised by complete detachment and is accompanied by a unique form of delight, the two are described as similar. But there is one vital difference between them. It is the lack in the former of the knowledge of ultimate reality, which is essential to the latter (a deficiency which is made good here by assuming grades of aesthetic intuition that progressively reveal reality). To this, they trace the lapse from art experience which takes place sooner or later when, to speak generally, all the tensions of ordinary life return. There is a reversion to common life from the experience of *jīvanmukti* also; but it can by no means, be regarded as a 'lapse', since the philosophic conviction endures then with all its expected influence upon life's conduct. In other words, there is according to the Indian view, no direct connection between aesthetic and absolute experience, as seems to be supposed here. The discipline of the fine arts, particularly of music, is not however, excluded from religion; but it is explained as only a useful aid to success in meditation upon the highest."[142]

Hiriyanna demarcates between the art experience and the religious experience from the standpoint of their influence on the reality of life. The *yogins* comeback to the imperfect reality of the world, when their trance is over. Similarly, the connoisseurs see the reality of the worldly life when the momentary relish of *rasa* comes to an end. But this difference alluded do not affect the conclusion that the relish of *rasa* is different from the realisation of *Brahman*. One's feasibility can be deduced from the other. The art experience is not a temporary luxury. A momentary relish of *rasa* infuses the desire for its further realisation and pleasure. In latter days Pt. Jagannātha has critically analysed the pleasurable aspect of *rasa* and *Brahman*[143]. Thus it is clear that the monistic concept of *rasa* which is hinted in the *Dhvanyāloka* has been saturated into a philosophical doctrine at the hands of Abhinavagupta and Paṇḍitarāja Jagannātha.

Speaker's intention and *vyañjanā*

Ānandavardhana has stated in many places that speaker's intention is *vyañjanā* 'suggestion'. While refuting the views of *Naiyāyikas,* he states that suggestion depends on speaker's intention[144]. He does not consider the speaker's intention as a separate function like the *Mīmāṁsakas.* He does not use the term *tātparaya* 'import' to denote it, rather he uses the maxim of 'words and sentence meaning' *vākyārtha-padārtha-nyāya*[145] to connote the idea of *tātparya.*

The poetic language is regulated and modelled by the intention of the poet. It communicates the sentiments to the readers by the suggestive power of language. If a poet attempts to communicate the aesthetic relish through denotative power of the language, the effect is less powerful[146]. The *rasa* can be communicated by the *dhvani* language[147]. The poetry is flourished and the particular *rasas* are displayed by the intention of the poet[148]. Ānandavardhana has repeatedly remarked that the suggestion is based on denotation (*DL*.I.10-11). The denotative elements of speech are constant whereas the suggestive elements are accidental. The suggestion cannot be considered as a variety of denotation because of its adventitiousness. The *Mimāṁsakas* admit the adventitiousness as a criterion to make distinction between human utterance and Vedic utterance. By this attribute, they establish the eternal relation between words and senses. Thus they indirectly admit suggestion, so far as adventitiousness is concerned. The adventitious power of suggestion is very common in human speech[149]. A problem crops up at this stage that if the adventitiousness is the common attribute, both in ordinary language and in *dhvani* language, then what should be the basis to identify a particular language? Ānandavardhana meets with the above objection. According to him, the suggestive element remains not only in the *dhvani* language but also in ordinary speech to reveal the desire of the speaker. The suggestive elements which remain in ordinary speec are of different nature. These are not different from denotative elements. They remain inside the denotative meaning. The suggestive elements are not mainly expressed here. They exist in a subordinate position in common speech[150]. Ānandavardhana states that suggestion is a special type of intention of the speaker. Any ordinary intention cannot be suggestion. The special type of intention is that in which suggestive elements are predominant. It is revealed by the function of suggestion[151]. As the speaker's intentions are limitless, the *dhvani* language, whose life is suggestion, is also limitless. The speaker's intention brings about the suggestive meaning in different ways and in many varieties. The suggestive elements and denotative elements are organically associated on the basis of speaker's intention. Because of this nature of suggestion *Mīmāṁsakas* cannot abandon it[152].

Import of the sentence and suggestion

The *tātparyavādin* hold that the denotative function expresses the primary sense of the sentence. After that the special meaning is conveyed by the intention of the speaker. In other words, to know the speaker's intention a function like suggestion is not essential. The denotative function in its wider capacity reveals the speaker's intention Thus according to *tātparyavādins,* the speaker's intention is denoted and not suggested. On the contrary, Ānandavardhana claims that the speaker's intention is suggested. It can never be denoted. In order to justify his propositions, he analyses the semantic problems of poetic language. Ānandavardhana states that a sentence is built of words and the sentence meaning is built of world meanings[153]. The words and word meaning help in the cognition of the sentence and sentence-meaning. But they are fictitious. The relation between the parts (words and word-meanings) and whole (sentence and sentence-meaning) may be similar to the relation which exists between *ghaṭa* 'a pitcher' and its primary cause, i.e. clay. The clay is essential as long as the *ghaṭa* is not built. Once it is built the raw clay loses its significance. Similarly, until the sentence meaning is understood wholly, the word-meanings continue to raise it. But when the sentence meaning is cognised as an indivisible whole, then the word-meanings are no more required. If one attempts to know the sentence-meaning by separately analysing the word-meanings, then the import of the sentence is lost[154]. But this analogy cannot be applicable to determine the relation between *vācya* 'denotation' and *vyaṅgya* 'suggestion'. Ānandavardhana explains it with the analogy of *ghaṭa* 'a pitcher' and light. The denotative meaning helps the cognition of suggested meaning. But the former is not useless when the latter is revealed. The denotative meaning is organically linked with the suggested meaning. Just as the light helps the perception of a jar and it continues its manifestation still further, similarly the expressed sense continues to reveal the suggested sense even though it is manifested[155].

The role of the the parts in the cognition of the whole sentence has already been discussed. Ānandavardhana further analyses whether parts denote or suggest the meaning of the whole. Stating the view of the *Mīmāṁsaka* he says that the words and meaning of words are cognised first in their individual capacity, and latter they give rise to the understanding of the sentence and meaning of the sentence. "According to them the meaning of the words are cognised by the denotative power of the word whereas the meaning of the sentence is understood by *tātparya*[156]. But Ānandavardhana is of different opinion. According to him, the meaning of the words are known by the power of denotation. But the meaning of the sentence is not the sum total of the meanings of words[157]. It is different. Its meaning is cognised by the intention of the speaker. Its comprehension is possible through suggestive power of language and not through the denotative power. This suggestive power remains more or less in all speech acts in the form of speaker's intention. But all intentions are not suggestions. When the intentions are pre dominant and special, they are suggested. When they are subordinate and minor, they are denoted[158]. According to Ānanda-vardhana, the special intention of the speaker is suggestion. This suggestive function is not an extension of denotative function. Though the reality of the *dhvani* language is the sentence whose meaning is brought about by the speaker's intention, yet the parts are not absolutely without any purpose. The speaker's intention is also manifested by parts. That is why Ānandavardhana accepts the working of *dhvani* in phonemes, words, suffix, prefix, particle, stem and roots etc. But according to the *Mīmāṁsakas,* the intention of the speaker is conveyed not by the parts, but by the whloe sentence. It has been stated earlier that both denotative and suggestive elements of speech remain organically associated with each other. When one element is primary, the other element is secondary and vice-versa[158].

In the poetic language, sometimes peculiarities and beauty lie in the parts and at other times they remain in the whole. The speaker's intention which reveal the beauty of the expressions, does its work for the part as well as for the whole. Thus the concept of *tātparya* of the *Māmāṁsakas* is to explain the linguistic peculiarities of the whole which is insufficient to explain the beauty of the parts. Ānandavardhana in the third flash of the *Dhvanyāloka* has shown a number of minute parts of the sentence which on the basis of speaker's intention can reveal wonderful poetic meanings. At the same time he never forgets the role of the whole expression. The whole is the reality of any language may it be common or poetic. Both whole and parts convey their meanings by speaker's intention through suggestion. Both in the ordinary and the poetic speech, the suggestive elements remain in the form of speaker's intentions. Its different ratios give particular status to particular language. When the suggestive elements are more, the language is called *dhvani* language; when it is less, the language may either be 'subordinate *dhvani* language' *guṇībhūtavyaṅgya* or ordinary language[159].

While arguing against the views of the *Naiyāyikas,* Ānandavardhana claims that suggestion exists in our human experience. Sometims it is expressed by sounds (in music) and sometimes it is manifested by gestures and other acrobatics. It is seen both in words and senses whereas denotation is found only in words[160]. By *vivakṣā* the *Naiyāyikas* mean speaker's intention which is nothing but suggestion. He states that the speaker's intention can be *vyañjaka*[161]. The *vyañjakatva* of the word is *anumāpaka* of the speaker's intention. Therefore the speaker's intention is liṅgatva. Since the speaker's intention is brought by suggestive power, the *vyañjakatva* is nothing but *liṅgatva.* It does not harm the fundamental concept of *dhvani*[162].

Ānandavardhana further states that there are two types of speaker's intentions *(vivakṣā)* which are treated by the *Naiyāyikas* as subjects of inference. The first type of speaker's intention is the desire to manifest the nature of the word, and the second type is the desire to convey the meaning through the words.

The desire to manifest the nature of the word is the intention to use or to utter the word. For instance, when there is desire of uttering the term *haraḥ,* the nature of the term is manifested. By this, the intention to convey special meaning does not arise. The import of the use of the word is this : The listener knows that the utterer is an animal[163].

The second type of speaker's intention is necessary for creative sentence meaning. The speaker here wants to use particular word for particular meaning. If a speaker wants to communicate the meaning of a sentence, and if the ideas of the sentence-meaning are expressed by a particular expression then that expression is generative of sentence-meaning. Though a temporary gap is created here by the word itself, yet the meaning is comprehended in a flash. In this case, the speaker's intention is cognised by the instrument of the word[164].

The implication of Ānandavardhana's discussion is that the language which is comprehended by speaker's intention has not only the scope of inference, but also it has the scope of suggestion. In admitting inference for the comprehension of language one faces difficulties.

On the basis of speaker's intention the denotative scope of language is divided into expressive and suggestive. Various shades of meanings of suggestion cannot be explained by inference[165]. The suggestion cannot be brought under the rules of inference. Logic is careful of its method and precision whereas suggestion is always fleeting and variable. In the *Nyāya* terminology, the *vyañjakatva* is not similar to *liṅgatva.* The nature of suggestiveness is not co-extensive with the nature of an inferential process since the former exists in objects like light where the latter is absent[166]. Thus the element of suggestion which poets use frequently is nothing but speaker's intention. Its comparative discussion follows in the fourth chapter of this book.

The *dhvani* theory of Ānandavardhana is studied in this chapter from a completely new angle. As it has been mentioned earlier that the evaluations of *sphoṭa, pratibhā* and *dhvani* are made to discover a common undercurrent between them, therefore, only some remarkable features are analysed. In this chapter the evolution of *dhvani* meaning shows that it is not a sudden phenomenon in the history of sanskrit poetics. The pre-*dhvani* rhetoricians, namely, Bharata, Bhāmaha, Vāmana, Daṇḍin, Udbhaṭa and Rudraṭa were well aware of it. They utilised the suggestive elements differently because of their bias to respective dogmas. Ānandavardhana has developed and given completeness to this therory of *dhvani.*

Ānandavardhana has proved that the *dhvani* language is not a self styled fabṛication without guarantee of facts. It is not extra linguistic. It is based on concerete language and expressed by solid language structures. It is purely linguistic in nature. It is a developed form of ordinary language preferably used by the great poets. It has special qualities which separates it from ordinary language. The ordinary language has limitations which is restricted to fixed structures whereas the *dhvani* language is elastic in nature. It can be manipulated in many ways by skilled persons. It is more generative than the ordinary language. The speaker's intention plays a major role in the *dhvani* language. But the difficulty with the *dhvani* language is that it has no direct medium of expression. It is expressed through the denotative and the indicative functions of language.

The realisation of *rasa* as explained by Ānandavardhana has some metaphysical traits. Abhinavagupta elaborates them. The *dhvani* language is the only means to delineate the metaphysical poetic experiences.

This most elastic, most reflective and most generative *dhvani* language of Ānandavardhana was originally discovered by the greạt grammarian-philosopher Bhartṛhari in his VP. Both Bhartṛhari and Ānandavardhana have many common ideas on the philosophy of language and metaphysics. They are discussed in the preceding chapters separately. It seems that Ānandavardhana has borrowed the philosophy of language and metaphysics directly from

Bharthari and refashioned them for *dhvani* language. Thus the *dhvani* theory of Ānandavardhana which is the meeting point of all disciplines[167] of poetics owes its inspiration from the philosophy of grammar. This will be analysed elaborately as we proceed.

References

1. *Kāvyālaṁkāra* of Bhāmaha, Patna, 1962, 2.87 :
gato'stam arko bhātīndu
yānti vāsāya pakṣiṇaḥ ।
ity evam ādi kiṁ kāvyaṁ
vārtām enāṁ pracakṣate ॥
2. *Ibid.*, 6.23 :
vakra vācāṁ kavīnāṁ ye
prayogaṁ prati sādhavaḥ ।
prayoktuṁ ye na yuktāś ca
tad viveko 'yam ucyate ॥
3. *Ibid.*, 2.85 :
saiṣā sarvaiva vakroktir
anayārtho vibhāvyate ।
yatno'syāṁ kavīnā kāryaḥ
ko 'laṁkāro 'nayā vinā ॥
4. Mathurānātha on *Tattvacintāmaṇi*, Calcutta, 1892-1901, p. 481:
śaktigrahaṁ vyākaraṇopamāna
kośāptavākyād vyavahārataś ca ।
vākyasya śeṣād vivṛter vadanti
sāṁnidhyataḥ siddhapadasya vṛddhāḥ ॥
also *Tattvacintāmaṇi*, p. 649; *Siddhāntamuktāvali*, p. 266.
5. *VP*. II. 317
6. *DL*. I.4
7. *Raghuvaṁsam*, ed. K.M. Tripathy, Varanasi, 1979:
iv. 73, *kīcakadhvanihetavaḥ;*
iv. 56, *abhyabhūyata..... vanadhvani;*
vi.56, *mandradhvanityājitayām atūrya;*
vii.41, *rathāṅgadhvanināvijajñee;*
ix. 97, *paṭupaṭahadhvanibhi vinitanidraḥ;*
x.35, *svareṇovāca bhagvān*
paribhūtārṇavadhvaniḥ;
xvi.13, *mṛdaṅga-dhīradhvanim anvagacchat;*

xvi. 32, *prabhuṇ prayāṇa dhvanimiśāratūryaḥ;*
xvi. 87, *divyas tùrya dhvani.*

8. (i) *kirātārjunīyam*, xiv,46;
vibhidyamānā iva dadhvanur diśaḥ c;
(ii) *Śiśupālavdham*, vi.49 :
śruta tad īritakomalagitaka dhvaniḥ.

9. *Uttararāmacaritam*, vi.17 :
dhvani na iva baddhapulakam

10. *NŚ.* Vol.I, GOS, p. 288-90:
katham āsvādyate rasaḥ yathā hi nānā vyañjanasaṁskṛtam annam etc. :
For English translation see *NŚ.* Vol. I, ed. Manmohan Ghose, pp. 105-106.

11. *Ibid.*, p. 348:
tatrāṣṭau bhāvāḥ sthāyinaḥ ... evam ete kāvyarasābhivyaktihetavaḥ ekonapañcāsatbhāvāḥ pratyavagantavyāḥ ebhyaś ca sāmānya-guṇa yogena rasā niṣpadyante...yo'rtho hṛdaya-saṁvādī tasya bhāvo rasodbhavaḥ śarīraṁ vyāpyate tena śuṣkakāṣṭham ivāgninā;
For english translation see *NŚ.* Vol. I, ed. M.M.Ghose, pp. 120-121.

12. *Ibid.*, p. 349 :
atrāha yadi kāvyārtha saṁśritai etc.
For english translation *NŚ.* Vol.I, pp. 121-122.

13. *Abh.* on *NŚ.* Vol. I, GOS, p. 290 :
suddha tatsvarūpa etc.

14. *Ibid.*, p. 289 :
tathābhinayavyañjite, etc.

15. *DL.* I, ed. K. KrishnaMoorthy, 1974, p. 12, 9-10 :
vividhavācyavācakaracanāprapañca cāruṇaḥ kāvyasya sa evārthaḥ sārabhūtaḥ

16. *Ibid.*, III. p. 188, 12-15; also see pp. 138,140,142,162.

17. *Ibid.*, III. p. 188, 9-13.

18. *Abh. NŚ.* Vol.II.9, GOS, p. 297 :
iha kāvyārtha rasā ityuktam...etc :
also see *Ibid.*, pp. 297-298 :
evam arthasyāpi;

also see Bhāmaha and Bhaṭṭanāyaka's view on *lakṣaṇā, Ibid.*, p. 298

19. See footnote No.4, Ch. III.
20. S. Mukhopadhyaya. "*Dhvani* o' tadīya virodhi saṁpradāya" (in Bengali), *Our Heritage*, Vol. IV, part-I, 1956, p. 137.
21. Prahallad Kumar, Ṛgvede' laṁkārāḥ, Munshiram Manoharlal, Delhi, 1977.
22. *KL.* II. 34 :
    samānavastunyāsena
    prativastupamocyate ।
    yathevā nabhidhāne'pi
    guṇasāmyapratītitaḥ ।।
23. *Ibid.*, II.79 :
    yatrokte gamyate'nyo 'rthas
    tat samānaviśeṣaṇaḥ ।
    sā samāsoktirudd iṣṭā
    saṁkṣiptārtha tayā yathā ।।
24. *KL.* III. 8-9.
25. *DL.* III. p. 228, 5-15.
26. S.K. *De, History of Sanskrit poetics,* Vol. II, 1960, p. 53.
27. *KD.*, ed. D.Gupta, I.76-78.
28. *KD. II. 303.*
29. *KD.* I.193; II. 205.
30. *KD.* III.330, II.46.
31. *KD.* II.214.
32. *KD.* II.295.
33. *KD.* II. 340.
34. *KD.* I. 100.
35. *KLSV.* Nirṇaya Śagar edition, 1926, i. 2.6-8 :
    rītir ātmā kāvyasya viśiṣṭā padaracanā
    rītiḥ viśeṣo guṇātmā
36. *KLSS.*, ed., N.D. Banhatti, Poona, 1925, IV. 6 :
    paryāyoktaṁ yad anyena prakāreṇābhidhīyate;
    also see *Laghuvṛtti* of Indurāja below it, p. 55.
37. *DL.* II. p. 90, 4.7.
38. *Kāvyānuśāsanam* of Hemacandra, Kāvyamālā edition, 1901, p. 263 :
    vyaṅgyasyoktiḥ paryāyoktam;

also *Kāvyānuśāsanam* of Bāgbhaṭṭa ii, NirṇayaSāgar press, 1915, iii ch, p. 36 :
dhvanitābhidhānam paryāyoktiḥ

39. *KLSS* I.11, *cf*, *KD*. I.65, II.254.
40. *Ibid.*, iv. 2
41. *Ibid.*, iv.3-4.
42. *Alaṁkārasarvasva* of Ruyyaka, ed. Rewaprasad *Dwivedi*, 1971, p. 6:
iha hi tāvat ... etc.
43. S.K. De, *History of Sanskrit Poetics*, 1960, p. 58.
44. *KLR*, Delhi, 1965, XII.2
tasmāt kartavyaṁ yatnena
mahīyasā raser yutam ।
udvejanam eteṣāṁ śāstravad
evānyathā hi syāt ॥
also SV.21 :
ete rasā rasavato ramayanti puṁsaḥ, samyag
vibhajya racitās catureṇa cāru; yasmādim
ānanadhigamya na sarva ramyam, kāvyaṁ
vidhātum alam atra tad ādriyeta; also of. *NŚ*. I.21. *KL*. V.3. *KD*. I.18.
45. *KD*. I. 51, I.60.
46. *KLR*. vii. 38
47. *Ibid.*, vii.40;
cf. *DL*.I.p. 8, 7-9;
sarveṣu ca teṣu prakāreṣu tasya vācyād anyatvam
... hi kadācit vācye vidhirūpe pratiṣedharùpaḥ
48. *KLR*. vii.14; cf. *DL*. I. p. 8, 15-16.
49. *Ibid.*, vii. 42.
50. *Alaṁkārasarvasvam* of Ruyyaka, ed. Rewaprasad Dwivedi, 1971, p. 11 :
evam api... etc. ;
Also *Ibid.*, p. 12 : *yad vā dvidheti* ... etc.
51. *Ibid.*, pp. 17-18.
52. *Ibid.*, p. 6 :
rudra tenāpi bhāvālaṁkāro ... etc.
53. S.K. De., *History of Sanskrit Poetics*. pp. *60-61*, *fn. No. 34.*
54. *DL*. I. p. 14, 10-14.
55. *DL*. I. 13.

56. *DL.* p. 18, 9-10 (Meaning of *upasarjana);* Also *DL.* p. 296, 22-23 :
'When a theme, even though it follows one already existing is utilised by a good poet with 'stylistic beauty' *bandhacchāyā* which consists in using words capable of conveying the desired literal and suggested sense, he does not become blameworthy'.;
Also *DL.* p. 202. 3-5 :
'For sometimes the suggested meaning is predominant and the literal meaning is subordinate and sometimes the literal meaning is predominant and the suggested meaning is subordinate. When the suggested meaning is predominant then we have *dhvani.* When the literal meaning is predominant, then we have another variety (of poetry viz. *guṇībhūta-vyaṅgya*).'
57. *DL.* II. *kā.* 33 :
'The complete definition of *dhvani* involves the clear perception in all varieties (of *dhvani)* of the predominantly suggested sense'; Also, *DL.* p. 18, 6 :
jhaṭityevāvabhāsate;
DL. p. 114, 19 : *rasamatvena sphuṭam evāvabhāsate;*
DL. p. 146 16 : *sphuṭam eva vyañjakatvaṁ dṛśyate;*
DL. p. 262.2 : *sphuṭatvenāvabhāsanam;*
DL. p. 276.12 : *sphuṭam evāvabhāsate*
58. *DL.* p. 20, 13 : *vyaṅgyaprādhānye hi dhvaniḥ:*
DL. p. 28, 16.18 : *vācyavyatiriktasyārthasya vācyavācakābhyām tātparyeṇa prakāśanaṁ yatra vyaṅgya-prādhānye as dhvaniḥ;*
DL. p. 40.12 : *mukhyatayā prakāśamāno vyaṅgyo'rtho dhvaner ātmā*
DL. p. 40, 16-17: *sa cāṅgitvenāvabhāsamāno dhvaner ātmā;*
DL. p. 48, 10-11 : *yaḥ punar aṅgīraso bhāvo vā sarvākāram alaṁkāryaḥ sa dhvaner ātmeti :*
DL. p. 206, 16 : *tatra vyañjakatve yadā vyaṅgyaprādhānyaṁ tadā dhvaniḥ*
DL. p. 244.19 : *vyaṅgyasyārthasya prādhānye dhvani sañcjitaḥ kāvyaprakāraḥ*
DL. p. 250, 20; *kāvyādhvani dhvanir vyaṅgya prādhānyaika nibandhanah*

59. *DL.* II. p. 42, 3-5: 'The word *dhvani* is used when in a poem figures of speech related to meaning and figures of speech related to words as well as qualities which are mutually separate and distinct from *dhvani,* and where they subordinate themselves to the main suggested sense, consisting of *rasa, bhāva, rasābhāsa, bhāvābhāsa* and *bhāvaśānti.*
60. *DL.* I.9 :

    'Just as a man interested in seeing (some object in the dark) concerns himself with the flame of a lamp, because it is a means to his seeing, in just this manner does a man (really only) interested in the (suggested) sense, none the less turn his attention to the explicit sense'.
61. *DL.* I. 10-11:
62. For details see K.K. Raja, Indian theories of Meaning, Madras, 1977, p. 289-303.
63. *Locans* on *DL,* ed. J. Pathak, 1965, pp. 104-5 :

    sa iti artho vā śabdo vā, vyāpāro vā artho' pi
    vācyo vā dhvanatīti, śabdo 'pyevam vyaṅgyo vā
    dhvanyata iti vyāpāro vā śabdārtha yor dhvananam iti ।
    kārikayā tu prādhānyena samudāya eva kāvyarūpo
    mukhyatayā dhvanir iti pratipāditam ॥

    'Either the meaning or the function (is *dhvani*). If it is meaning it can be the literal meaning because it suggests. The (denotative) word too (is *dhvani)* for the same reason, (i.e. because it suggests) *(dhvanati),* or the suggested meaning (is *dhvani*) because it is suggested *(dhvanyate),* or the suggestive function *(dhvanana)* of both words and meaning (is *dhvani).* In the *kārikā,* however, the collection (of word and literal meaning, suggested meaning and suggestive function) in the form of poetry characterised by its prime importance, has been put forth as *dhvani* in the strict (conventional) sense of the term'.
64. *DL.* I. 12.
65. *DL.* I.6.
66. *DL.* III.232, 3-5 :

    'There is by no means any form of poetry which will entrance the sensitive critic where the beauty is not caused by association with a suggested sense. This is the highest secret of poetry which should be meditated on by the wise'.

67. *DL.* III. *kā.* 37 :
'This beauty resulting from a suggested sense is the main ornament of the speech of great poets even when that speech comprises figures of speech, just as bashfulness is the highest ornament of a women even otherwise adorned'.

68. (i) *DL.* III. p. 262, 11-12 :
vaikāṭikā eva hi ratnatatvavidaḥ
sahṛdayā eva hi kāvyānāṁ rasajñā iti
'For only jewellers really know the (true) value of gems, and only sensitive critics really appreciate the *rasa* of poems'.
(ii) *DL.* III. p. 250, 18-19.

69. A. Amala Dass, *Philosophical Implications of Dhvani* Unpublished Ph. D. dissertation, Department of Sanskrit, Madras University, August, 1980, p. 66.

70. (i) *DL.* I. pp. 26-28, 16-17, 1-2; also see Chapter IV. fn.No. 6.
(ii) *DL.* III. p. 214, 15-16.
(iii) *DL.* IV, p. 278, 8 :
nirṇītaścāyam arthaḥ
śabdatatvavidbhir eva

71. DL. III. *kā* - 2.

72. See P. 6 of this book.

73. *DL.*III.*kā*.3-4

74. *Locana* on *DL.* III. ed. J.Pathak, pp. 329-330, 7-13, 1 :
'Although the cause of aestetic enjoyment is the richness of apprehension of the *vibhāvas, anubhāvas* and *vyabhicāribhāvas,* none the less, it is self evident that the *vibhāvas* etc. bring about such apprehension since only if they are conveyed by specific phonetic sounds. Therefore even the peculiar character of letters which are soft, harsh, etc. and which is grasped by the ear the moment they are heard, whether or not their meaning has been understood, is only helpful to aesthetic appreciation. In fact, it was just in order to convey the fact that letters are helpful, that the locative of cause was used in the expression. It is not that *rasa* is suggested just by letters, for we have said many times that aesthetic experience arises from the presentation of the *vibhāvas* etc. But (letters) which are grasped only by the ear, quite on their own, can give rise to a flow of aesthetic experience just like music without words (which can also give rise to aesthetic pleasure), or like the

imitation of the sounds of particular *jāti*, 'postures' *karaṇa* and fanciful gestures, all of which are regulated by a musical instrument such as a drum etc.'

75. *DL*.III.*kā*.16 and its *vṛtti* pp. 146-148.
76. *Locana* on DL, p. 379, 2-5.
77. *DL*.II.*kā*.6 :
    tamartham avalambante ye'ṅgīnam te
    guṇāḥ smṛtāḥ
78. *Veṇisaṁhāra* of Bhaṭṭa Nārāyaṇa I.21.
79. *Ibid.*, III.32.
80. *DL*. II.*kā*.9.
81. *KP*. ed. Ch. viii, V.Jhalakikarsa, 1965, pp. 463-465.
82. G.N.Jha, english translation of *KP*, 1967, pp. 299-300.
83. *DL*. III p. 156, 11-16 :
    'It was said that *rasas* etc. are suggested through the power of the meaning (of whole sentence). It is therefore unreasonable to show in a varied manner how declensional markers etc. can be suggestive. We have already replied to this objection when we explained how words can be suggestive. Moreover, even if we admit that *rasas* etc. are suggested through the force of the meaning of a sentence, the knowledge of the nature of suggestivity as already shown in a detailed manner, is (of course useful), because sentence meanings cannot exist without suggestive words. The beauty of a particular word that has been explained in a detailed manner elsewhere (i.e. in other works on poetics) should also be understood to be dependant on the suggestiveness of words alone (inspite of what has been written on this subject)'.
84. See P. 66 of this book.
85. *DL*.I.13.
86. *Nyāyaratnamālā* of Pārthasārathi Miśra,
    ed. K.S. Ramaswamy Shastri, GOS, Baroda, 1937, p. 106 :
    nanu evam abhidhāyakatvaṁ padānām na syāt
    padārtha svarupāgateḥ smaraṇāt avaśiṣṭatvāt
    smārakatvam evāstu, nābhidhāyakatvam
87. *DL*. III, p. 110, 19-20.
88. *DL*. III, p. 112, 15-20 :
    'You said earlier that *dhvani* was a type of poetry. How then can it be revealed by (isolated) words? For any type of poetry

is a particular collection of words that gives rise to a particular meaning. This cannot be the case for suggestion through words, for words do not directly express meanings, but only serve to remind us of them (nor do individual isolated words convey the sense of an entire sentence, which is essential for poetry).

Our reply to this objection is as follows : This would indeed be a serious objection were the force of direct expression a deciding factor in conferring the name of *dhvani* (on a poem). But this is hardly the case, for *dhvani* is determined through the power of suggestion. Moreover, though actually beauty is achieved through the sum total (of the different parts of the body) characterised by particular configurations, we admit it in individual parts, because the beauty of the whole, or its absence, depends on the presence or absence of the individual parts. Since the same is true of poetry, it is not unreasonable to say that certain words form part of the process of *dhvani* by means of their suggestive power.'

89. *DL.* I. 11.
90. *DL.* III., p. 110, 19-20, See fn No. 87 Chapter III.
91. *DL.* III., p. 114, 1-4 :

    'Therefore there is beauty in all the varieties of *dhvani,* which is revealed by mere words, even though words do in fact serve only as reminders'. 'Just as a woman appears lovely through a single ornament beautifully arranged so also the speech of a good poet appears lovely through *dhvani* revealed in a single word.'
92. See fn No.87,90 of Chapter III.
93. *DL.*III, p. 170, 3-5 :

    '(nor is it possible to say that the principle of subject and predicate is not valid in the case of *rasas*), because it is admitted that *rasas* are the ultimate sense of a sentence. If the subject and the predicate are found in the literal sentence meaning, why should they not be found in *rasas,* which are suggested by the (force) of the (literal) sentence meaning as a whole?'
94. *DL.*III, p. 116, 14-15 :

    'Since this sentence shows how their mutual love has grown, the entire sentence conveys the highest *rasa*';

Also. cf. *Locana* on *DL.* p. 334.

95. *DL.*III.p. 108, 3-4 :

'During what is night for all other creatures, the controlled man is wide awake. When all other creatures remain awake this is the night of the visionary sage'.

In this sentence, surely the usual meanings of 'night' and 'awake' are not intended. What is then? The saga's deep concern for the final truth and a corresponding aversion to whatever is not the final truth. Thus the sentence is suggestive of the variety of *dhvani* where the literal meaning completely disappears.

Also see *DL.*III, p. 108, 11-14 :

In this example the literal meaning of the sentence attracts suggested meaning. For some, time seems made of poison. For some, it seems made of nectar. For others, time seems a combination of both; and for still others it seems made of neither poison nor nectar. Here the sentence poison and nectar stand for pain and pleasures;

Also see *DL.*III. p. 112, 7-8.

96. *DL.*III.p. 200, 4-13.
97. See 2.2.3, 2.2.4, 2.2.5, 2.2.6, 2.2.7.
98. S.K.De, *Some problems of Sanskrit Poetics,* Calcutta, 1959, p. 189.
99. *DL.*III. p. 188, 18-20 :

'For the *vṛttis,* if they are introduced with *rasas* as their major object, will impart a most wondorous beauty to poetry. For *rasas* etc. are the life breath of both of them. The plot, etc. are merely the body'.

100. *DL.* III.p. 190, 192, 15-16, 1-2 :

'What is the point in imagining a sequence, since words alone, as determined by context etc. give rise to the apprehension of both the literal meaning and the suggested meaning at one and the same time? It is not true that only an understanding of the literal meaning of a word gives rise to suggestiveness. For we find that *rasa* is manifested from the (mere) sounds of singing even when the sounds (have no meaning) or even their meaning is not understood.'

101. *DL.* III. p. 188, 9-11.

102. *DL*.III. *kā*-33.
103. *NŚ*. GOS. Vol.I, Second edition, 1956, Ch.VI, 15-16.
104. *V*.Raghavan, *Number of Rasas*, Adyaer Library, xxvi, 1967.
105. K.A.S.Iyer, *Bhartṛhari*, p. 99.
106. See 1.3.6, 2.1.
107. *VP*.I.1-4.
108. S.N. Ghosal, *Elements of Indian Aesthetics*, Vol.I, 1978, 9 p. 59 : also see sections of 'Non-dualism in sound and sense', 'The concept of dual entity and the dual world in Indian Aesthetics and Esoterics', 'Mono-sentimentalism and Multi-sentimentalism' pp. 59-64.
109. *Sṛṅgāraprakāśa*, 1.7 :
 baṭayakṣa iva vibhāti.
110. S.N. Ghosal, *op. cit.*, p. 63.
111. *DL*.II. *kā*-28.
112. See fn.110.
113. For details see S.N. Ghosal. *Studies in Divine Aesthetics*, part II, Santiniketan, 1974.
114. *Uttararāmacaritam* III.47:
 eko rasa karuṇa eva nimittabhedāt
115. *Sāhitya Darpaṇa* of Viśvanāthakavirāja,
 ed. Satyavrata Singha, Varanasi, 1976, p. 106 :
 tasmād adbhutam evā ha kṛtī Nārāyaṇo rasam.
116. For details see V.Raghavan, *Number of Rasas*, Tenth Chapter, *Rasa*-Synthesis.
117. S.Kuppuswami Sastri,
 Introduction to Āścarya Cuḍāmaṇi : A drama by Śaktibhadra, pp. 13.14, Madras, 1926.
118. *NŚ*. *Vṛtti* on VI.31 :
 na hi rasād ṛte kaścid arthaḥ pravartate.
119. *Abh.* on *NŚ*. Vol.I, GOS, p. 272 :
 pūrvatra vahuvacanam atra ... etc.
120. *Ibid.*, p. 267 :
 tena rasa eva nāṭyaṁ yasya vyutpattiḥ ... etc.
121. *VP*.I.1.
122. Pt. Yogendranath Tarka Sāṁkhya Vedānta Tirtha,
 Bhāratīyadarśanaśāstrer samanvaya (Bengali),
 Adhar chandra Mukherji lecturers, Calcutta University, 1952, pp. 80-89.

In this book he has shown how Vedantic monism passes and develope through *ārambhavāda, saṁghātavāda, pariṇāmavāda, vivartavāda.*

123. *DL.* II.*kā.7 :* III.p. 250, 3-4; III.kā.28-29.
124. *DL.*IV. pp. 272, 274, 276, 278; *Ibid.*, p. 278, 10-12.
125. *DL.* III.*kā.*21, 22, 24, 29.
126. *Ibid.*, II.*kā.*7-9; III. p. 176, 8-1; iv.p. 272-278; 280, 8.
127. *Ibid.*, ii.*kā.* 7-9.
128. *Ibid.*, iii.p. 176, 8-11.
129. *Ibid.*, iv. pp. 272-278.
130. Singular use of the term *rasa :*
DL. ii. *kā.*17; iii. *kā.* 21, 22, 24, 29, p. 250, 3. iv. pp. 272, 27.
Plural use of the term *rasa* :

*DL.*ii.	p. 40,16	:	*rasādir artho*
	p. 42.2	:	*rasādiparatā yatra*
	p. 42.9	:	*rasādyas te*
	p. 44.15	:	*rasādayo vākyārthibhūtā*
	p. 46.1	:	*rasādibhiś cārutvaniṣpattiḥ*
	p. 48.10	:	*rasādinām alaṁkāratā*
	p. 52.6	:	*yat tu sarvarasān prati*
DL.iii.	p. 164.1	:	*sukavīnāṁ rasādayaḥ*
	p. 155.11	:	*rasādaya ity uktam*
	p. 170.3	:	*na ca raseṣu*
	p. 170.5	:	*tadākṣiptānāṁ rasānām*
	p. 176.8	:	*nanu yeṣāṁ rasānām*
	p. 174.15	:	*nanu rasāntareṣu bahuṣu*
	p. 182.27	:	*nivartata hi rasayo*
	p. 186.19	:	*vijñāyetha rasādīnām*
	p. 188.4	:	*evaṁ rasādiṣu*
	p. 188.7	:	*rasādi viṣayenaitat*
	p. 188.12	:	*etac ca rasāditātparyeṇa*
	p. 188.14	:	*rasādyanuguṇatvena*
	p. 188.18	:	*rasādi tātparyeṇa*
	p. 188.19	:	*rasādayo hi*
	p. 190.2	:	*rasādimayaṁ hi vācyam*
	p. 190.3	:	*yadi rasādimayam eva*
	p. 190.5	:	*rasādayo 'pi*

	p. 190.8	:	*rasādirūpatvam iti*
	p. 190.13	:	*rasādīnāṁ pratīti*
	p. 190.14	:	*rasādipratītiḥ*
	p. 192.9	:	*rasādipratītiḥ*
	p. 192.15	:	*rasādau na pratīyate*
	p. 246.11	:	*cittavṛttiviśeṣo hi rasādayaḥ*
	p. 256.7	:	*yā vyāpāravati rasān rasayitum*
DL.iv.	p. 272.12	:	*rasādimaya ekasmin*

131. *VP*.I.73; *DL*.i. *kā*.10-11; 2.2.5, 2.2.6, 4.3, 4.3.1.
132. (i) *Abh.* on *NŚ.* Vol.I, GOS, p. 333 : *iha tāvat dharmādi* ... etc.
(ii) *Ibid.*, p. 339 : *tasmād asti śānto rasah.*
133. *DL*.iii. p. 182, 5-6 :
'The pleasure of love, as well as the great pleasures of heaven, do not equal even the sixteenth part of the happiness that succeeds the destruction of desire'.
of. *Locana*, DL.p. 431 :
iti Bharatavākyam dṛṣṭavantaḥ sarvarasa-
sāmānyasvabhāvṁ śāntam ācakṣāṇā anupajāta-
viśeṣāntara cittavṛttirūpam śantasya
sthāyībhāvaṁ manyante
'Having taken their stand on the Bharata's aphorism (that various feelings, because of their particular respective causes, arise from *śānta* (a state of mental calm) but when these causes disapper, they melt back into *śānta).* Others claim that *śānta* is common to all *rasas* and consider the permanent of *śānta* to be that state of mind which has not been particularised into any other mood.'
134. *Taittirīya Upaniṣad*, ii.7.
135. Bhaṭṭanāyaka's lost work *Hṛdayadarpaṇa* quoted in the *Vyaktiviveka of Mahima Bhaṭṭa*, ed. Rewaprasad *Dvivedi*, 1964, Varanasi, p. 100:
pāṭhyād atha dhruvāgānāt
tataḥ saṁpūrite rase ।
tadā svādabharaikāgro
hṛṣyatyantarmukha kṣaṇam ॥
tato nirviṣayasyāsya
svarūpāvasthitau nijaḥ ।
vyajyate hlādaniṣyandau
yena tṛpyanti yoginaḥ ॥

136. *Abh.* on *NŚ.* GOS, Ch.vi.
137. *RG.* BHU, Vol. I, 1963, p. 120;
iyaṁ ca parabrahmāsvādāt samādher vilakṣaṇā vibhāvādiviṣayasambalita-cidānandālambanatvāt bhāvyā ca kāvya vyāpāra mātrāt
138. Bhaṭṭa Nāyaka quoted in *Locana, DL*, p. 93; *vāg dhenur dugdha etaṁ hi* ... etc.
139. *Locana* on *DL*.iii.p. 543;
evaṁ prathamam eva paramesvara-bhaktibhājaḥ kutūhala ... etc.
'This stanza is the utterance as the author (Ānandavardhana), who began by first being a devotee of god, and then, simply out of curiosity, adopted both the view points of the poet and the philosopher (but found them ultimately unsatisfying) and once again came to believe that rest in devotion to God was inevitable. For we have already explained that the happiness which results from (conceptual understanding of) both Sun and unseen objects which are ascertained by all the means of valid cognition (i.e. philosophy) or even that transcendant joy which consists in relishing an aesthetic experience...to both of these the bliss that comes from finding rest in God is far superior; and that aesthetic pleasure is only the reflection of a drop of that mystic bliss. But ordinary worldly happiness is for the most part inferior to even that aesthetic delight, because it is mixed with abundant suffering as well. This is the essence of what he means.'
140. Kumārasvāmin on *Pratāpraudrīya yaśobhūṣaṇa* of Vidyānāth, ed. V. Raghavan, The Sanskrit Education Society, Madras, Mylapore, 1970, p. 196 :
ata evāyaṁ brahmānanda eva iyāṁs tu viśeṣaḥ brahmānando yoga-gamyaḥ ı ayaṁ tu vibhāvādy anusaṁdhānagamya iti ı idam api tenaivoktam - 'sarvatraikaivānandavyaktir laukikaṁ sukham iti vyavahriyate ı alaukikavibhāvādy abhivyaktyā kavisamayamātra prasiddhy anusārād alaukiko rasa iti kathyate nānāvidhavimala-karma nirmalāntaḥkaraṇeṣu samadamādisādhanasaṁpanneṣu śravanamanananididhyāsanapareṣu paramayogiṣu nirvikalpaka-samādhy abhivyaktyā brahmeti paramātmeti iśvara iti śabdyata iti uktaṁ ca svātmayogapradīpe ı yā sthāyībhāva ratir eva nimitta-

bhedāḥ ı śṛṅgāramukhyanavanāṭyarasi bhavanti ı sāmāikān sahṛdayān naṭanāyakādīn ı ānandayet sahahja pūrṇaraso 'smi so'ham.

'So it is (*rasānanda)* is similar with *(brahmānanda).* The difference between them is, the *brahmānanda* is attained by *yoga,* whereas it *(rasānanda)* is realised by excitants etc. It is *rasānanda* one and characterised by uncommon happiness. Poetic tradition proclaims that *rasa* is an unworldy experience as it is manifested by unearthly causes viz. excitants etc. (on the other hand) the Supreme *Brahman* who is called *Īśvara* is revealed in the *nirvikalpaka samādhi* of *yogins,* whose hearts are pure because of many suspicious actions, and who practise hard penance, viz. *śama, dama,* etc. and occult practices such as *śravaṇa manana* and *nidhidyāsana.*

In my *Yoga pradīpa* it has been mentioned, 'that which is manifested as *śṛṅgāra* etc. by permanent moods *rati* etc., and to which the audience, connoisseurs, actors, heroes etc. relish in the form of enjoyment, and that which is absolute bliss is known as *rasa.* This *rasa* is the (Supreme *Brahman*).'

141. *Pañcadaśī,* Nirṇaya Sāgar ed. 1949, xi, 85-86 :
also for the concept of *ānanda* (bliss) in the *Vedānta* see *Pañcadaśā* Ch. xi-xiv; also see the *Pañcadaśī* of Bhāratī Tīrtha Vidyāraṇya pp. 175-266, ed. by T.M.P. Mahadevan, Centre of Advanced Study in Philosophy, University of Madras, 1969.

142. M.Hiriyana, Art Experience, First and Final, Kāvyālaya Publishers, Mysore, 1954, p. 86:
For details see chapters i.e. Art Experience-i, ii, pp. 25-42 of this book.

143. *RG.* BHU, 1969, pp. 117-121;
also see K. Krishna Moorthy, *Studies in Indian Aesthetics and Criticism,* "Vedantic idea of aesthetic experience", Mysore, 1979, p. 206. For the nature of *ānanda* of *Vedānta* and its interpretation as neuro-paychological instinctual urges, see *Ānanda, and experience,* by M.Sivaram, Vikas Publishing House, 1976 ;
also by the same author, *Ānanda and the three great ācāryas,* 1976.

144. *DL.* iii. p. 216, 12-13.

145. *Ibid.*, p. 200, 4.
146. *Ibid.* p. 248, 1-3.
147. *Ibid.*, p. 248, 7-8.
 cf. *Ibid.*, p. 250, 1-6.
148. *Ibid.*, p. 250, 7-11.
149. *Ibid.*, pp. 210-212, 8-16, 1-9.

"Moreover, nobody should entertain any doubt but that the property of words and meanings in the form of suggestiveness conforms to a wellknown relationship that exists between words and their meanings known as *vācyavācakabhāva*, (but) it is contingent upon the various factors that lead to the suggestive function, (i.e. the speaker, the context, the audience, intonation etc.). and this is why it is distinct from deontation. For denotation is the fixed nature of a particular word, and it is well known that it remains invariably associated with this word right from the moment we learn its lexical meaning. But suggestiveness is not fixed, because of the fact that it is contingent (upon other factors). For the suggested sense is apprehended as conditioned by context, etc. In their absence it will not arise. If it is really not fixed then what point is there in examining its nature? This is no fault. For it is not fixed so far as the form of the word is concerned, but it is fixed with regard to its own sphere, namely the suggested sense. One can apply the analogy of the middle term *(liṅga)* to suggestiveness. Because the state of being an (operative) logical reason *(liṅga)* is uncertain in its appearance, but it does invariably lead to the conclusion (e.g. the presence of fire) in its own province, (e.g. the mountain), provided the desire to construct a proper syllogism is present.

The same is case with this suggestiveness that we have already explained (i.e. it can become operative only if there is desire and capacity to appreciate it). And because it is uncertain with regard to words, it is not possible to consider it as denotation. For if it were same as denotation, then it would be fixed with regard to the form of the words, the way denotation is.

Now this contingent property (of words, viz. suggestiveness) must necessarily be acceepted by the *Mīmāṁsakas (vākyatatvavit)* who claim that there is a primordial connection between words and their meanings, when he asserts that there is a difference (with regard to validity) between human and divine utterances. For if it is not accepted, although the relationship between words and their meanings is eternal (in the case of both human and divine utterances), there would be no difference (between the two kinds of utterances) so far as the conveyance of sense is concerned. But if that property (i.e. suggestiveness) is accepted, then since human utterances have a contingent function, (i.e. suggestiveness) conferred on them (i.e. since human utterances acquire such a conditioned function), as they are always in keeping with their desire, human utterances can be untrue (for the *Mīmāṁsakas),* although the relation between words and meanings is eternal.'

150. *Ibid.,* iii, pp. 212-214, 16, 1-6 :
'Human utterances principally reveal only the intention of the speaker. And this (intention) is suggested, and not directly stated, because the words actually used are not connected with it (i.e. the intention of the speaker) by the relation of the expressed sense and the expressive word. If we follow this reasoning all worldly utterances will have to be designated as *dhvani,* for all worldly utterances, if we follow this reasoning, will carry suggestion. That is true but the suggestiveness in the form of revelation of the intention of a speaker is equally common to all worldly utterances. Nor does it differ from denotation, for a suggested meaning is invariably present (in such utterances). But (the difference is that in such cases) it is not especially intended.'
151. *DL.*iii.p. 214, 7-8.
152. *Ibid.,* p. 214, 8-14.
153. See pages 157, 63, 66, 71 of this book.
154. *DL.*iii.p. 200, 4-8.
155. *Ibid.,* p. 200, 8-12.
156. See pp. 29-30.
157. See p. 71 of this book
158. *DL.*iii.p. 202, 1-6.
159. *Ibid.,* p. 214, 4-6.
160. *Ibid.,* p. 216, 1-2.

161. By this Prabhākara's opinion is admitted.
162. *DL*.iii. 218, 1-6.
163. Ibid., iii. 218, 9-12.
164. *Ibid.*, iii.218, 12-14.
165. *Ibid.*, iii, 218-220, 15, 1-2.
166. *Ibid.*, iii, 220, 12-13.
167. K.KrishnaMoorthy, *Studies in Indian Aesthetics and Criticism*, "*Dhvani* as the basic principle of Sanskrit criticism", Mysore, p. 128 ff. : "*Dhvani* as the meeting point of all principles of Sanskrit literary theory" in *Principles of literary criticism in Sanskrit*, ed. R.C. Dwivedi, Motilal Banarsidas, Delhi, 1969, 201 ff.

4

Synthesis of Sphoṭa, Pratibhā and Dhvani

The Sanskrit grammarians did not avoid the problems of semantics. Actually, a large portion of grammatical works deals with the descriptions of the semantic aspects. According to the Sanskrit grammarians, the descriptive and the semantic systems are closely knit together and do not exist separately. The *dhvani* theory of Ānandavardhana offers almost parallel analysis of content that we find on the expression side. According to Bhartṛhari, the distinction between *dhvani* and *sphoṭa* is that the latter appears to be different from sound as class from individual. *Sphoṭa* is characterised as a class of sounds related to *dhvani* through phonetic similarities. The sounds may vary widely but the *sphoṭa* remains the same. The later grammarians hold that there are two different aspects which concern the nature of meaningful linguistic unit. One is *akhaṇḍavākyasphoṭa*, according to which, a sentence is not taken into account in terms of a series of meaningful units. As opposed to this, the approach advanced by the theories of *varṇasphoṭa* and *padasphoṭa* is analytical and tries to dissolve the utterance into its constituent elements. The theories of *abhidhā* and *lakṣaṇā* try to dissolve the meaning of utterance into constituent meaning elements. The theories of *abhidhā* and *lakṣaṇā* are more concerned with "how the language functions" and 'how the language is used?' Their value lies in presenting formal account of language and in building up the *dhvani* theory of language. The *abhidhā* and *lakṣaṇā* advanced by later philosophers mainly lay emphasis on the formal treatment of meaning-analysis. The teaching put forward by the *varṇa-sphoṭa, pada-sphoṭa* and the *abhidhā* and *lakṣaṇā* need not be looked upon as true from the point of view of communication. The analysis furnished by the above theories is undoubtedly a fiction, because the listener, while understanding the meaning, does not grasp the existence of linguistic units and their meanings. The views of *varṇa-sphoṭa* and *pada-sphoṭa* and *abhidhā* and *lakṣaṇā* put together form the theory: "The words can be isolated from a sentence and each isolated word denotes its distinct meaning". On the same line the theory of *abhihitānvayavāda* maintains that the individual words have meaning in themselves.

In Bhartṛhari's theory of *pratibhā* and in Ānandavardhana's *dhvani* theory, meaning is attached to a sentence, because only the flash of meaning or emotional overtones can be understood from a sentence. We set side by side sentences in which only one word is different and then we decide that difference in meaning should correspond to the difference in words. Thus we take for granted that recurring words are capable to convey some meaning. But language cannot be reduced to the purely referential use. The linguistic expression often indicate the speakers' attitude namely fear, anger, pity and love etc. According to Ānandavardhana, the imaginative and poetic power of linguistic form cannot be assigned to the referential value of language. The *vākya-sphoṭa* maintains the indivisibility of sentences unit. According to this theory, the entire sentence is endowed with denotative function. Bhartṛhari maintains that the meaning of a sentence is grasped as the instantaneous flash of insight *(pratibhā)* which is indivisible into word meanings. The expression not only accounts for actual contents but also dynamic, emotive and aesthetic values. The use of language talks about the speaker and his state of mind. Thus in literary forms, the imaginative and poetic power *(dhvani)* comes into play. Thus, according to Bhartṛhari and Ānandavardhana, the language cannot be reduced to the referential value only. The grammarians assume that the cognition of the series of phonemes finally leads to the cognition of the *sphoṭa* word. Similarly, according to Ānandavardhana, the cognition of meaning through the *abhidhā* and *lakṣaṇā* leads to the cognition of *dhvani.* The grammarians hold that the relation between *dhvani* and *sphoṭa* is *vyaṅgyavyañjakabhāva* 'revealer-revealed'. Similarly, according to Ānandavardhana, the formal relation that exists between *vācyārtha* and *pratīyamānārtha* is *vyaṅgyavyañjaka bhāva* 'revealer–revealed'. Thus, Ānandavardhana has extended all the theories regarding the nature of *śabda* and its meaning to the concept of *dhvani.*

This semantic philosophy stated above mainly forms the foundation to correlate the *dhvani* concept of Ānandavardhana with *sphoṭa* and *pratibhā* concept of Bhartṛhari which were discussed in the preceding chapters separately. All the statements and arguments to be mentioned aim at showing that Ānandavardhana owes his inspiration from grammarians to formulate his new semantic theory, namely *dhvani.*

Development of the *dhvani* theory from Patañjali to Ānandavardhana

The *dhvani* concept was analysed in connection with speech act by the ancient grammarians. Sphoṭāyana[1] (P. 6.1.123), Audumbarāyaṇa and Vārtākṣa were ancient thinkers in this field (*Nir.* 1.1; *VP.* II.342). But their views are available in excerpts. We find mythical and magical speculations on speech and sound in the *Vedas* and the *Upaniṣads,* which can be characterised as constituting the prescientific stage. However, the *Brāhmaṇas* (C. 800 B.C.) while attempting 'peculiar exercises in etymologies *(parokṣa-vṛttis),* tried to analyse words into their elements and to assign meanings to these elements. The *Śikṣās* (general phonetics, C.500 B.C.) describe the mechanism of articulation, and offer amazingly precise sound classification into such features as voicing/unvoicing, aspiration/non-aspiration, nasality, vocal quality etc. P (C. 350 B.C.) who mentions a number of predecessors, can be viewed as the final regulator of earlier grammatical tradition which has started some centuries before him. But Pāṇini's grammar does not concern philosophical problems of language. Its main aim is to offer a structural description of the Sanskrit language but not the exposition of the nature of language. Kātyāyana and Patañjali brought some philosophical discussion into the fold of grammar. In India, there are various philosophies of language which have been advocated by various schools of science. Among them, the grammarians' philosophy of language is most famous and it has a long history. In order to describe the language fully the grammarians took into account emotiveness and affectivity of language. This philosophy of language finally culminated in Ānandavardhana's *dhvani* philosophy of language.

The systematic discussion of *dhvani* and *sphoṭa* begins with Patañjali. He has assimilated the philosophy of language of his predecessors and has given a concrete shape to the concept of *dhvani*. Patañjali makes an important statement about the nature of *śabda* (*Mbh.*Vol.1, p. 18). He says *śabda* is that which is perceived by the auditory organs, grasped through intellect, revealed by the sounds, pertaining to the region of the sky. The term perceived auditorily stands for the sound *(dhvani)* which passes from the speaker to the listener. According to the first definition, *śabda* stands for a meaning sound. According to the second definition, *dhvani* 'sound' is designated as *śabda*. According to Patañjali, the language *(śabda)* has two aspects, i.e. *sphoṭa* and *dhvani*. The *sphoṭa* refers to the permanent element in the sound whereas *dhvani* refers to the non-permanent element of speech i.e. physical articulated sound. *Dhvani* manifests *sphoṭa. Dhvani* is associated with various peculiarities of the individual speaker. *Dhvani* refers to the articulate sound which differs in phonetic value with reference to different speakers. Patañjali further states that (on P.8.2.18) *dhvani* stands for ordinary sound and *sphoṭa* represents class sounds or phonetic pattern of sounds. According to Patañjali, the *sphoṭa* is not necessarily meaning-bearing segment of the word as it is generally believed. Its operation is restricted within the phonetic level of sound.

The concept of *dhvani* is exhaustively treated by Bhartṛhari. He has utilised the earlier possible sources. He has collected earlier possible views prevalent at his time on *dhvani.* Bhartṛhari identifies *dhvani* with articulated sound. But its relation with *sphoṭa* is highly controversial. Since isolated sound units cannot communicate meanings, a binding power is postulated to put them together. On the one hand this binding power *(sphoṭa)* juxtaposes the disjoined sound-impressions, and on the other hand it starts communicating elements of language. According to traditional scholars, *sphoṭa* represents the meaning bearing unit of language. But Patañjali and Bhartṛhari nowhere clearly say that meaning bearing unit of language is called *sphoṭa.*

The *dhvani,* according to Bhartṛhari, is an articulated sound. It is a revealer of *sphoṭa* (*VP.* I.97). The primary sound reveals *sphoṭa* whereas the secondary sound continues its further manifestation (*VP.*I.76-77). The process is similar to the mother flame from which other flames are generated and continues their existence *(VP.*I.106). The *dhvani* does not represent the permanent element whereas *sphoṭa* stands for constant element (*VP.*I.49, 75, 77). Bhartṛhari gives three views on the nature of *sphoṭa* (*VP.*I.102, 104, 93). The third view which states that *dhvani* represents individual sounds whereas *sphoṭa* represents the class sound, is considered to be the opinion of Bhartṛhari. According to this view, *sphoṭa* is sound pattern of individual sounds *(dhvani).* It strictly operates in the phonetic level. It is related to the articulated sound and not to the meaning. The *sphoṭa* to be meaning bearing entity is a later developed theory which identifies *sphoṭa* with the meaning-bearing elements of language. It is a wrong interpretation. Really speaking, *sphoṭa* can be an auditory image of the sound (1.3.71). Nowhere is it stated in the *VP* that *sphoṭa* is indivisible (1.3.8.1) and self-revealing entity (1.3.8.2).

When a speaker desires to say something, before the actual production of utterance, the articulatory image of the sound remains in the mind of the speaker. This image is manifested when the physical sound is heard. So the physical sound is called the manifester of *sphoṭa.* This image of the sound cannot be denoted or indicated. It can only be suggested. In this respect *dhvani* is a suggester of *sphoṭa.* Because *sphoṭa* remains in the mind in the form of sound-image, it is called *antarbuddhirnirgrāhya* (fn.No.34, Ch.I). It is not clearly suggested when the first sound is heard, but in a vague form. As the subsequent sounds are perceived, its comprehension becomes clearer and clearer. Thus *sphoṭa* is progressively revealed which represents the conceptual entity of the sound, it has nothing to do with the meaning.

The later grammarians, the *Mīmāṁsakas,* and the *Naiyāyikas* interpreted *sphoṭa* differently from the view held by Patañjali and Bhartṛhari. They think that *dhvani* is the crude articulated sound from which *sphoṭa* emerges as a meaning conveying entity. Keeping this view in mind, the *Mīmāṁsakas* and the *Naiyāyikas* refute *sphoṭa.* All of them identify meaning bearing *śabda* with *sphoṭa*. This is erroneous, because Patañjali and Bhartṛhari have never used the term *sphoṭa* in the concept of meaningful speech unit.

Ānandavardhana takes his inspiration from the grammarians to formulate his *dhvani* theory[2].

Abhinavagupta states that the source of Ānandavardhana's *dhvani* theory is the *sphoṭa* concept of Bhartṛhari[3]. Abhinavagupta's supposition is correct. Ānandavardhana has borrowed many things from Bhartṛhari. Similarities of ideas and nomenclature are very intimate among both the great thinkers. Ānandavardhana has successfully assimilated the ideas of Bhartṛhari and fitted them to the poetic speech.

Further, both in *sphoṭa* and *dhvani* the elements of sound *(dhvani)* play an important role. The *sphoṭa* represents the class sound whereas *dhvani* represents the individual sound. The first represents the phonematic level of language whereas the second represents the phonetic level of language. The term *dhvani* losely refers to the distinctive level of language.

Taking the cues from the early and later grammarians Ānandavardhana specially selected the term *dhvani.* Following the earlier grammarians, the term *dhvani* is used by Ānandavardhana in the sense of suggester. According to him, the suggested meaning is manifested by *dhvani,* i.e. by a phoneme, a stem, a suffix, a word or sentence. Just as the speaker wants to manifest the meaning-bearing element *(sphoṭa)* through the articulated sound, similarly, according to Ānandavardhana, *dhvani* reveals the suggested meaning. The term *dhvani* is used to represent the articulate sound which is the conveyer of *sphoṭa,* and it is also used for the conveyed *sphoṭa.* Similarly, the term *dhvani,* according to Ānandavardhana, represents both the suggester sound and the suggested meaning. Thus the stylistic begins with the notion of *dhvani* 'sound'. The speaker uses sounds once the hearer understands the speaker's intention. Thus the function of sound is not to convey the grammatical meaning only but something more than it. Sounds cannot be devoid of emotion. The affectivity may be due to the choice of sounds or words or sound of words. Ānandavardhana has deliberately chosen the term *dhvani* to show that the whole material of language has to be reconsidered from the new stand point of *dhvani.* The great master Ānandavardhana wants to show that rhetoric can be traced to the *dhvani* symbols. We cannot communicate something beyond the symbols i.e. sounds.

Apart from the *sphoṭa* concept, the concept of *pratibhā* of Bhartṛhari has much influenced the linguistic philosophy of Ānandavardhana. This *pratibhā* covers a wide range of communicative activity. It is a cause of origin of speech. It is the cause of all activities of human beings and animals. It is the same as what we know by instincts. It activaties the impression of the previous existence. It makes us to grasp the meaning of the sentence intuitively which is integral and indivisible. This *pratibhā* which is based on words represents the reality of language (Ch.II).

Both *sphoṭa* and *pratibhā* which are based on essential elements of language deals with certain devices of linguistic functions. The *sphoṭa* investiagtes the facts of sounds whereas *pratibhā* concentrates on the contents of expressions. The *sphoṭa* operates in the phonetic level of language whereas *pratibhā* operates in the semantic level. These two concepts describe the two sides of expression. Thus Bhartṛhari takes into account all the aspects of language in which Ānandavardhana's *dhvani* theory is included.

Ānandavardhana has picked up Bhartiṛhari's concept of *pratibhā* as the guiding instinct in understanding all meanings including emotive values. He has profusely used both these concepts in the treatment of *dhvani* language. This is treated in what follows.

Source of the *dhvani* theory of Ānandavardhana in the *sphoṭa* and *pratibhā* concepts of Bhartṛhari

Ānandavardhana propounds the *dhvani* theory to describe the poetic language. The *dhvani* theory has a long tradition which has been orally handed down[4]. The emotive and affective values of speech have been accepted by the earlier scholars[5]. Twice Ānandavardhana admits that he is indebted to the grammarians. But his precision and economy conceal the actual facts about the nature of his debt. The following passages bring out the similarity between the grammarians' theories and that of Ānandavardhana :

"The first and foremost among learned men are the grammarians, for all knowledge is based on the grammar. They have given the name of *dhvani* to letters that are (actually) heard. And so other wisemen, who had understood the true essence (i.e. the suggested sense) of poetry, following the footsteps of the grammarians, applied the name *dhvani* to the significative function, viz. *vyañjanā,* which is the soul (essence) of poetry to the literal sense and the word expressing it together with the suggested sense and deserves to be called poetry, because in both cases there is suggestiveness."[6]

Another passage runs as follows :

"The doctrine of *dhvani* was first conceived and promulgated by relying on the views of those who fully know the *śabdabrahman* which is without any change and so there is no question of considering whether our doctrine is in conflict with theirs or not."[7]

From the above passages the following points emerge :

(i) Ānandavardhana does not mean that the expression *dhvani* as understood by the literary critics is as old as Patañjali. He tries to establish that the name *dhvani* is not a casual thing brought up in a moment of leisure, but rather has the backing of the grammarians, famous for their seriousness and learning. Here Ānandavardhana has not suggested that the doctrine of *dhvani* is as old as the *Mahābhāṣya,* but only that the name and the function of suggestion had been already accepted by the grammarians in connection with their doctrine of *sphoṭa.*

(ii) The views of the grammarians given by Ānandavardhana match with that of Bhartṛhari.

In the *VP-I,* the *dhvani* is described both as suggester and suggested. As the suggester, it suggests *sphoṭa* (*VP.* 1.93. 97). Again *dhvani* is described as the suggested according to a particular school of grammarians whose views are mentioned in the *VP.* Āccording to this view, *dhvani* is produced from *sphoṭa.* So it is suggested. The idea is, the initial sound of any utterance is *sphoṭa,* and the succeeding sounds which are generated from the (initial sound *(sphoṭa)* in the same manner as reverberation of the bell is *dhvani.* (*VP*.I.102, 106)

Ānandavardhana adopts this (as sugester) feature of *dhvani* from the grammarians.

(iii) The element of suggestions in connection with *dhvani* is common to both the *VP* and the *Dhvanyāloka.* As the sound uttered by the speaker progressively reveal the word form, similarly, *dhvani* progressively reveal the *vyaṅgyārtha* 'emotive and affective meaning'. Often the attitudinal meaning and speakers' intention are not beyond the element of sound.

(iv) The second passage quoted, undoubtedly refers to the famous principle of eternal verbum (*VP*.I.1) of Bhartṛhari on the basis of which Ānandavardhana has framed the *dhvani* theory. According to Bhartṛhari, *śabdabrahman* which assumes various forms due to *avidyā* is expressive of meaning. To the grammarians it is the supreme reality. It is devoid of all qualities and distinctions. The supreme word gives to the object its existential status.

Following the same line, Ānandavardhana mentions that the *rasadhvani* is the supreme reality. It is devoid of all qualities and distinctions. The *rasadhvani* is indentified with the supreme meanings *vyaṅgyārtha.* The *rasadhvani* remains over and above the constituent meaning. Both Bhartṛhari and Ānandavardhana maintain that the undivided utterance conveys undivided meaning. Like the later grammarians, Ānandavardhana has shifted the earlier conception of *dhvani* from the feature level of language to the semantic level. The discussion on the nature of *dhvani,* according to Ānandavardhana, essentially deals with emotive and affective aspects of language. And, finally, following Bhartṛhari, Ānandavardhana has attributed the metaphysical aspect of *śabdabrahman* to *dhvani.*

(v) According to Bhartṛhari, *sphoṭa* is sound-image which operates in phonetic level of language. The *dhvani* in relation to it can only suggest the sound. Had *sphoṭa* been the conveyer of meaning, *dhvani* would have been the suggester of meaning. But this is not so. The *dhvani in VP* is treated as *vyañjaka* of *śabda* (sound) and not as *vyañjaka* of *artha* (sense).

But in the *Dhvanyāloka, dhvani* is used in both the senses i.e. *vyañjaka* of *śabda* (sound) as well as *vyañjaka* of *artha.* In this respect he follows the later grammarians, who maintain that the relation between the feature level of language *(dhvani)* and semantic level of language *(sphoṭa)* is *vyaṅgyavyañjakabhāva* 'revealer and revealed'. It seems that Ānandavardhana has taken the nomenclature of *vyañjakatva* 'suggestiveness' of Bhartṛhari and extended it to both suggestiveness of sound and sense[8].

Source of *dhvani* theory of Ānandavardhana according to Abhinavagupta

Abhinavagupta in his commentary on the *Dhvanyāloka* has expounded the cryptic statement of Ānandavardhana as to the nature of relation between his new theory and the grammarians' views. Abhinavagupta thinks that the *dhvani* theory of poetics has been styled after the *sphoṭa* concept of Bhartṛhari. He holds that Ānandavardhana has used *dhvani* in four various ways. It may be suggester *(dhvanati iti)*, or suggested *(dhvanyata iti)*, or the process of suggestion *(dhvananam iti)*. It may stand for the whole poetry which is composed of *dhvani* elements *(dhvani samudāya)*[9]. Abhinavagupta thinks that the term *dhvani* used in these four senses are traceable in the *VP* of Bhartṛhari[10]. His exposition of Ānandavardhana's *dhvani* theory in terms of *sphoṭa* concept of Bhartṛhari can be summarised in the following way :

Abhinavagupta argues that both in the *VP* and the *DL*, *dhvani* is suggested *(vyaṅgya)*. He states that *dhvani* is suggested by *sphoṭa* (1.3.1.1). According to this view, the first articulated sound produced by the contact and separation of articulatory organs is called *sphoṭa*. The succeeding sounds which are produced from the *sphoṭa* as children waves from the mother wave are called *dhvanis*. These *dhvanis* are *śabdajā śabdā* as they are created from the sound. Their creation is in the fashion of reverberation (*VP*.1.102). Because the subsequent *dhvanis* are generated from the initial *sphoṭa*, these are said to be suggested by *sphoṭa*. Thus, according to this opinion, *dhvani* is suggested of which *sphoṭa* is suggester.

Taking cue from this, Ānandavardhana treats *dhavni* as suggested *(vyaṅgya)* one. According to the above mentioned opinion, *dhvanis* are treated as *vyaṅgya* of *sphoṭa* which is initial sound. But Ānandavardhana uses the *dhvanis* for *vyaṅgya* of sound *(śabda)* and sense *(artha)*.[11] On the basis of *vyaṅgya-artha* 'suggested sense' he has classified *dhvanikāvya* into three main types, namely *vastu*, *alaṁkāra* and *rasadhvani*[12].

It may be noted that Abhinavagupta in this connection does not clarify whether suggested sense *(vyaṅgya-artha)* is traceable back in the discussion of the *VP*.

Abhinavagupta further states that both Bhartṛhari and Ānandavardhana use the term *dhvani* in the sense of 'suggester' *(vyañjaka)*. In the *VP*, *dhvani* as suggester has been referred to in more than one verse which are stated in the following lines:

"Through previous cognitions unnameable but favourable to the final clear cognition (just as Vedic passage is got by heart through repetition, *VP*.1.82), the form of the word, manifested by the last sound is perceived[13].

Again, "some believe that the *sphoṭa* (stands for) the universal (concept) which is manifested by many (i.e. varied) individual (sounds), and corresponding individual (instances) are what one imagines to be sounds *(dhvanis)*[14].

Further, "Just as there is a fixed eternal relation between a thing which enables one to perceive (i.e. sense organs) and the thing to be perceived (i.e. objects), similar is the relation of manifester and manifested between the sounds and the *sphoṭa*"[15].

In all these three passages of the *VP*, *dhvani* is treated as a manifester of *sphoṭa.* Similarly, the *locana* states, "so also the sounds which we hear and which are otherwise called *nāda,* suggest the *sphoṭa* which is comprehended when one hears the last letter in a word, and to these sounds, the grammarians call *dhvani.*"[16]

With reference to the suggestiveness of *dhvani,* Abhinavagupta evaluates the nature of *sphoṭa* of the grammarians. He believes that *sphoṭa* is an entity which is comprehended through the intellect. The *dhvani* reveals it.[17] Thus, according to the grammarians, *dhvani* is the suggester or revealer of *sphoṭa.* In the same manner the term *dhvani* is used as *vyañjaka* of the meaningful element viz. stems, verbal bases, suffixes, prefixes, particles, words and sentences, and the whole composition[18]. Ānandavardhana in this connection rightly remarks:

"In this manner the nature of *dhvani* alongwith its varieties has been shown with respect to what is suggested. Now this something will be expounded from the point of view of the actual words etc. which achieve the suggested effect."[19]

One controversial point is noteworthy here. Ānandavardhana believes that the grammarians use the term *dhvani* as *vyañjaka* of *śabda*[20], whereas Abhinavagupta uses this term as *vyañjaka* of *śabda* and *vyañjaka* of *artha*[21].

In this connection he follows the later grammarians according to whom the term *sphoṭa* is derived from the verbal base *sphuṭ* which means 'to burst forth' and it is defined in two ways : It is normally defined as that from which the meaning bursts forth *(sphuṭati artho yasmāt)* i.e. 'the element denoting meaning'. Secondly, it means 'an entity manifested by *sphoṭa' (sphuṭyate varṇaiḥ yaḥ* i.e. *varṇābhivyaṅgyaḥ)*.

But Bhartṛhari uses the term *dhvani* as *vyañjaka* of *śabda,* which may not be necessarily meaningful. His term *dhvani* does not stand for *vyañjaka* of *artha* 'sense'. We have discussed in detail that both *sphoṭa* and *dhvani* of Bhartṛhari represent the phonetic feature of language. The sound which we hear in the course of revelation of the *sphoṭa* appears to be present in the the *sphoṭa* itself, only because of our inability to distinguish the *sphoṭa* from the sounds. In reality, according to Bhartṛhari, the sounds are regarded only as manifesting agencies, and have no function other than that of revealing *sphoṭa.* The *sphoṭa* is regarded as meaning conveying unit of language by the opponents and the later grammarians, but not by Bhartṛhari.

Under such circumstances one cannot argue that Bhartṛhari uses the term *dhvani* as suggester of meaning *(vyañjaka* of *artha)*. Abhinavagupta thinks *dhvani* to be the suggester of sense because he believes *sphoṭa (śabda)* represents a meaningful unit[22]. According to Abhinavagupta, just as *sphoṭa* is meaningful element, similarly *dhvani* reveals suggested meaning. But this is not Bhartṛhari's view. Nowhere has Bhartṛhari state that *sphoṭa* conveys meaning and *dhvani* is revealer of meaning[23].

The term *dhvani* as explained by Ānandavardhana has two sides : significant and signifie. Thus *dhvani* is a two sided entity. On the one hand *dhvani* (as *vyañjaka)* reveals the sound elements, and on the other hand *dhvani* (as a *vyaṅgya)* stands for the suggested sense which is connected with the elements of language. The sounds *(dhvanayaḥ)* uttered by the speaker reveal the meaningful elements like stems, suffixes, words etc. to the listener. Therefore *dhvani* is *vyañjaka*. These elements convey the suggested meaning which is also called *dhvani*. So the relation between the elements of language and signified suggested sense is also *vyaṅgya-vyañjakabhāva* 'revealer-revealed'. Thus the term *dhvani* stands for both the suggestive elements and suggested meaning. In this connection it may be noted that non-verbal activities, i.e. movement of hands, eyes etc. and sounds in music and dance etc. are also suggesters of sense. We have discussed them in the third chapter of this book.

Abhinavagupta states that Ānandavardhana refers to the process of suggestion by the term *dhvani*. In the *VP* the same term *dhvani* is used to refer to the process *(vyāpāra)* of the sound communication.

According to Bhartṛhari, *dhvani* is of two types, i.e. *prākṛta* 'primary' and '*vaikṛta* 'secondary'[24]. The *prākṛta dhvani* is the initial cause of manifestation of *sphoṭa*, whereas *vaikṛta dhvani* brings about the continuity of the perception of the already manifested *sphoṭa* (*VP*.I.77). The differences in the speed of utterance are caused by *vaikṛta dhvani*. These differences do not affect the continuous perception of *sphoṭa* (*VP*.I.76).

The process[25] which brings about difference in the speed of utterance does not affect the primary sounds. It is something over and above the articulated sounds. When a word is uttered in a low voice it may either be heard absolutely or may not be heard totally. 'There is no part-recognition and part-ignorance'[26]. The effect of the process of articulation is an absolute whole. The fastness and slowness of the continued sounds do not affect the nature of *sphoṭa*, which is revealed by the primary sound. The differences associated with the secondary sounds are falsely felt to be associated with the meaningful *sphoṭa*.

Metaphorically the process of continuous manifestations which include these different *dhvanis* of *vaikṛta* variety is also styled by the term *dhvani*[27].

In the same way Ānandavardhana applies the term *dhvani* to imply the process of suggestion which is an extra-function added to the wellknown functions of the word namely *abhidhā* 'denotation', *lakṣaṇā* 'indication' and *tātparya* purport[28]. The suggestive function is responsible for the continued appearance of various meanings after the denotative and secondary meanings are conveyed by *abhidhā* and *lakṣanā*. The above process is similar with that of secondary sounds which are responsible for difference in duration of sounds. Just as the differences in suggested meanings do not affect the denotative meanings, so also the differences in the durations of the secondary sound do not affect the *sphoṭa*. Again just as secondary sound is different from the primary sound, so also the suggested meaning is different from primary meaning[29].

Abhinavagupta has not clarified one point in which Bhartṛhari and Ānandavardhana share.

According to Bhartṛhari, there is an order *(kramaniyama)* of the process of realisation of suggestor and suggested. This order is just like the definite stages of milk which passes through to become curds. Similarly the rice grains pass through certain inevitable stages of transformation to become a plant. In the same fashion the hearer grasps the sounds *(vaikṛta)* gradually in definite sequence to perceive *sphoṭa.*[30]

Ānandavardhana seems to accept this idea of order *(krama)* from Bhartṛhari in connection with the realisation of suggester and suggested. He says, "It is clear, therefore, that even as the apprehensions of denotative word and denoted sense involve a cause-effect relation and consequently temporal sequentiality, so also the apprehensions of the expressed and suggested involve a cause-affect relation as well as temporal sequentiality. As has been already illustrated, sometimes it is noticed and sometimes it is not"[31].

Thus Abhinavagupta has proved that how Ānandavardhana and Bhartṛhari follow the same line of thought on *dhvani* as suggester, suggested and the process of suggestion or revealation.

Monistic concept of *Śabda Brahman* versus the concept of relaisation of *rasa*

Apart from the similarities drawn by Abhinavagupta, there are number of similarities in ideas and nomenclature that we find in Bhartṛhari and Ānandavardhana. One such similarity is the idea of the realisation of *śabdabrahman* of Bhartṛhari, and realisation of *rasa* of the followers of *dhvani* school. In the third chapter we have analysed the monistic aspect of the relish of *rasa*. Ānandavardhana has given hints about *śabdabrahman* in his work[32]. Presently an attempt is made to bring out the similarities on the metaphysical philosophy of the realisation of *Brahman* according to the grammarians and the relish of *rasa* according to Ānandavardhana and his followers. This will highlight on the fact that how much Ānandavardhana is indebted to the grammatical philosophy to formulate his theory of *dhvani* whose soul is *rasa*. The *Vedānta* is the philosophy of the *Vedas* and of the *Upaniṣads*. According to *AdvaitaVedānta*, from the ultimate point of view, *Brahman* is the only reality (*sat)* and all else is non-real *(asat)*. Saṅkara makes this doctrine of non-dualism popular in the 8th century A.D. Bhartṛhari has inducted the concept of *Brahman* directly from the monistic tradition. The same term *Brahman* is used in different places, i.e. the *VP* I.1, the *Hṛdayadarpaṇa,* the *Abhinava Bhārati,* the *Locana,* the *Sāhityadarpaṇa* and the *Rasagaṅgādhara*. Though Ānandavardhana does not use the term *Brahman* in the *Dhvanyāloka,* he utillises the essence of the concept in it. No doubt he receives inspiration from monistic saivsim of Kashmir because he uses one important term *pratyabhijñā* in his *DL*. 1.8. But it seems that his affinity to the *VP* is more than any work on the *Vedānta* or the

Śaivisim. He declares his debt to the grammarians unequivocally. So it is probable that he accepts the idea of oneness and its predominancy over all multiplicity, from the metaphysical concept of *śabdabrahman* of the *VP*.

Bhartṛhari's philosophy of language and metaphysics go hand in hand. He states that *śabdabrahman* 'word-principle' is the ultimate reality. It is the source of entire cosmos which is characterised by numberless peculiarities. It has different forms of powers. But initially it is one. It contains the seed of all multiplicity. It manifests itself as the experiencer, the experienced and experience itself (*VP*.I, 1-4). All the manifestations of *Brahman* are intertwined with the word. So their source *(Brahman)* is rooted in the nature of word[33]. The word principle is the ultimate source of the universe consisting of *vācya* and *vācaka* (*VP*. I.118 with *vṛtti).* This *Brahman* is the ultimate reality. Its oneness is real and its different manifestations are imaginary (*VP*.1.2).

In ordinary life this ultimate reality is not directly comprehended. People understand all kinds of things having all kinds of forms. Through these manifoldness and difference of forms, the ultimate reality is comprehended. As these forms are congnised different from one another, people apply different words to identify them. It is the word which expresses the things or ideas cognised. The changing and unreal forms of the object are congnised through words. Through these differences the ultimate reality is expressed. The ultimate reality is the meaning of all kinds of things and ideas. Bhartṛhari states that words are not capable of expressing the ultimate reality directly, because of their formlessness. People do not cognise them directly in ordinary life. There is something which runs through all these differences. The object of the differences are unreal forms *(asatyopādhi)*. That thing exists when these forms disappear. That is *Brahman,* the ultimate reality. This is the expressed meaning of 'all the words[34].

The import of Bhartṛhari's statement is that, the

ultimate reality is realised through a series of unreal things. The *Brahman* is congnised through manifold differences which are unreal. He gives an analogy of crow (a non-permanent element) that sits on the house (a permanent element). The crow may not sit on the house always. But its presence helps to identity that particular house from other houses[35]. Similar idea is explained by another analogy. The metal gold is one which can be converted into number of ornaments having different shapes. But when the different ornaments are dissolved the substance gold reappears which is the ultimate reality[36]. This view appears to be similar to *satkāryavāda* held by *sāṁkhya* school.

Likewise all words in language denote particular forms. Through these particular forms, the ultimate reality is comprehended. Thus, according to Bhartṛhari, the ultimate reality is cognised directly in ordinary life through words which are not different form *Brahman.* It is comprehended through limiting factors *(upādhi).* These limiting factors represent the phenomenal world which are unreal or false. But the unreal factors (phenomenal world) which are transitory and impermanent helps to cognise the permanent and ultimate reality which is one, and which has the form of meaning. Bhartṛhari states that this ultimate reality is free from all differentiations. It differentiates itself into unreal forms as subject, object and experiencer etc. But *Brahman* is only real[37]. This is the central idea of the doctrine of *vivarta*[38].

Process of cognizing *śabdabrahman*

The oneness of *śabdabrahman* is discussed in the foregone section. Now we will discuss how the eternal reality is comprehended.

Vṛṣabhadeva states in the *vṛtti* of the *VP*.I.14 the various stages of realizing *śabdabrahman*[39]. In his words[40], "one who with a previous knowledge of the correct form of words, realises the unity of the real word, goes beyond sequence and attains union with it. By acquiring special merit through the use of correct word, he is united with the great word and attains freedom from senses. After having reached the undifferentiated state of the word, he comes to the source of all differentiations : 'Intuition' *pratibhā*. From that intuition in which all being is latent and which due to the repetition of the union tends to produce its result, he reaches the supreme source in which all differentiation is completely lost."

Thus, the *vṛtti* refers to the three stages of attaining *Brahman*. The first stage is known as *śabdapūrvayoga*. In this stage there is no diversity or sequence in any form. The mind is concentrated on the undifferentiated reality. The second stage is known as *vaikaraṇya* in which religious merits are accrued by the study of correct forms of the words as given in the grammar. The third stage is entitled as *pratibhā* or *prakṛti*. This stage is free from all distinctions. In this stage union with word principle takes place.

These three stages of attaining *brahma* correspond to three stages namely *vaikharī, madhyamā* and *paśyantī*, through which language passes for externalisation. The *vaikharī* is the name of any externalised form of human speech and ordinary sounds of the drum, flute and axles of cart etc. It is associated with temporal sequence. It forms the domain of ear.

The next internal stage is the *madhyamā*. It is a stage just before the externalisation of speech in which sequence remains in subtle form. It is located in the heart. At the *vaikharī* stage speech remains in the articulatory organ whereas in *madhyamā* stage it remains in the intellect 'mind' or in the heart.

The next innermost stage is *paśyantī*. It is beyond ordinary communication. According to *vṛṣabha*, this *paśyantī* is same as *pratibhā*. In ordinary life one starts from *paśyantī* and goes upto *vaikharī*, whereas in *śabdapūrvayoga*, one starts from *vaikharī* and goes upto *paśyantī (prakṛti)* and sometimes upto *parāprakṛti*[41]. This *paśyantī* stage is the ultimate state of *śabdabrahman*. This speech is self revealing.

The following conclusion emerges from the above discussion. Through the knowledge of unreality, the reality is achieved. The idea of differentiation is an essential factor for the cognition of the unity. The vague perception always leads to the clearer perception. The vague perceptions are unavoidable factors for correct perception. This perception of *śabdabrahman* through a series of unreal means is similar to the perception of *sphoṭa*. In the comprehension of *śabdabrahman* and *sphoṭa*, the same principle holds true, i.e. through the vagueness and differentiation, the reality and unity is achieved.

The devices employed by the grammar, although unreal from the point of the ultimate reality, are still helpful because they enable us to realise the ultimate reaity. These devices are viewed as unreal means to the realisation of the ultimate reality.This idea, in fact, is derived from the *Vedānta*. It holds that at the initial stage of the realisation of *Brahman*, the differentiations and disturbances of the mind are chastened by knowledge progressively, when knowledge is awaken, the ignorance is vanished which gives rise to the idea of oneness.

According tos Sadānanda, an aspirant adopts the method of superimposition and negation after recoursing to strenuous chastenment. Then he develops a consciousness (mental state) by supressing the nescience. He thinks himself to be a reflection of supreme *Brahman*. At this stage the consciousness is identified as similar to supreme *Brahman*. It is eternal, pure, intelligent, free, infinite and one. It is of the nature of supreme bliss.

The next stage is characterised by absolute identification of the aspirant with supreme *Brahman*. At this stage, the idea of 'reflection' *pratibimba* vanishes. The consciousness submerges into the infinite. Gradually, the knowledge of duality dwindles away and the cognition of oneness of the ultimate reality emerges[42].

Bhartṛhari was the first to formulate the philosophy of *śabdabrahman* wherein the essence of word is regarded as the essence of reality and the source of cosmic revolution. All the words denote primarily pure existence. That which cannot be subjected to the expression of articulated sound cannot be the context of thought and must therefore be regarded as illusion. These metaphysical contributions of Bhartṛhari are quite forgotten in the light of Śaṅkara.

It is evident that one point is common in the realisation of *śabdabrahman, sphoṭa* and *brahman* in the *Vedānta*. In each of the cases the duality is false and unit is reality. Through duality or vagueness, oneness and reality are achieved.

The influence of Bhartṛhari's philosophy is discernible in many ways in Ānandavardhana's theory of *dhvani*. Ānandavardhana suggests the ieda of oneness in the *Dhvanyāloka* while dealing with the problems of *aṅgīrasa*. He says that when many *rasas* are displayed one is chief among them. The minor *rasas* help the chief one to flourish at their own cost[43]. In the fourth *udyota* he establishes the mono-rasa cult in relation to the *śāntarasa*[44]. In the *Mahābhārata* all *rasas* aim to flourish the *śāntarasa* which runs as undercurrent in the whole work. Similarly, in the *Rāmāyaṇa karuṇarasa* is considered to be the chief sentiment.

Thus the monistic concept of *rasa* is the reality in poetry. It claims the oneness of the soul of *dhvani* which is the essence of poetry. This oneness is achieved through diverse factors, i.e. excitants etc. and many *rasas*. Every diversity aims to bring oneness of sentiment and oneness of poetic experience. All the writers on *alaṁkāra* base their metaphysical contributions on *vivartādvaita* which was masterfully presented by Śaṅkara in his *Brahmasùtrabhāṣya*.

The experiences of the realisation of *śabdabrahman* and *Brahman* of the *Vedānta* are similar to the experiences of the relish of rasa. Followers and critics of Ānandavardhana reveal this aspect and connect the metaphysical experience of *Brahman* with the relish of *rasa.* By this act they elevate the *rasa* experience to the supermundane plane. They identify the *rasa* experience with supersensous experience. This attempt of connecting the experience of *rasa* with the experience of *Brahman* provides a philosophical status to the new theory of Ānandavardhana. Though an opponent of Ānandavardhana, Bhaṭṭa Nāyaka introspects into the super sensuous nature of the realisation of *rasa* for the first time in Sanskrit poetics. The idea of supersensuous experience of *rasa* which was concealed in Ānandavardhana was expounded by Bhaṭṭa Nāyaka and Abhinavagupta.

Bhaṭṭa Nāyaka's concept of *brahmānanda* (supreme bliss)

According to Bhaṭṭa Nāyaka, the bliss that emerges from the relish of *rasa* is equivalent to the pleasurable experience of realising *Brahman.* He does not account suggestion, but supports *rasa.* He holds that in poetry and dramatic performance, the denotative meaning is first comprehended. Then by *bhāvakatva,* the permanent mood with its accessories are generalised which gives to *sattva* 'goodness' suppressing *rajas* action and *tamas* 'ignorance'. This leads to illuminate the inner luminosity or bliss, a kind of unstained consciousness, full of happiness in which all other consciousness freeze completely. This peculiar kind of experience is called *bhoga* 'enjoyment'.

This *bhoga* is described as a process of enjoyment similar to the enlightened, self-sufficent and blissful knowledge. This experience arises from the predominance of *sattva* 'attribute of goodness'.

This is a type of bliss. It is different from the personal and worldly happiness. It is different from 'feeling' *anubhāva* and 'remembrance' *smaraṇa.* It is characterised by the qualities of melting, pervading and expansion of the mind. It is compared to the bliss of 'divine contemplation' *brahmāsvādasavidha.* This bliss is divine and disinterested. In the *Abhinavabhāratī,* Abhinavagupta refers to this idea[45].

Abhinavagupta's interpretation

Abhinavagupta crystalises the process of realisation of *rasa.* Ānandavardhana cliams the existance of *rasa* in all poetic elements. According to him, the *rasadhvani* is the highest form of poerty. In orher to bring the true spirit of *rasadhvani,* Abhinavagupta expiains the process of the realisation of *rasa.* In this connection, he actually extends the findings of Bhaṭṭa Nāyaka without mentioning it. Instead of admitting two additional functions, i.e. *bhāvakatva* and *bhojakatva* of Bhaṭṭa Nāyaka to bring out *rasa,* he argues in the favour of suggestion of Ānandavardhana for that purpose.

He takes the process of generalisation of permanent moods, the awaken *sattva,* the concept of 'disposition' *vāsanā,* the necessity of 'connoisseurs' *sāmājika,* the identification of the cognition of *rasa* with an extraordinary cognition, the affinity of the relish of *rasa* with the bliss of attaining supreme *Brahman,* the nature of melting, and the oneness and repose of *rasa* in the consciousness at the time of relish from Bhaṭṭa Nāyaka. He maintains that the permanent moods inferred from the worldly causes i.e. women, garden, etc. remain in the hearts of the connoisseurs in the subtle form of 'predisposition' *vāsanā.* It is left in our mind through *saṁskāra* of previous birth. Sometimes it is acquired by study and experience in the present birth. The grammarians and the philosophers admit its necessity. When one reads a poem or sees a drama, these latent impressions are aroused by suitable *vibhāvas* etc. which are generalised and impersonalised by the power of suggestion, through skilful use of poetic merits and figures in poetry and dexterous representation. The permanent mood is generalised because its seeds are hidden in the minds of the readers and audience in the form of latent impressions. This generalisation wards off the temporal and spatial limitations. The readers and audience go beyond their narrow personal limitations and think that the pleasure and pain of the person described belongs to everybody. This is a subjective relish equivalent to the philosophic 'bilss' *ānanda.* It is beyond the level of worldly joy. This divine joy of *rasa* is attainable only by the function of suggestion and not by the other functions.

Mammaṭa explains this process of the relish of *rasa* systematically but cryptically. He states that the relish of *rasa* is of mixed nature like beverage. When it is relished it appears as if it were vibrating before the eyes, entering the inmost recess of the heart, inspiring the entire body and eclipsing everything else. It makes one feel, the rapturous bliss of *Brahman*[47].

From the analysis of *rasa* it appears that he compares *rasānubhuti* 'realisation of *rasa'* with *brahmānubhuti* 'realisation of *Brahman'* on the basis of the findings of Bhaṭṭa Nāyaka. Though both these experiences are equivalent, Bhaṭṭa Nāyaka puts the rasānubhuti at a higher plane than the *brahmānubhuti*[48].

Abhinavagupta maintains that though both the realisations are similar[49], the *rasānanda* 'pleasure out of the relish of *rasa'* is better than *brahmānanda* 'bliss of Brahman', because the earlier is natural whereas the latter is artificial and attained by hard penance[50].

Again the term *vyakti* of *abhivyaktivāda* of Abhinavagupta suggests the idea of *Brahman.* According to Paṇḍitarāja Jagannātha the term refers to conscicusness whose veil of ignorance is broken or removed[51].

In the *Vedānta* the dismissal of ignorance and removal of desire leads to detachment. This detachment results in the identity of self with *Brahman.* This identification brings supreme bliss. Thus in the *Vedānta,* the removal of ignorance leads to the 'manifestation' *abhivyakti* of knowledge.

Abhinavagupta seems to take the idea of his theory of manifestation of *rasa* from the *Vedānta*. According to him, suitable poetic conditions i.e. excitants etc. are conducive to reveal the predisposed propensities that remain in everyone in embryonic stage. It may have been accrued from the actions of the previous birth or present existence. When these past impressions are revealed and saturated, *rasa* appears.

Thus, Abhinavagupta's theory of the manifestation of *rasa* is conditioned by the doctrine of the *Vedānta*.

Paṇḍitarāja Jagannātha expounds the ideas of Abhinavagupta and states the similarities between *brahmāsvāda* 'the realisation of *Brahman*' and *rasasvāda* 'the relish of *rasa*'. In both the realisations, ego-centric attitudes are crumbled down and the separate identity is dissolved into unity. Both are extraordinary in nature. Just as in the *brahmāsvāda*, the mind is free from any external contact and contemplates only *Brahman*, similarly, in *rasāsvāda*, one's consciousness is free from any external contact and it is absolutely merged in the pleasure of *rasa*[52]. Both are marked by the nature of supreme ecstasy. Both of the experiences are unitary in nature[53].

Strictly speaking both the experiences of *brahmānanda* and *rasānanda* are different[54]. The *rasa* experience is one of the *citsvabhāva* 'pure contemplation detached from personal interest' which results in 'composure' *viśrānti*. But the experience of *Brahman* is absolute segregation from pleasure, pain and egoistic impulses. The realiser becomes impersonal by transcending his *buddhi* 'intelligence'. Further, though the element of *sattva* remains in both the experiences, its nature is different in the realisation of *Brahman*. The aspirant modifies his own nature of 'goodness' *sāttvika* by intelligence which contains the seeds of *vāsanā* 'acquired impulses'. The egoistic attitudes are purged by this *sāttvika* qualities and the idea of unity emerges from it.

This absolute detachment is not possible in case of the

realisation of *rasa.* It describes the pleasure obtained in association of worldly objects whereas the *Vedānta* deprecates these worldly joys. In a sense the poetic joy is different from the worldly joy. It is a joy of idealised type which is purely impersonal. It is not affected by ego-centric behaviour. It is distinterested in worldly joy. But it is momentary. When the elements i.e. excitants etc. conducive to evoke *rasa,* disappear, the connoisseur is thrown down to the lower plane of natural world from the higher level of impersonalised exuberance. It is temporary in this sense. But the aspirant who enjoys the pleasures of *Brahman,* does not return to the empirical realities of the world. Thus the enjoyment of *rasa* is spoken of as akin to the bliss of highest reality *(brahmāsvādasahodara).* When the spectator or the reader witnesses a world in the drama, he knows that it is not the real world but something similar to it. At this time he is freed from the selfish attitude and practical ego. His involvement is aesthetic and not practical. Since at the time of aesthetic enjoyment he is detached from the phenomenal world, his attitude is compared with the stage of the realisation of *Brahman.*

Inspite of these discrepancies, according to Bhaṭṭa Nāyaka and Abhinavagupta, the pleasure of the realisation of *rasa* is greater than that of the realisation of *Brahman.*

Synthesis of the cognitions and experiences of the *Brahman,* the *śabdabrahman* and the *rasabrahman.*

In an attempt to connect the concept of *śabdabrahman* with *rasa* referred to by Ānandavardhana (*DL,* 214, 15-16), the nature of cognition and experience of *Brahman* of the *Vedānta, śabdabrahman* of Bhartṛhari and the relish of *rasa* equivalent to the bliss of *Brahman* are discussed independently in the earlier sections. Presently an interrelation between them is attempted to justify the declaration of Ānandavardhana that he has inducted the ideas of *śabdabrahman* to his theory of *dhvani.* When

Ānandavardhana states that his *dhvani* theory is based on the nature of *śabdabrahman* which is eternal and indestructible reality, he certainly refers to Bhartṛhari. But because of the brevity of the statement one fails to identify the common natures between the realisation of *śabdabrahman* and *rasa.* Though Ānandvardhana is silent in this respect Bhaṭṭa Nāyaka, Abhinavagupta, Viśvanātha and Jagannātha explain it in the context of *rasa*-experiences. On the basis of their interpretations of *rasa*-cognition and *rasa*-experiences, the *rasadhvani* of Ānandavardhana can be traced back in the concept of *śabdabrahman* of Bhartṛhari and *Brahman* of the *Vedānta.*

Inspite of certain differences, the nature of the experiences of *Brahman, śabdabrahman* and *rasa* is similar. Each of them is a singular experience. In each case the multiplicity is lost and the idea of unity emerges. This is monism. This idea of unity is the principal nature of the ultimate reality. All pluralities are helpful to bring about the singular reality.

The *Upaniṣads* declare *Brahman* similar as *rasa*[55]. The *Vedānta* propounds that the avoidance of ignorance brings this single reality which is supreme *Brahman.*

In grammar, the correct knowledge and the use of correct words dispel ignorance. It awakes goodness *'sattva'* which leads to the experiences of *śabdabrahman* (*Vṛtti* of *VP*.I.14). At this stage, all diversities are merged and one enjoys the ultimate reality.

In case of literature, especially in poetry, the excitants, ensuants and accessories bring about the experiences of *rasa.* These different elements essential to bring out *rasa* symbolise multiplicity. But *rasa* itself is devoid of multiplicity. The diverse elements bring a united *rasa*-experience simultaneously. It is just like the taste of the beverage in which various spices lose their respective identity to bring about one taste which arises from different ingredients. In this connection the nature of the three experiences are somewhat similar.

Another point to be noted in this connection is the experience of *Brahman* as well as of *rasa* bring unfailing joy. The experience of *śabdabrahman* leads to the full knowledge of word principle which brings all prosperity and pleasure *(abhyudaya)*. The experience of *rasa* in poetic work is characterised by supreme ecstasy and divine pleasure. The only differences with *brahmānanda* is that the *brahmānanda* is permanent, but the *rasānanda* is temporary. But the nature of bliss in both cases is similar. The *brahmānananda* is characterised by absolute attachment to *brahman* and absolute detachment to the objects other than it. Similarly, in the case of *rasānanda,* one is absolutely meged in *rasa* which can be termed as purgation, and also he is absolutely detached to objects other than *rasa.*

In all these three experiences the element of 'goodness' *sattva* brings the knowleges of ultimate reality.

The foregone pages go to prove that the main intention of Ānandavardhana is to put old theories in proper perspective, although we cannot deny the importance of his own contributions on many topics. According to Ānandavardhana and Abhinavagupta, the *rasāsvāda* 'relish of *rasa'* is *alaukika* 'non-worldly', similar to *brahmāsvāda* 'realisation of *Brahman'*. The aesthetic experience is realised when one comes over the bondage of the ordinary world. Thus the aesthetic experience has bearing on the *Vedāntic* theory of illusion or on the *vivartavāda* of Bhartṛhari. All words in literature have their denotative base in language. But they do not remain denotative only in poetry. The denotative words in the context of poetry suggest some meaning *(dhvani)*. Ānandavardhana uses the analogy of lamp and the jar to explain the relationship between *vācyārtha* 'denotative' meaning' and *vyaṅgyārtha* 'suggested meaning'. The lamp functions as the stated meaning while the jar functions as the suggested meaning. The aesthetic experience is different from the experience of the phenomenal world just as the cognition of *śabdabrahman* is different from the cognition of phenomenal world. The world of literature is not the same as the phenomenal world.

Similarly, the aesthetic experience is similar to the state of 'spiritual emancipation' *samādhi.* The attitude of the dramatic spectator is similar to the attitude of spiritually emancipated person. Both have realisation of one supreme reality (i.e. either *Brahman* or *rasadhvani.*)

On the basis of these similarities discussed above it may be supposed that Ānandavardhana's experience of *rasa* concept is fashioned on the nature of the experience of *Brahman* of the *Vedānta* on the one hand, and *śabdabrahman* of Bhartṛhari on the other hand. Ānandavardhana has fitted the nomenclature and ideas of both these concepts to his *dhvani* theory very skilfully.

Reality of language : Bhartṛhari and Ānandavardhana

In the preceding chapters the concept of *sphoṭa* and the concept of *pratibhā* of Bhartṛhari have been discussed exhaustively. His concept of *sphoṭa* deals with conceptual idea of the sound whereas the concept of *pratibhā* deals with the organisation of isolated parts of the meaning situation into a structured whole of meaning language. Both the concepts are complementary to each other and are essential for communication of ideas. But *sphoṭa* operates at the phonetic level of language, whereas *pratibhā* works at the semantic level. Both of them provide fullness to the language used for communication.

In connection with the concept of *sphoṭa*, Bhartṛhari's ideas on reality of language have been analysed briefly. By reality we mean the permanent feature of language which is not affected and divided into further smaller units shunning its indivisibility by any adverse elements and agents.

Bhartṛhari has discussed the nature of ancient Indian

semantics in the second *kāṇḍa* of the *VP*. He gives many views prevalent in different disciplines including grammar. (*VP*.II.1) Bhartṛhari says that a word meaning represents a mental image or conception of an external concrete object (*VP*.II.132). It is not even necessary that the mental image must have a corresponding external object. The mental conception of non-concrete things is also conveyed by words (*VP*.II.133). Bhartṛhari says that the nature of meaning is not fixed. The speaker will make reference to something and a listener may grasp something totally different. Even the same person understands the different meaning from the same word at different times. The congnition of meaning varies from person to person. The same word may not mean the same thing to the same man or to different people at different time (*VP*.II.133-140). The meaning of a sentence is not grasped from the knowledge of word-meaning but from the whole utterance. The sentence meaning is grasped by *pratibhā*. Both the theories of *sphoṭa* and *pratibhā* maintain unity of utterance and unity of meaning. The preference for unity is charac-teristic not only to Bhartṛhari but also to Ānandavardhana. According to both, we critically divide the utterance into their parts. But this division is useful for understanding units. We get into the unity through artificial diversity. According to Bhartṛhari, the criteria to decide what is real are : oneness, simultaneity, being indivisible, being without sequence, being something to be intuited and inexpressible. On this side comes the intellectual word, indivisible speech unit (sentence), indivisible word meaning suddenly grasped by intuition. This is ultimate reality. Whatever exists in words is real. There is no reality beyond language. This clearly indicates how much Ānandavardhana has borrowed from Bhartṛhari's philosophy. The language is only a means to describe reality. The language must subserve only to give a faithful account of reality. The poetic language also describe reality. The reality is manifestation of *pratibhā* which is caused by several factors.

The concept of *pratibhā* envisages the reality of language. Accordingly, the sentence and sentence meaning are chief realities of speech. In this connection Bhartṛhari analyses the views of the *Mīmāṁsakas*.

According to them, words are realities of speech. The words are actual constituents of language. Each word has a fixed sense. The words act as part of the sentence. They give rise to unitary sense of sentence meaning.

Whether the unitary meaning of the sentence emerges directly from the collection of words or from the recollection of word meanings, two schools of thoughts, namely, *abhihitānvayavāda* and *anvitābhidhānavāda* differ. These two schools are very ancient but Kumārila Bhaṭṭa and Prabhākara Bhaṭṭa respectively developed and popularised these theories.

According to *anvitābhidhānavāda*, both the individual word meanins and their mutual relation are conveyed by the words themselves.

Accoring to *abhihitānvayavāda*, the words only convey the individual word meanings. The mutual relation is conveyed by the word meanigs and not by words[56].

According to *anvitābhidhānavāda*, meanings of the sentence are directly conveyed by the words. While conveying its own meaning a word also conveys the syntactical relations with other meanings also. In the expression *gām ānaya* 'bring a cow', the word *gām* conveys the isolated meaning 'cow' as well as its relation with *ānaya*. According to this theory, the sentences has a unitary meaning of its own. The constituent words posess meanings of its own. The constituent words possess meaning only as they are related to this unitary sentence meaning[57].

The *abhihitānvayavādins* object to this view. They argue that if the first word in a sentence can convey the meaning of the whole expression, then the other words are redundant. They say that when a sentence is heard, at first the separate meanings of words are understood one after another. Then these separate meanings of the parts are put together by the three factors, viz. *ākāṅkṣā, yogyatā* and *saṁnidhi* which ultimately give rise to the sentence meaning[58].

Śabara seems to agree with this theory. This theory holds that without a previous understanding of words no one can understand the meaning of a sentence. It says that if the meaning of a sentence is quite independent of the meanings of the constituent words, then any sentence could convey any meaning. When a new verse is understood, it is on the basis of separate knowledge of words and their separate meanings. Thus the meaning of the sentence is synthesis of separate meanings of words[59].

It is believed that *anvitābhidhāna* theory is an extension of *abhihitānvaya* theory. The meaning of the sentence is the supreme reality over the meanings of the words.

Mukula Bhaṭṭa synthesises that since both the theories contain partial truth, both are essential for the meaning of the sentence[60].

In modern linguistics[61] parallel theories to the above two theories are found. The *anvitābhidhāna* theory is comparable to the views of Wilhem Wundt. Inspite of this the differences, one point is common to all schools of thought on the nature of relation of words and sentence. That is, the sentence is some sort of linking of a succession of words and concepts.

According to Wundt, the sentence is not a mere association of concepts. It has two forms, i.e. outer form and inner form. Every articulation of the parts of the sentence influences the succession of words in a sentence.

The word spoken at a particular moment is a focal point of attention. Yet from a wider perspective, other parts of the sentence are there. The sentence consciousness is one. Each part of the sentence consciousness is related to the whole consciousness. On account of this fact one can be aware of the principal parts of the sentence with the rest of others.

The outer form of the sentence is the result of inner form. The inner psychological construction proves that the nature of the sentence is a simultaneous and a sequential one.

From the psychological point of view the sentence is both a simultaneous and a sequential structure. It is simultaneous because at each moment it is present in consciousness as a totality even though individual subordinate elements may occasionally disapper from it.

It is sequential, because the configuration changed from moment to moment in its cognitive condition, as individual constituents move into the forms of attention and out again one after the other. The simultaneous existence of the sentence is revealed by sentence unity. Its sequential course is revealed in the successive prominence of particular components. Both the analytic and synthetic elements are necessary for the construction of the sentence.

But Wundt believes the meaning of a sentences as a unity like Bhartṛhari. Wundt holds that the sentence is a linguistic representation of a voluntary sequential ordering of a simultaneous mental impression into logically connected segments. The words are the parts of the whole sentence structure. The words again can be diffused into further parts. Generally the sentence formation is materialised by the words. The words arranged in a particular order form the sentence. But the whole sentence is taken as a unity, so far as the communication of ideas are concerned. No isolated parts can convey meaning. It is similar to the spirit of *anvitābhidhānavāda.*

In contrast to this view Paul[62] holds that a sentence is a linguistic expression. A linguistic expression is a combination of several ideas. These ideas are joined together in the minds of the speaker and the listener. The ideas are connected by the frequency and intensity of events. But this association of ideas is not a mechanical mixture. It is an internal juxtaposition. Paul has analysed the above definition of sentence from the standpoint of hearer whereas Wundt does it from the standpoint of the speaker. This view of Paul is comparable to *abhihitānvayavāda.*

But this comparison is based on a loose similarity rather than a strict one. The *Mīmāṁsakas,* analysis of language is more linguistic than psychological whereas both Paul's and Wundts' analysis are more psycholinguistic.

Reality of languages according to Bhartṛhari

Bhartṛhari's idea on reality of languages has been briefly discussed. When he refers to *akhaṇḍavā-kyasphoṭa* 'indivisible sentence *sphoṭa'* as the real form of *sphoṭa* he indirectly suggests his idea of reality of language. A reality is that which cannot be divisible into parts.

The words have no reality of their own. The sentence is an indivisible, integral unit of language. Its meaning is *pratibhā* which appears as an instantaneous flash in the form of understanding. An unbroken sentence may be broken into words, and words into roots, stems and suffixes etc. One word can have many inflectional forms. So it can appear in indefinite forms. Again some words may be constant without any change in a form. Different grammarians analyse the same word differently. One who cannot understand one word in a sentence, for instance *vanāt pikaḥ ānīyatām,* he cannot understand the whole sentence (*VP*.II.72,92; cf.II.55)[63]. The individual words may give positive meaning, but a negative particle at the end of the sentence can change the whole meaning into negative one (*VP*.II.240-249). Under such conditions how words can be the reality of language. The reality of language is determined from the communicative ability of language. The communication is possible only by the sentence and not by the words or its parts. The sentence is not the sumtotal of words and the sentence meaning is not the sumtotal of word meanings, though the syntactical relation is established between the sentence and the words, and the sentence meaning and word meanings (*VP*.II.239,310,312,313,321).

Bhartṛhari does not believe in the reality of parts. He thinks that without the whole the communication is not possible.[64]

If a word is isolated from a compound word, for instance, *brāhmaṇa kambala* (2.2.4), the whole meaning of the compound is lost. Similarly, if a word is taken away from a sentence then that word loses its significance and the meaning of the sentence is not comprehended (*VP*.II.11-14). Bhartṛhari states that the meanings of the parts are seen by fools. The fools see the parts of indivisible atom. They believe in the multiplicity of *Brahman* which in fact is one. But this idea of divisibility is unreal. It is misleading to the ignorants (*VP*.II.235-38).According to Bhartṛhari, the word and sentence serve two purposes : they are subjected to grammatical operation and they are used for communication. But for the purpose of communication only sentence is useful and not words. That is to say when the communication is to be performed the sentence cannot be broken into words and stems etc. If it is broken communication cannot take place.

But when the sentence is to be analysed for grammatical purposes, it can be broken into parts. Bhartṛhari's insistence on indivisibility of sentence suggests that the sentence as unbroken unit is used for the purpose of communication only. Bhartṛhari states that isolated words and their further subdivisions are unreal or fictitious. "Being wellknown, only shortened forms like *udvami* and *kari* are used in the *śāstra.* All grammatical derivations are meant to serve practical puposes. It is only nescience which is described in the science of grammar through the different modes of derivation. But knowledge arises spontaneously free from the alternatives of tradition." (*VP*.II.232-33)[65]. The words are not used to communicate ideas. In this respect they are fictitious. But for grammatical purpose they are essential (*VP*.II.235). Stating the role of the words in the sentence Bhartṛhari says that the individual words are the means to an end. They help to know the meaning of the sentence.[66]

Bhartṛhari believes that words build the sentence and the word meanings construct the sentence meaning. But when the sentence is finally built and sentence meaning has fully emerged, the words and word meanings lose their significance respectively. Their importance remains as long as the sentences and sentence meanings are not constructed. The indivisible sentence and indivisible meaning of the sentence only represent reality of language[67]. Their natural property is the function of communication. Their divisibility is artificial which is approved by P (*VP*.II.27). When a compound is analysed, it is explained with separate words. A verb mentioned in a sentence is related to all elements in a *dvandva* compound together, yet it is connected with each item, because different elements form parts of the compound word.[68]

According to Bhartṛhari the sentence is sequenceless (*VP*.II.19) though at the time of utterance it appears to have sequence. The sentence meaning does not rest anywhere. At the time of communication it is the soul of word meaning (*VP*.II.437). In the process of communication the hearer does not pay any attention to the division and structure of language. He concentrates on the whole expression.[69]. The division of the sentence into parts does not exist at all.[70]. This idea of indivisibility is suggested by Bhartṛhari in the indivisible sentence *sphoṭa*[71].

There are some single words which give the meaning of the whole sentence. In that case those words are regarded as single word sentence which are reality of language. It is because the idea of complete utterance is comprehended from the implied meaning of word. For instance, when a master orders his servant *dvāram* 'door' at the departure of a guest, the servant understands that master wants to say *pidhehi* 'close' which is not mentioned. This item *dvāram* is a one-word-sentence because it gives the idea of the whole sentence. So it represents the reality of language[72].

The ancient authorities, namely, *vārtākṣa* and *Audumbarāyaṇa* approved the indivisibility of the sentence as reality of language[73].

According to Bhartṛhari, as the sentence is indivisible, so also its meanins is indivisible which appears as a flash. It is *pratibhā*. It is not gradually built up by word meanings. It is grasped by the hearer instantaneously as a flash of insight. It is indefinable and is comprehended in the mind (*VP*.II.146).

Thus, according to Bhartṛhari, the reality of language is indivisible sentence and indefinable 'meaning of the sentence' *pratibhā*. The sentence is the only reality of language[74]. The words and their meanings help to grasp the form of a sentence and sentence meaning. When the higher linguistic units are formed the lower ones lose their significance.

Ānandavardhana takes a cue from Bhartṛhari's philosophy of sentence and sentence meaning for his new interpretation of *dhvani* language. Following Bhartṛhari, Ānandavardhana states that sentence and sentence meaning are the reality of speech; words and their meanings are unreal. They only help to arouse the sentence and its meaning. They are regarded to have some lower reality as compared with actual language used in everyday life. Just as the sentence meaning is cognised through word meanings, similarly, the suggestive sense is comprehended through denotative sense[75]. The denotative function and the indicative function have also lower reality because they are dependant on words which are abstracted by us from actual sentences in the same way as the grammatical elements are abstracted. Ānandavardhana says, "Just as through the sense of individual words the sense of an entire sentence is understood, so also one understands that (suggested) idea by first understanding the explicit meaning : Just as the meanings of individual words that convey through their own power the meaning of the whole sentence, when their function (of conveying the sentence-sense) is achieved, are no longer separately cognised."[76]

Thus Ānandavardhana denies the absolute reality.

There are some more points of similarities of ideas between Bhartṛhari and Ānandavardhana which are stated below :

(i) Just as according to Bhartṛhari, the words and word meanings render themselves secondary to the indivisible sentence and indefinable sentence meaning, similarly, according to Ānandavardhana, the primary meaning (denotative sense) renders itself secondary to the other meaning (suggested meaning).

(ii) Just as the sentence meaning appears as a sudden flash, *pratibhā* (*VP*.II.143), similarly, the suggested meaning appears as a sudden flash (*DL*.1.4;).

(iii) Both Bhartṛhari and Ānandavardhana treat *pratibhā* as a creative anergy.

(iv) Just as the sentence meaning is different from the sum total of word-meanings, similarly, *dhvani* sense is over and above the sumtotal of word-meanings.

(v) On the reality of word Ānandavardhana follows Bhartṛhari's analysis of one-word-sentence (4.3.1). When a word is suggestive and contributes its property to the whole expression then it is a reality. Its reality is determined by its association with the whole. He says, "you said earlier that *dhvani* was a type of poetry. How then can it be revealed by (isolated) words? For any type of poetry is a particular collection of words that gives rise to a particular meaning. This cannot be the case for suggestion through words, for words do not directly express meanings, but only serve to remind us of them (nor do individual isolated words convey the sense of an entire sentence, which is essential for poetry).

Our reply to this objection is as follows : This would indeed be a serious objection were the force of direct expression a deciding factor in conferring the name of *dhvani* (on a poem). But this is hardly the case, for *dhvani* is determined through the power of suggestion. Moreover, though actually beauty is achieved through the sum total (of the different parts of the body) characterised by particular configurations, we admit in individual parts, because the beauty of the whole, or its absence, depends on the presence or absence of the individual parts. Since the same is true of poetry, it is not unreasonable to say that certain words form part of the process of *dhvani* by means of their suggestive power."[77]

(vi) According to Bhartṛhari, the function of the whole cannot be explained as sum of the function of its parts.

Similarly, according to Ānandavardhana, the reality of *dhvani* language lies in its whole. The function of *dhvani* cannot be reduced to the function of its parts. The parts, i.e. words, phonemes, stems, participles, etc. may bear some properties of the soul. They contribute to the whole poetry and not to the parts. In other words the suggested meaning cannot be explained as the sum of the functions of its parts. Just as the beauty of a particular limb contributes to the excellence of the whole, and thereby merges its identity to enhance the charm of the entire body, similary, the words with their individual suggestive capacity bring charm to the meaning of the whole *dhvani* poetry. And when the unified suggested meaning is comprehended the individual words or parts thereof, lose their suggestive significance[78].

This idea is similar to the ideas of reality of language of Bhartṛhari.

Abhinavagupta has clearly elaborated this idea of Ānandavardhana which is stated below:

"And poetry consists in a sentence that is able to give a cognition which is complete in itself. Individual words cannot do this. (we reply) : This is true. But we too never said that an individual word is *dhvani*. We (too admit) that *dhvani* is just a well-organised community of words. This is why when we talk of *dhvani* that is revealed by a word we do, in fact, stress the word 'revealed'. Objection : how can a word have such a power (namely the ability to reveal *dhvani*), since the process of apprehension is an undivided one. Anticipating this objection, he says : 'of poetry'[79].

(vii) According to Bhartṛhari, *pratibhā* is the guiding instinct in our acting including of animals'. Similarly, Ānandavardhana holds *pratibhā* as a guiding instinct for poetic creation.

Thus it may be concluded that Ānandavardhana not only takes the nomenclature like *dhvani* and *pratibhā* etc. from Bhartṛhari's philosophy of language, but also the exact ideas inherent in it. The whole is real, the parts are false. This is the central theme of ordinary and poetic speech according to these two great thinkers. The *pratibhā* is the guiding principle which sparks through all speech activities. The concept of *pratibhā* of Bhartṛhari has, thus, galvanised the new poetic theory of Ānandavardhana in many ways.

Bhartṛhari and Ānandavardhana on the concept of *saṁskāra*.

The concept of *saṁskāra* has many connotations. In this connection both Bhartṛhari and Ānandavardhana seem to be influenced by the *sāṁkhya* and the *vedānta* systems of thought. According to these systems, the *saṁskāra* 'disposition' is an impression left by a past cognition. It is revived by certain conditions and gives rise to recollection[80].

The *saṁskāras* remain in the 'intellect' *buddhi*[81]. They do not remain in the external senses, *manas* and *alaṁkāras*. Even blind and deaf persons can remember things seen and heard in the past. Even when *manas* and *ahaṁkāras* are desroyed by right knowledge of reality, there is recollection. So *saṁskāras* are modes of *buddhi* and subsist in it.

Indian philosophers believe in the transmigration of the soul and the deeds. The deeds of the previous birth of the creatures regulate the deeds of the present existence. The deeds of the past and present existence are deposited in the intellect. If one does good deeds, then the impressions turn up to be good which control further activities. The deeds of the previous existence are forgotten. But their impressions are manifested in the present life and regulate every activity of life. These dispositions are manifested through body. If one has done good deeds in the previous life, his good dispositions are manifested through *sāttvika* body. If one has done bad deeds in the previous life, he gets *tāmasika* body or *tīryak yoni* to exhaust the past deeds. The dispositions are not annihilated because this process goes beyond our life. They are enjoyed *(bhoga)* as we bring with us at the time of our birth all the *saṁskāras* of our past birth. As long as the dispositions are not exhausted there is no emancipation. When they are exhausted liberation comes. The *mokṣa* 'liberation' is the cessation of *saṁskāras*[82].

The *saṁskāra* generates *smṛti* 'remembrance'. It is different from *pratyabhijñā* 'recognition' by which one tries to recall and reunite the former states of consciousness.

The *saṁskāra* 'disposition', instinct, *vāsanā* 'predis-postion, desire' and *bhāvanā* 'residue, feeling' are taken as synonyms in Sanskrit poetics. They are the psycho-spiritual conditions which remain in the mind. They are referred to by the term *sthāyībhāvas* 'dominant feelings'[83].

The poet's imaginative faculty is also a kind of *saṁskāra*. When the *saṁskāras* as dominant feelings are elevated to the conscious stage of mind by appropriate stimuli 'condition', the *rasa* is relished. It is a powerful mental function which regulates all activities namely spontaneous, reflective and voluntary. Because of the powerful function of *saṁskāra,* Bhaṭṭa Nāyaka proposes *bhuktivāda* for the realisation of *rasa.*

Bhartṛhari has mainly used the term *saṁskāra* in the above sense. He says that *pratibhā* is directly caused by words in this life or impressions or traces left by words on the mind, either in this or in a previous life (*VP*.II.151).

The concept of *saṁakāra* denotes three different senses in the *VP*. The term occurs six times in the *VP*. i.e. I.78, 79, 80, 113(121), 123(131), 139(147).

Saṁskāra in the sense of fitness

Just as collyrium brings fitness to the eyes, sunshine to the oil and water to the earth, similarly ear brings fitness to the 'sound' *dhvani* which reveals *sphoṭa*[84].

Saṁskāra in the sense of purification

The term *saṁskāra* is used to refer to the correct forms of the words distinguished from corrupt forms[85]. The use of the correct form brings the cognition of word principle and leads to the attainment of immortal *Brahman*[86].

Saṁskāra as disposition

Bhartṛhari explains the *saṁskāra* as disposition in connection with *śabdabhāvanā.* Every knowledge is revealed by language 'words'. Bhartṛhari states that the speech activities of the past existence are transformed into impressions which in favourable conditions are manifested, and take the shape of articulated speech. These impressions are called *saṁskāra* or *bhāvanā* in the *VP.*[87]

This property of *saṁskāra* is an important element in his concept of *pratibhā.* Beyond the production of all activities and all creative abilities the *saṁskāra* 'disposition' remains as a governing force. It activates *pratibhā* and *pratibhā* as a spark reveals it. The power of acquisition of language of the newborn child remains hidden in the subtle impression accrued in the previous birth, or in this life through various circumstances. These 'impressions' *saṁskāras* are the seeds which induce to further actions and speech activities[88].

Saṁskāra according to Maṇḍana Miśra

The scope of *saṁskāra* of Bhartṛhari has further been extended by Maṇḍana Miśra in his *Sphoṭa Siddhi*. He states that *saṁskāra* is a power. It remains in the soul. It is brought by previous cognition. Its work is to produce further cognitions[89]. This *saṁskāra* may be of two types, i.e. (i) That those when awakened cause remembrance, (ii) that those cause an effect other than remembrance. This *saṁskāra* which causes the cognition of *sphoṭa* is known as *bhāvanā*[90] and the *saṁskāra* which reveals the meaning is known as *vāsanā*[91]. Thus *saṁskāra* has two functions according to him.

While refuting the views of the *Mīmāṁsakas* regarding the nature of phoneme as reality of language Maṇḍana Miśra utilises Bhartṛhari's concept of *saṁskāra* as disposition. The *Mīmāṁsakas* hold that the last phoneme accompanied by the impression of the previous phonemes express meaning[92]. They believe that *saṁskāra* originates from the cognition of phonemes. This *saṁskāra* resembles with 'residual force' *apūrva* produced by the performance of the sacrifice[93].

In connection with *sphoṭa,* Maṇḍana Miśra explains the role of *saṁskāra*. Here the *saṁskāra* is similar with the *bhāvanā*. The revelation of *sphoṭa* is a gradual perception. At first we have a vague perception of *sphoṭa*. Gradually the vagueness is removed and *sphoṭa* is perceived little by little till we get a clear perception[94]. The erroneous perception of *sphoṭa* is a similar type of perception of a rope to be a snake or a stream[95]. But the false cognition becomes progressively clearer by *saṁskāra* of previous cognition[96]. Thus both the vague and clear perception of *sphoṭa* are caused by *saṁskāra*[97].

Maṇḍana Miśra's concept of *saṁskāra* as *vāsanā* may be taken into account to explain the child's acquisition of language. The *saṁskāra* deposited in the previous existence of the child are suddenly sparked by *pratibhā*, and he utters his first speech (2.4)[98].

As to the question whether Bhartṛhari's concept of *saṁskāra* is inherited from the previous experience or it is deposited in this life, he is very obscure. There are evidences in favour of two alternatives. The phrase *sākṣāt śabdena* refers to the idea of linguistic knowledge which is directly acquired in this life, and the phrase *bhāvanānugamena* suggests to the cognitions, inherited through impression of the previous life[99].

In relation to *pratibhā*, the *saṁskāra* can be directly or indirectly accrued. According to Bhartṛhari, the *pratibhā* is a creative impulse and guiding force of all activities that is activated by certain conditions. These conditions are either *āgama* 'tradition' or *bhāvanā* 'predisposition'. By *āgama*, we mean continuity or tradition which is a type of direct knowledge. But this continuity is incomplete without *bhāvanā*. It is indirect and is latent in every creature in the form of predisposition. It activates *pratibhā*[100]. Iyer has gone a step further and shows the cause-effect relation between them. The reaction can be presented in this manner : *bhāvanā>āgama>pratibhā*[101]. This *bhāvana* or *saṁskāra* of Bhartṛhari embraces everything in this universe, since *śabdabhāvanā* 'word principle' is the medium through which all cognitions are revealed[102]. As the *pratibhā* is all pervasive, the *bhāvanā* which activates it is also all pervasive. As the *pratibhā* is indefinable in nature, *bhāvanā* is also indefinable. Only from unusual effects, namely, nestling before germination, cuckoo's song in the spring, command of the elephant etc. the existence of *pratibhā* can be inferred. The *pratibhā* is the creative instinct or impulse and *bhāvanā* is its activating force. It is an imaginary force to explain certain irregularities of law of speech and action. Thus it should be indirect. It seems that Bhartṛhari used the term *saṁskāra* and *bhāvanā* as activating force of *pratibhā* which would have been inherited from the past existence.

Though Maṇḍana Miśra interprets Bhartṛhari's *bhāvanā* and *vasānā* as two types of *saṁakāras,* still the three terms denote the same idea of disposition. It is the dormant cause of speech activities. Ānandavardhana has taken this concept of *saṁskāra* from Bhartṛhari and fitted it to his *dhvani* theory.

Ānandavardhana has not used the term *saṁskāra* even once. But he uses the terms, i.e. *vāsanā*[103] and *bhāvanā*[104] once each. The *Locana* referes to the three terms *saṁskāra*[105], *vāsanā*[106] and *bhāvanā*[107] many times. Ānandavardhana uses the term *bhāvanā* in the sense of poetic thought and *vāsanā* in the sense of *saṁskāra* 'disposition'. His idea on *saṁskāra* is implied from his use of the term *pratyabhijñā* (*DL.* 1.8). This concept of *pratyabhijñā* is an important item in Kashmir Śaivism. The *saṁskāra* 'disposition' is very intimately associated with this concept of *pratyabhijñā.*[108].

Ānandavardhana suggests the role of *saṁskāra* 'disposition' without mentioning it while analysing the creativity of the poet. He says, "the creative ability of good poets is indeed the outcome of the fruition of excessive merit amassed by them in their past births and such men will neighter be eager in borrowing ideas invented by others nor will they find any need of taking great pains over their work."[109] Ānandavardhana thinks that poetic genius is inherited from the previous existence. The residues of poets' strenuous practice of the past life are manifested in this life under certain favourable condition. When the impediments are removed, the genious sparkles.

Thus theoretically, Ānandavardhana speak in terms of *saṁskāra* without referring to it. It is similar to that of

Bhartṛhari and *sāṁkhya* as well as *Vedānta* systems. It is probable that Bhartṛhari has taken the idea of *saṁskāra* from the *sāṁkhya* and the *Vedānta* which further has been inducted and utilised by Ānandavardhana in connection with poets' genius[110]. In this respect he follows the doctrine of Bhartṛhari.

Speaker's process of conveying meaning : Bhartṛhari and Ānandavardhana

P does not deal with meaning directly. But the process of derivation as given in the *Aṣṭādhyāyī* involves a complete description of a semantic relation of the constituent parts of a sentence. Thus meaning plays a crucial role in the derivation. The meanings are of two types, namely lexical meanings given in the *dhātupāṭha* and *sūtrapāṭha* and categorical meaning which are used for grammatical purposes such as *vartamāna* 'present', *bhùta* 'past' etc. These lexical and categorical meanings are not defined by P but are assumed by him, because without them the derivative procedure cannot work. Apart from lexical meaning P but are assumed by him, because without them the derivative procedure cannot work. Apart from lexical meaning P has to take into account attitudinal meanings. P commentators believe that meaning of an expression is determined by the intention of the speaker[111]. There are a number of instances in the *Āṣṭādhyāyī* where the intended meaning of the speaker is different from the lexical meaning of the same expression[112]. P was aware that the intention of the speaker determines the meaning of an expression. This intended meaning of the speaker has fixed relation with the linguistic form. In modern terminology, this intended meaning can be known through content. The meaning and content may refer to different facts. One may know the meaning of an expression, but he may not understand the content. The content presupposes meaning, but meaning does not presuppose the content. For instance, from a particular sentence, 'the sum of the angles of a traingle is 180 degree', the layman having no knowledge of geometry can understand the meaning of the expression, but not the content. Only persons having the knowledge of geometry can understand the content[113]. For the knowledge of the content, specialised knowledge is required. This knowledge of content cannot work without linguistic knowledge. It refers to the unsatisfactory nature of lexical meaning to explain the intended meaning of the expression.

Bhartṛhari explains this type of meaning other than linguistic meaning in the *VP* with various instances.

According to Bhartṛhari, meaning of an expression is determined by the intention of the speaker. In conversation words and sentences do not determine the meaning of an utterance. It is the speaker's intention that determines the meaning. The meaning cannot appear independently of the context. The contextual factors which determine the special meaning of an utterance are enumerated by Bhartṛhari (*VP*.II.315,316). A particular expression provides two types of meanings, i.e. lexical meaning and intended meaning of the speaker. Sometimes both the meanings go together. Sometimes one may be different from the other. Although a sentence is regarded as a basic meaningful unit, sometimes its meaning cannot be fixed without understanding the speaker's intention. Bhartṛhari states, "without its application, a word does not convey its meaning. That is why it has been declared that the relation between a meaning and the word is through *ukti,* that is application. Just as it is when the eye is directed towards an object that it perceives, in the same way, a word denotes an object when deliberately applied to it."[114] Again when a word imply several meanings, the speakers' intention determines the actual meaning. In such cases, even the context cannot decide the meaning. In this connection Bhartṛhari says, "some scholars who believe in the sameness of the word (in all its meaning) declare that at the time of the practice (of learning the words of the Veda) they are without a meaning, that they stand for their form only when they are taught to others but that (at the time of the performance of a sacrifice) they are expressive of different meanings because of difference of expressive power based on difference of intention".[115] It states that Vedic words are devoid of meanings when they are learnt by heart, but when they are employed with specific purposes by the ritualists, they appear to be meaningful. This truth also holds good in the case of words used in ordinary discourse. Both in Vedic and ordinary speech, the meanings are determined by the intention of the speaker. The words and sentences, taken into account independently of the speaker's intention, have only artificial meanings.

In this connection Patañjali on P.1.4.24 states that the objects referred to by the speaker are one thing and his way of presenting them is something else. For instance, we may say *alomikā edikā* 'a wool-less ewe', *anudarā kanyā* 'a bellyless girl'. Here the existence of the wool and the belly is not intended by the speaker. The speaker may also refer to the things which do not exist in reality. For instance, *samudraḥ kuṇḍikā* 'the ocean is a jug', *vindhyo vardhitakam* 'the Vindhya mountain is a heap of rice'. Here the issue is basically the relation between fact and statement. The statement is more dependant on the speaker's intention than on fact, especially in more or less in poetic mode of speech.

Bhartṛhari further observes that a verb which is a principal element in a sentence, and its accessories, and the relation existing between them, are motivated by the speaker's wish. The speaker can present the object as he likes[116]. The intended meaning of the speaker, according to Bhartṛhari, is over and above the lexical meaning of the expression. He has given some specimen of sentences where the intended meaning is sometimes variable and sometimes invariable. That is, the meaning determined by the speaker sometimes follows the lexical meaning and sometimes does not follow it. This feature of meaning is an essential property of suggestion, in which manifold meanings do not necessarily follow the linguistic meaning. Ānandavardhana seems to develop this intended meaning of the speaker as discovered by Bhartṛhari to suggestive meaing of poetic language.

In order to know the exact nature of meaning, Bhartṛhari's specimen of the examples would be worthwhile to examine. In all his examples the lexical meaning is one whereas the intended meaning of the speaker is other. All these intended meanings can be subsumed under suggestive meaning of Ānandavardhana.

One of the examples analysed by Bhartṛhari is as follows : "one has to go, look at the Sun' through this sentence says something about the sun, it really indicates time, because it says, with a hint at the 'means' *upāya* that time should be ascertained."[117] The expression 'one has to go, look at the Sun' has fixed lexical meaning. But the desired meaning is different from it. The intended meaning is that it is time to go. It does not mean that the listener is being ordered to look at the Sun. The term 'ṣun' particularly suggests that the time is very short. Thus here the intended meaning of the expression is determined by the intonation of the speaker. This desired sense is different from literal or denotative sense. The *Ambākartrī* (a commentary on VP) finds *ajahat lakṣaṇā* in this example. The *ajahatsvārthāvṛtti* maintains that the whole expression may have specialised meaning whose connection with constituent meaning may not be clear although the constituent elements do not abandon their meaning.

From this example it will be clear that it is difficult to draw a boundary between linguistic meaning and non-linguistic meaning. The intonations, strees and paralinguistic features (like loudness) convey different types of semantic information. The suggested meaning as in the present case can be indicated by intonation.

The speaker's intention determines the actual meaning of the expression is shown in another example. Here also the desired meaning is different from lexical meaning : "When a boy is told, 'save the butter from the crow', he does not refrain from protecting it from dogs etc. knowing that the order refers to destructive agents in general."

The lexical meaning of the verse is that a child is instructed to save the butter from the crow. But the desired meaning is that he should not only protect it from crow, but also from other destructive agents like dogs, cats etc. The desired meaning is determined by the intention of the speaker and not from the lexical meaning. The *Dhvanikāra* in this case would say that the desired meaning is suggested. The term 'crow' suggests all destructive agents who can contaminate the butter.[119]

Still in another example, similar idea is more clear : "Just as a crying child is refrained when he is threatened that a tiger would eat him, in the same way, some bad consequence though unreal, is held up (before one who does some prohibited act)."[120]

In this verse, the linguistic meaning is that the mother says to the child, if he cries the tiger will eat him. But the intended meaning is to present a fearful picture of a tiger. So that the child may stop crying. No mother wants that her child should be swallowed by a tiger. The speaker wants to communicate fear represented by the term tiger[121].

This type of intended meaning has similarity with the suggested meaning described in the *Dhvanyāloka* in connection with *vastudhvani.*[122]

Sometimes meaning of an expression denoting a particular thing stands as a symbol for other similar things. For example, *vidhyatya adhanuṣā* (P.4.4.87) 'he pierces with something other than a bow', the particular weapon stands for any weapon in general which has the substratum of power of being a weapon.[123]

Bhartṛhari further states that the described meaning of the speaker is motivated by certain factors[124]. When the literal meaning is obscure these factors help to determine the intended meaning of the speaker. In this respect they are complementary and not contradictory to the actual meaning. In poetics these factors are utilised to explain the various natures of suggested meanings in case of *abhidhāmūlāvyañjanā* 'suggestion based on denotation' and *guṇībhūtavyaṅgya*, 'subordinated suggestion *(KP)* respectively.

There are certain non-verbal actions which denote one thing whereas the intended meaning implied from the action is different. For instance, the cleaning of dishes and plates imply that the food is ready for eating.[125]

Again, there are some one-word sentences. These one-word sentences require accessories or an 'action-word' *kāraka* to complete the syntactic meaning. For example the single word *dvāram* 'door' requires *pidhehi* 'close'[126] and *sat* 'being' requires *tad abhūt* 'it was' or *tad asti* 'it is' or *tan nābhūt* 'it was not', *tan nāsti* 'it is not' for completion.[127] The missing word need not be supplied in a sentence. They are left to be understood. Certain things are implied on the basis of speaker's intention. If the single verb is uttered it would require some meaning to complete the idea. It is understood on the basis of speaker's intention. When a single word, noun or verb is uttered it brings to our mind any other meaning which is required to complete the sense.

Bhartṛhari further states that action and accessories require each other to furnish the complete meaning of the sentence and to make it fit for communication. In a sentence the action, accessories and their relation are determined by the speaker[128]. For instance, the action of cooking is expressed by the verb *pacati* in *pacikriyām karoti* 'he performs the act of cooking'. Here the actual act of cooking is understood as a process *(sādhyakriyā)*[129]. Here the sentence does not mention what he cooks. An object is understood as the speaker wishes it. It is presented by different speakers differently as *odanam, yavāgum* etc. Similarly, the action of cooking can be presented by different expressions, i.e. *pākaṁ karoti, pacati, pākasya nirvṛttiṁ karoti* etc. In all these different sentences, the objects of cognition are presented as desired by the speaker. Bhartṛhari rightly says, "an object has all powers, it is presented as rendering whatever service the speakers think of."[130]

Thus, according to Bhartṛhari, meaning, that is content, is a property which remains in the speaker. In this respect he follows Pāṇini *(kā* on P.8.1.8, 8.1.10; 4.3.1). This intended meaning sometimes may follow the lexical meaning, and other time may differ from it. Bhartṛhari has given specimen of sentences where intended meaning of the sentence is different from literal meaning. The force which brings the desired meaning into cognition is speaker's intention.[131]

Ānandavardhana develops this concept of speaker's intention in the *Dhvanyāloka.* He claims that the speaker's intention is the cause of suggestion which brings the *dhvani* meaning into cognition (3.6). Just as according to Bhartṛhari the speaker's intention brings the desired meaning into knowledge, so also according to Ānandavardhana, the same speaker's intention brings suggestion into force which brings suggestive meaning into cognition. Thus the idea of *dhvani* meaning of Ānandavardhana is shaped by the speakers intention of Bhartṛhari. Bhartṛhari saw certain irregularities of common speech where intended meaning does not follow the lexical meaning. Here the duality of meaning is discovered. (*VP*.II.310-312, 321). This is extended by Ānandavardhana in poetic speech. The lexical meaning is 'denotative meaning' *vācyārtha* and the intended meaning of the speaker is nothing but *pratīyamānārtha* 'suggested meaning.' It has been discussed that the speaker's intention is the soul of *vyañjanā* 'suggestion'. All examples given by Bhartṛhari can be interpreted in favour of *dhvani* meaning.

The speaker in the poetry is poet himself. He is the

dictator of his creation (poetry). He can shape his creation as he likes. In other words his intention is supreme over verbal expressions. This creativity of the poet which depends on his intention is activated by the spark of *pratibhā*. It brings the residual traces of the previous existence and manifest them through verbal and non-verbal expressions. The verbal expressions are poetic speech and non-verbal expressions are movements of the body, eyes, hands and legs etc.[132]

Ānandavardhana is very clear as to the role of speaker's (poet's) intention in the poetry. The suggestion is the force which brings about poetic intention. He can manipulate and mobilise anything and everything as he desires. Ānandavardhana's famous statements are noteworthy in this respect:

"For in the cases of mature poets, it would not be seemly for them to engage (in writting poetry) that is devoid of exclusive emphasis on *rasa* etc. where importance is given to *rasa*, etc. There is no subject matter, which being brought into subservience to the desired *rasa* will not be endowed with beauty. For even insentient objects, introduced suitably either as *vibhāvas* of the appropriate *rasa* or by ascribing to them the qualities of sentient creatures, will act as auxiliary to a *rasa*...In this limitless world of poetry, the poet is the unique creator. All things in the world assume that character he wishes to attribute to them. If the poet is emotionally moved (lit. in love) in his poems, then the whole world is infused with *rasa*. But if he be without an interest in the senses then everything will become dry."

"A great poet, at his own will, causes even inanimate objects to behave as if they were animate objects and animate objects to behave as if they were inanimate."[133]

It is obvious that the concept of *vyañjanā* in the form of intended meaning of the speaker was latent in the *VP*. It was meant for ordinary speech. Ānandavardhana takes cue from Bhartṛhari and developed this intended meaning of the speaker to a fullfledged theory of literary language known as *dhvani* theory. Thus he is totally indebted to Bhartṛhari to formulate his new theory.

References

1. *Sphoṭavādaḥ* of Nāgeśa Bhaṭṭa,
Adyar Library, 1977, p. 102 :
vaiyākaraṇanāgeśaḥ
sphotāyanarṣer matam ।
pariṣkṛtyoktavāṁs tena
prīyatāṁ jagadīśvaraḥ ॥
2. *DL*. I. pp. 26, 28, 16-17, 1-2.
3. *Locana* on *DL*, pp. 138-141.
4. *Ibid*., p. 11:
avicchinnena pravāheṇa tair etad uktam vinā'pi
viśiṣṭapustakeṣu viniveśanād ity abhiprāyaḥ
"He now explains this : 'uninterrupted succession'. They have said this in an unbroken succession, without however putting it down in any particular book. This is what he means."
5. *Ibid*., *loc. cit*. :
budhasaikasya prāmādikam api tathābhidhānaṁ syāt
na tu bhūyasā tadyuktam । *tena budhair iti*
bahuvacanam...na ca budhā bhȳāṁso
nādaraṇīyam vastvādareṇopadiśeyuḥ ॥
"should (only) one scholar have made such a statement (i.e., *dhvani* is the soul of poerty) it is quite possible that he could be mistaken. But this could not be the case of many (wise men make such a claim). Therefor (Ānandavarhana) uses the plural in "scholars"...For many scholars could not teach, with great respect, something that really did not merit such respect."
6. *DL*. I.pp. 26, 28; 16-17, 1-2:
prathame hi vidvāṁso vaiyākaraṇāḥ । *vyākaraṇa-*
mūlatvāt sarvavidyānām । *te ca śrūyamāṇeṣu*
varṇeṣu dhvanir iti vyavaharanti । *tathaivānyais*
tan matānusāribhiḥ sūribhiḥ kāvyatattvārthadarśibhir
vācyavācakasammiśraḥ śabdātmā kāvyam iti
vyapadeśyo vyañjakatvasāmyād dhvanir ityuktaḥ

7. *DL.* III. p. 214, 15-16 :
pariniścitanirapabhraṁśasabdabrahmaṇāṁ vipaścitāṁ matam āśritya iva pravṛtto'yaṁ dhvanivyavahāra iti taiḥ saha kiṁ virodhāvirodhau cintyete
8. *DL.* III. p. 202, 10-12 :
itaś ca vācakatvād vyañjakatvasyānyatvaṁ yad vācakatvaṁ śabdaikāśrayam itarat tu śabdāśrayam arthāśrayaṁ ca । śabdārthayor dvayor api vyañjakatvasya pratipāditatvāt
"And another reason for holding suggestiveness to be different from the power of denotation is that the power of denotation depends solely on words, whereas the suggestive power depends on meaning as well as words, as it has been shown already that both words and meanings can carry suggestion."
9. *Locana* on DL. I. pp. 141-142:
tena vācyo 'pi dhvaniḥ । vācako'pi śabdo dhvaniḥ । dvayor api vyañjakatvaṁ dhvanatīti kṛtvā । sammiśrayate vibhāvānubhāvasaṁvalanayeti vyaṅgyo'pi dhvaniḥ । dhvanyata iti kṛtvā śabdanaṁ śabdaḥ śabdavyāpāraḥ । na cāsāvabhidhādirūpaḥ । api tvātmabhūtaḥ so'pi dhvananaṁ dhvaniḥ । kāvyam iti vyapadeśaś ca yo'rthaḥ so, pi dhvaniḥ । uktaprakāradhvanicatuṣṭayamayatvāt...vyaṅgyavyañjakabhāvaḥ sarveṣu pakṣeṣu sāmānyarūpaḥ sādhāraṇa ity arthaḥ ।।
"Therefore the literal sense too is *dhvani*, and the expressive word is also *dhvani*, since both suggest (i.e. since both of them are suggestive). The suggested sense is also *dhvani*, since it is suggested, and it is called (a mixture) because (it is blended by combining the *vibhāvas*, and *anubhāvas*, (and the *vyabhicārībhāvas*, as Bharata states in the *Nāṭya Śāstra)*. The *śabda* is used here in the sense of *śabdana*, (i.e. the significative function of words). It is not the function of denotation, etc. but rather it is the function which is vital (to poetry), (i.e. it is *vyañjanā)*. That too, in so far as it is *dhvanana* (the act of suggesting), is *dhvani*. That sense which is fit to be called

'poetry' is also *dhvani,* because it is a combination of the four ideas conveyed by the word *dhvani* mentioned already. So he gives the general reason (for calling all the five as *dhvani*)".

10. K.Krishna Moorthy, *Dhvanyāloka and its critics,* Mysore, 1968, p. 42 :
also Nagendra, *Dhvanyāloka,* introduction, Varanasi, pp. 3-5;
Ramaranjan Mukheruji, *Literary Criticism in Ancient India,* Calcutta, 1966, pp. 386-388.
Mukunda Madhav Sharma, *Dhvani theory in Sanskrit poetics,* Varanasi, 1968, pp. 33-34,
Vyañjanā prapañca Samīkṣā, Varanasi, 1979, pp. 78 ff;
Bholasankar Vyāsa, *Dhvani Sampradāya aur uske siddhānta* (Hindi), Vol.I, Varanasi, 1959, pp. 320 ff., (I do not agree with his relation between *sphoṭa* and *dhvani);*
Krusnakumar Sharma, *Dhvani siddhānta kā kāvya-śāstrīya aur samāja manovaijñānika adhyayana,* (Hindi), Allahabad, 1975, pp. 1-6;
Satyadeva Choudhari, *Śabdaśakti aur dhvani siddhānta,* Hindi, Delhi, 1973, pp. 14.23,
Viswanath Pandeya, *Dhvanisampradāya kā vikāsa,* Hindi, Delhi, 1971, pp. 105-6;
Ravisankar Nagar, *Vyañjanāvimarśa,* (Sans), Delhi, 1977, pp. 16 ff.
11. *DL.* III, p. 198, 11-12.
12. *Locana, DL,* pp. 138-139 :
śrotraśaṣkulīṁ santānenāgatā antyaḥ śabdāḥ śrūyanta iti prakriyāyāṁ śabdajāḥ śabdāḥ śrūyamāṇā ityuktam । *teṣāṁ ghaṇṭānuraṇanarūpatvam tāvad asti* । *te ca dhvaniśabdenoktāḥ yathāha bhagavān Bhartṛhariḥ* .. *VP* I.101.
evaṁ ghaṇṭādinirhlādasthānīyo, nuraṇanātmopalakṣito vyaṅgyo'py artho dhvanir iti vyavahṛtaḥ
"The last sounds are heard as they reach the orifice of the ear in a continuous wave. In this hypothesis, it has been said that it is the secondary sounds that are heard. They are of the form of the resonance of a bell, and are called by the name of *dhvani* (by the grammarians). As the great Bhartṛhari has said :
Others say that whatever is produced by the conjunction and disjunction with the points of articulation is the sphoṭa; while

the sounds originated from the (initial) sounds are the dhvanis'.

In the same way, the suggested sense (of perceptible process, *saṁlakṣyakramavyaṅgya)* which corresponds to the resonance of a bell, and the suggested sense (of imperceptible process) as well, are called *dhvani* (by those concerned with poetics).

N.B. (i) The verse VP.1.102 does not record the view of Bhartṛhari. *Iyer* wonders how Abhinavagupta refers to it to justify the source of *dhvani* theory. The view recorded in this verse goes against the grammarians view. It states the non-eternality of sound (see K.A.S.Iyer, 'who are *anitya-sphoṭavādins", POC,* 1035;

also Iyer discusses various views under the exposition of the translation of the *VP*.1.102 in this connection.

(ii) Bishnupada Bhattacharya states an objectionable view in this regard. He states that *sphoṭa* is eternal, indivisible word which is termed as *dhvani* by the grammarians; see *DL*.ed. by him, Firma KLM, 1968, p. 191; also 1.3.3.

(iii) I desagree with Bhāmaha who states that *sphoṭa* is meaning conveying segment of the word : *KL*. VI.7-15; See Ch. I.

13. *VP*.I.83.
14. *VP*.I.93.
15. *VP*.I.97.
16. *Locana* on *DL*. p. 139 :

    tathā śrūyamāṇā ye varṇā nādaśabdavācyā
    antyabuddhinirgrāhyasphoṭabhivyañjakās
    te dhvani śabdenoktāḥ

    "So also the sounds which we hear and which are otherwise called *nāda,* suggest the *sphoṭa* which is comprehended when one hears the last letter in a word, and these sounds the grammarians call *dhvani."*
17. In this passage, quoted above, Abhinavagupta uses the terms *dhvani* and *nāda* as synonyms. But according to Bhartṛhari these stand for different things :

    nādair āhitavījāyām antyena dhvaninā saha, VP.1.84;

    also see Satyakam Verma, *Bhāṣātatva aur Vākyapadīya* Hindi, Bharatiya Prakasana, 1964, pp. 50-51.
18. *DL*. III.*kā*.2, p. 114 :

yastv alakṣyakramavyaṅgyo dhvani varṇapadādiṣu ।
vākyasaṅghaṭanāyāṁ ca sa prabandhe'pi dīpyate ॥

19. *DL*.III. p. 106, 1-2:
evaṁ vyaṅgyamukhenaiva dhvaneḥ pradarśite saprabhede svarūpe punar vyañjakamukhenaitat prakāśyate
"In this manner the nature of *dhvani* alongwith its varieties has been shown with respect to what is suggested. Now this something will be expounded from the point of view of the actual words etc. which achieve the suggested effect."
20. *DL*. III.202, 10-11:
yad vācakatvaṁ śabdaikāśrayam itarattu śabdāśrayam arthāśrayaṁ ca
".. that the power of denotation depends solely on words, whereas (the suggestive power) depends on meaning as well as words..."
21. *Locana* on *DL*. p. 140:
tena vyañjakau śabdārthāvapīha dhvani śabdenoktau
"Therefore suggestive words and suggestive meaning are both called *dhvani* in poetics."
22. Mukunda Madhava Sharma in the *Dhvani theory of Sanskrit poetics*, pp. 37-38, thinks that the term *śabda* (*VP*. I.55) stands for *sphoṭa* as meaning bearing segment of language. I disagree.with him.
23. See K.A.S.Iyer, "Bhartṛhari on *dhvani, ABORI*, Vol. XLVI, 1965.
24. Vyāḍi, *vṛtti* on *VP*.I.76, p. 142 :
śabdasya grahaṇe hetuḥ
prākṛto dhvanir iṣyate ।
sthitibhede nimittatvam
vaikṛtaḥ pratipadyate ॥
25. K.KrishnaMoorthy, *Dhvanyāloka and its critics*, pp. 39-40.
26. *Ślokāvārtika, Sphoṭa*. V.10, p. 615, quoted in *Locana*, p. 140; also B.Bhattacharya's ed. of *DL*., p. 194 :
alpīyasā pi yatnena śabdam uccāritam matiḥ ।
yadi vā naiva gṛhṇāti varṇaṁ vā sakalaṁ sphuṭam ॥
"If a sound is uttered with a degree of effortless than the minimum that is required for its being heard, the mind does

not grasp it at all; or else (i.e. if the sound is uttered with necessary degree of effort), the mind grasps the whole of it clearly."

27. *Locana* on *DL.* P.140 :
teṣu tāvatsv eva śrūyamāṇeṣu vaktur
yo'nyo drutavilambitādivṛttibhedāt mā
prasiddhād uccāraṇavyāpārād abhyadhikaḥ
sa dhvanir uktaḥ
"Since sounds are heard only when uttered with the requisite degree of loudness, that activity of the speaker, different from the well known articulatory activity which is responsible for the different speeds of utterance such as quick slow etc. is called *dhvani* (by the grammarians).
28. *Ibid.* p. 141 :
asmābhir api prasiddhebhyḥ
śabdavyāpārebhyo'bhidhātātparya-
lakṣaṇārūpebhyo'ti rikto vyāpāro
dhvanir ity uktaḥ
"We have also given the name *dhvani* to that function which is different from the well-known functions of *abhidhā, tātparya* and *lakṣaṇā'*
29. Maitreyi Choudhuri, *A Critical and Historical study of the function of vyañjanā*, unpublished Ph.D. dissertation, Jadavpur University, 1966, p. 60.
30. *VP.* I.91.
31. *DL.*III.p. 196, 3-5
tasmābhidhānābhidheyapratītyor iva vācya-
vyaṅgyapratītyor nimittanimittibhāvān
niyamabhāvī kramaḥ । sa tūktayuktyā
kvacil lakṣyate kvacin na lakṣyate
32. *DL.*III.p. 214, 15-16.
33. K.A.S.Iyer, *Bhartṛhari*, p. 100; also *VP.*I. p. 14, 3-4; VP.I.115(123), 116(124);
cf. *Īśvarapratyabhijñākārikā* of Utpaladeva, āhnika, *kā.* 11,13.
34. *VP.*III, pt.i, p. 107.
satyaṁ vastu tadākārair
asatyair avadhāryate ।
asatyopādhibhiḥ śabdaiḥ
satyam evābhidhīyate ।।

35. *VP.* III. p. 108
adhruvena nimittena
devadatta gṛham yathā ।
gṛhitaṁ gṛha śabdena
suddham evābhidhīyate ॥
cf. Mbh. Vol. I, p. 85:
itaratrāpi ya eṣa manuṣyaḥ
prekṣāpūrvakārī bhavati so'dhruveṇa
nimittena dve ubhaṁ nimittam
upādatte vedikā puṇḍarīkaṁ vā
36. *VP.*III.p. 109 :
suvarṇādi yathābhinaṁ etc.
37. *VP.*III.p. 118 :
vikārāpagame satyam
suvarṇaṁ kuṇḍale yathā ।
vikārāpagame satyam
tām āhuḥ prakṛtiṁ parām ॥
also *VP.* III.p. 173 :
yatra dṛṣṭā ca dṛśyaṁ ca
darśanaṁ vā vikalpitam ।
tasyaivārthasya satyatvam
śritastrayyanta vedinaḥ ॥
cf. *VP.* I
bhedodgrāha vivartena
labdhākārā parigrahā ।
āmātā sarvavidyāsu
vāgeva prakṛtiḥ parā ॥
38. *VP.* 111, pt.i, p. 48 :
na ca pariṇati śabdābhiprāyeṇāyaṁ
vikāraśabdaḥ । *anityatvaprasaṅgāt*
api tu vivartaparyāyo'yam
39. K.A.S.Iyer, Bhartṛhari, pp. 142-145.
40. *Vṛtti* on *VP.*I.14, pp. 47-48, 7-8, 1-3
41. Iyer, *op. cit.*, p. 145
42. *Vedāntasāra* of Sadānanda, ed.M.Hiriyanna, Poona Oriental Book Agency, 1929, p. 58
43. *DL.* iii. *kā*, 21-23
44. *DL.* iv. pp. 272-278.

45. *Abh.* Vol. I, GOS, 19 :
tasmāt kāvya doṣabhāvaguṇālaṁkāramayatva-lakṣaṇena nāṭye caturvidhābhinayarupeṇa niviḍanijamohasaṁkaṭakāriṇā vibhāvādi-sādhāraṇīkaraṇātmanā 'bhighāto 'dvitīyenāṁśena bhāvakatvavyāpāreṇa bhāvyamāno rase 'nubhava-smṛtyādivilakṣaṇena rajas tamo'nubedha-vaicitryavalāt drutivistāravikāśalakṣaṇena sattvodrekaprakāśānandamayanijasamvid viśrāntilakṣaṇena parabrahmāsvāda-savidhena bhogena paraṁ bhujyate

46. (i) *Abb. NS.* Vol.I, Ch Vi, p. 284
tatra lokavyavahāre kāryakāraṇa-sahacārātmaka liṅgadarśane sthāyyātmapara-cittavṛtty anumānābhyāsapātavād adhunā tair evodyānakaṭākṣavīkṣādibhi laukikīṁ kāraṇatvād:ɔhuvam atikrāntair vibhāvanānubhāvanā samau parañjakatvamātraprāṇaiḥ ata evā-laukikavibhāvādivyapadeśabhāgbhiḥ prācya-kāraṇādirūpasaṁskāropajīvanakhyāpanāya vibhāvādināmadheyavyapadeśyair bhāvādhyāye'pi vakṣyamāṇasvarūpabhedair guṇapradhānatā-paryāyeṇa sāmājikadhiyi samyag yogaṁ sambandham aikāgrayaṁ vā sāditavadbhir laukikanirvighna-saṁvedanātmakacarvaṇāgocaratāṁ nīto 'rthaścarvyamāṇataikasāro na tu siddha-svabhāvaḥ ı tātkālika eva na tu carvaṇātiriktakālāvalambi sthāyivilakṣaṇa eva rasaḥ.

"The effect, cause and accessories are known from the worldly use. The permanent mood remains in the minds of persons who because of practice can study the thoughts of other's mind. Those permanent moods in the form of ordinary causes namely the garden, side glances etc. are transformed into extraordinary excitants, ensuants and accessories (in poetry and drama). Thus, the extraordinary excitants etc. latent in the deeds of the previous birth which are discussed in *bhāvādhyāya*, are again discussed here because of their secondary and primary nature. The *rasa* is different from the

permanent moods. It is extraordinary, without hindrance, compassionate, comprehended and expressed through relish. (It is) not achieved. (It is) temporary and not permanent. (It is) relished in the concerntrated intellect of the connoisseures."
(ii) *op. cit.* p. 284
tenālaukikacamatkārātmā rasāsvādaḥ
smṛtyanumānalaukikasamvedana-
vilakṣaṇa eva
"Thus, the relish of *rasa* which is uncommon and expanding by nature, is distinguished from ordinary cognitions namely remembrance and inferrence."
(iii) *Locana, DL.* p. 50 :
yastu (rasa) svapne'pi na svaśabdavācyo na
laukikavyavahārapatitaḥ ı kiṁ tu śabda-
samarpyamāṇahṛdayasaṁvādasundara-
vibhāvānubhāvaśamucitaprāgviniviṣṭa-
ratyādivāsanānurāgasukumārasvasaṁvidānanda-
carvaṇāvyāpārarasanīyarūporasaḥ ı
sa kāvyavyāpāraikagocaro rasadhvanir iti ı
sa ca dhvanir eveti sa eva mukhyatayātmeti.

47. *Kāvyaprakāśa* of Mammaṭa, ed. Vamana Jhalakikara, 1965, p. 934 :
pānakarasanyāyena carvyamāṇaḥ pura iva
parisphuran hṛdayam iva praviśan
sarvāṅgīṇam ivāliṅgan anyatsarvam iva
tirodadhat brahmāsvādam ivānubhāvayan
alaukikacamatkārakārī śṛṅgārādiko rasaḥ
48. Quoted in *Locana, DL.* p. 93
See fn No. 148, Ch.II.
49. *Locana* on *DL.* p. 200 :
parabrahmāsvādasabrahmacāritvaṁ
cāstvasya rasāsvādasya
50. *Ibid.*, p. 93 :
tadāveśena vināpyākrāntyā hi yo
yogibhir duhyate.
51. *RG.* p. 107 :
vyaktiś ca bhagnāvaraṇā cit.
52. S.K.De, *Sanskrit poetics*, Vol. II, 1960, pp. 136-137.
53. *RG.* pp. 118-12 :
vastutastu vakṣyamāṇaśrutisvārasyena etc.

54. M.Hiriyanna, "Indian Aesthetics", POC of 1919, Vol.II, 1922, pp. 238-42.
    cf. S.K. De, *Sanskrit poetics*, Vol. II, p. 126.
55. *Taittirīya Upaniṣad*, 2.7 :
    raso vai saḥ rasaṁ hevāyaṁ labdhvā nandī bhavati
56. K.K. Raja, *Indian theories of Meaning*, p. 194.
57. *Ibid.*, p. 200;
    cf. *vākyārthamātṛkā vṛtti*, p. 2;
    bhuyāṁso yady api svārthāḥ padānāṁ te
    pṛthak pṛthak prayojanatayā tva eka-
    vākyārthaṁ saṁpracakṣate
58. *Ibid.*, pp. 203-204.
59. *Ibid.*, p. 211
60. *Abhidhāvṛttimātṛkā* of Mukulabhaṭṭa, Varanasi, 1973, p. 46 :
    anyeṣāṁ tu mate padānāṁ tat tat
    sāmānyabhūto vācyo'rthaḥ vākyasya tu
    parasparānvitāḥ padārthā iti
    padāpekṣayābhihitānvayaḥ vākyāpekṣayā
    tu anvitābhidhānam । evam caitayoḥ ॥
61. L.A. Blumenthal, *Language and Psychology*, John Wiley & Sons, INC, New York, 1970, pp. 20-23.
62. *Ibid.*, pp. 34-38.
63. For reality of word see John Brough. *"Some Indian Theories of Meaning" TPS*, 1953, pp. 165-167.
64. *VP*. II.13.
65. VP.II.232-33.
66. *VP*.II.55
67. *VP*.II.438-440.
68. *VP*.II.225(a), 226.
69. John Brough, *op. cit.*, p. 116; cf. *VP*.II.14.
70. *VP*.I.73 :
    Śabdakaustubha, p. 7
    eakḥ pata iti vada ekaṁ padaṁ vākyaṁ vā
    ity avādhitapratītevarṇātiriktam eva padaṁ
    vākyaṁ vā akhaṇḍaṁ varṇavyaṅgyam
71. S.D. Joshi, *Sphoṭa Nirṇaya*, pp. 80-81.
72. *VP*.II.333,
    "When the word 'door' having the second case ending is heard, then according to the context one understands either 'shut' or 'give way'.

73. *VP*. II. 342.
74. *VP*.II.343-344.
75. *cf*. *DL*.III.p. 200, 4-13.
76. *DL*.I.10-11:
    yathā padārthadvāreṇa
    vākyārthaḥ saṁpratīyate ।
    vācyārthapūrvikā tad vat
    pratipat tasya vastunaḥ ॥
    svasāmarthyavaśenaiva
    vākyārthaṁ prathayann api ।
    yathā vyāpāraniṣpattau
    padārtho na vibhāvyate ॥
77. *DL*.III.p. 112, 14-20.
78. *DL*. III.p. 112, 15-20; See fn No.88. Ch.iv
79. *Locana* on *DL*.III. p. 325 :
    kāvyaṁ cānākāṅkṣapratipattikāri vākyaṁ na padam iti tatrāha satyam evaṁ । *tathāpi padaṁ na dhvanir ity asmābhir uktam api tu samudāya eva* ॥ *tathā ca padaprakāśo dhvanir iti prakāśapadenoktam. nanu padasya tatra tathāvidham sāmarthyam iti kuto'khaṇḍa eva partītikrama ity āśaṅkyāha kāvyānām iti* ॥
80. *Sāṁkhya Sūtra Vṛtti* ii.43, 44.
81. *Sāṁkhyapravacana Bhāṣya* ii.42.
82. Jadunath Sinha, *A History of Indian Philosophy*, Vol. II, Central Book Agency, calcutta, 1952, p. 38.
83. S.N.Ghosal Sastri, *Elements of Indian Aesthetics*, Vol.I, Varanasi, 1978, p. 53.
84. *Sphoṭa Siddhi* of Maṇḍana Miśra, ed. K.A.S.Iyer, 1966, fn.No.20, Introduction, p. 22.
85. *VP.I*.123 (131), 139(147).
86. *VP.I*.123(131).
87. *VP*. I.113(121),
    iti kartavyatā loke
    sarvā śabdavyapāśrayā ।
    yāṁ pūrvāhita saṁskāro
    bālo'pi pratipadyate ॥
    "All knowledge what is to be done in this would depends

upon the word. Even the child, with its residual traces from the previous birth, has such knowledge."

88. *VP.* II.146, 151;
89. *SS.* p. 18, 4-5 :
jñānāntaropajanagocaraṁ sāmarthyam
evātmani prācīnavijñanāhitaniveśaṁ
saṁskāram ācakṣate dhīrāḥ
"Wise men give the name of 'impression' to that power, which exists in the soul, of producing another cognition and which has been brought there through a previous cognition."
90. *SS.* p. 32, 7-8:
sphoṭapalabdhinibandhanas tu
bhāvanābhidhāna eva saṁskāra iti vakṣyate
91. *Ibid., loc. cit,* 5-6 :
na tu praklṛptavāsanābhidhāna-
saṁskāranibandhano 'rthapratyayo'sya siddhyati
92. *Ibid., vṛtti* of *kā.*7.pp. 18-19.
93. *Ibid.,* p. 32, 4-5:
varṇavādī hi karmabhedajanyam apūrvam
ivātyantā paridṛṣṭam arthasamādhigamanimittaṁ
varṇavijñānajanmānaṁ saṁskāraṁ parikalpayati
94. *SS.* p. 43, 7-13; *cf. VP.*I.82-84; See 1.
95. *Ibid.,* p. 47, 1-2:
rajjvāṁ hi kaścit sarpa iti
viparyasyati kaścid dhāreti
VP. I.89, 90.
96. *Ibid., kā.* 19, with *vṛtti.*
97. *Ibid.,* p. 43, 21 :
anupākhyeyākārasphoṭopalabdhijanmānaś ca
saṁskārās tatraiva sphuṭataraparicchedām
98. *VP.* I. 151; *VP.*II.117.
99. *VP.*II.146.
100. *VP.*II.151:
"This intuition is the result of 'tradition' *āgama* accompanied by *bhāvanā.* The tradition is differentiated in as much as it is proximate or remote."
101. See note on the translation of *VP.*II.151, Iyer, 1977, p. 63.
102. *VP.*I.123 :

na so'sti pratyayo loke
yaḥ śabdānugamādṛte ।
anuviddham iva jñānam
sarvam śabdena bhāsate ॥

103. *DL*.II. p. 58, 15.
104. *DL*.I. p. 14.3.
105. *Locana*, p. 198, 214, 432, 450.
106. *Ibid.*, p. 50, 192, 198.
107. *Ibid.*, p. 40, 51, 199, 445.
108. K.C.Pandey, *Abhinavagupta*, Varanasi, 1963, p. 693 ff.
109. *DL*. IV. p. 298, 9-10 :
yeṣāṁ sukavīnāṁ prāktana-
puṇyābhyāsaparipākavaśena pravṛttā
vāk teṣāṁ paroparacitārthaparigraha-
niḥspṛhāṇāṁ svavyāpāro na kvacid upayujyate
110. Amala Dass identifies *saṁskāra* with *pratibhā*. But both are different entities. See his *philosophical implications of dhvani*, Unpublished Ph.D.dissertation, Dept. Sanskrit Madras University, 1980, p. 106.
111. *Kāśikā* on P. 8.1.8, 8.1.10:
ete ca prayoktṛdharmāḥ
nābhidheyadharmāḥ.
112. D.Kar, *Semantic basis of Aṣṭādhyāyī*, Unpublished Ph.D. dissertation, C.A.S.S.
Poona University, 1980, 32-33, 36-39, 39-45.
113. Laśzlo, Antal, *Content, Meaning and Understanding*, Mouton and Co., The Hague, 1964, pp. 10, 21-22.
114. *VP*.II.399-400.
115. *VP*.II.403-404.
116. *VP*.II.426-427; 430-433.
117. *VP*.II.310 :
gantavyaṁ dṛśyantāṁ sūrya iti kālasya lakṣaṇe ।
jñāyatāṁ kāla ity etat sopāyam abhidhīyate ॥
118. *VP*.II.312:
kākebhyo rakṣyatāṁ sarpir iti
bālo'pi coditaḥ । *upaghāta pare vākye*
na śvādibhyo na rakṣati ॥
119. cf. Nāgeśabhaṭṭa's *Paramalaghumañjuṣā*, ed. Alakhadeva Sharma, Varanasi, 1981, p. 39;

Vaiyākaraṇa Siddhānta laghumañjuṣā, ed. Sabhapati Sharma Upadhyaya, Varanasi, 1963, p. 101.

120. *VP*.II.321 :
vyāghrādivyapadeśena yathā bālo nivartyate ।
asatyo'pi tathā kaścit pratyavāyo vidhīyate ॥
121. cf. John Brough, "Some Indian Theories of Meaning", *TPS*, 1953, p. 172.
122. *cf. DL*.I. p. 8, 10-11, 15-16.
123. *VP*. II.311 :
vidhyaty adhanuṣety atra viśeṣeṇa nidarśyate ।
sāmānyam āśrayaḥ śakter yaḥ kaścit pratipādakaḥ ॥
124. *VP*.II.315-316.
125. *VP*.II.313 :
prakṣālanaṁ śarāvāṇāṁ sthālināṁ mārjanaṁ tathā ।
anuktam api rupeṇa bhujyaṅgatvāt pratīyate ॥
126. *VP*. II.333, 335, 338.
127. *VP*.II. 424-427.
128. *VP*.II.428.
129. *VP*.II.429.
130. *VP*.II.430.
131. cf. C.K.Ogden and I.A.Richards, *The Meaning of Meaning*, Routledge & Kegan Paul Ltd. London, 10th edition (fifth impression), 1960, pp. 192 ff.
132. (i) *DL*.III.p. 198, 10-12 :
na hi yaivābhidhānaśaktiḥ saivāvagamana-śaktiḥ avācakasyāpi gītaśabdāder rasādi-lakṣaṇārthāvagamadarśanāt । *aśabdasyāpi ceṣṭāder arthaviśeṣaprakāśanaprasiddheḥ* ॥

(ii) *DL*. III. 206, 9-12 :
tathā hi gītadhvanīnām api vyñjakatvam asti rasādiviṣayaṁ na ca teṣāṁ vācakatvaṁ lakṣaṇā vā kathañcil lakṣyate । *śabdād anyatrā'pi viṣaye vyañjakatvasya darśanāvācakatvādiśabdadharmaprakāratvam ayuktam*

(iii) *DL*.III.220, 12-13:
na ca vyañjakatvam liṅgatvarùpam eva ālokādiṣv anyathā dṛṣṭatvāt.

133. *DL*.III.248-250, 11-15, 1-6;
cf. *DL*.III. 248-50, 11-15, 1-6, p. 256 7;
fn.No.48, Ch.IV; fn.No.148, Ch.II;
also cf. Byron "Childe Harold" 111, 6:
its to create, and in creating live
A being more intense, that we endow with form
our fancy, gaining as we give
The life we imagine, even as I do now;
also P.B.Shelly, "Prometheus unbound"
Act I, Sc. i,
But from these create he can
Forms more real than living man,
Nurshiling of immortality.

5

Conclusion

There are many striking similarities between Bhartṛhari's philosophy of language and Ānandavardhana's *dhvani* semantics. Both recognise indivisibility of sentence and its meaning. Both recognise that *pratibhā* is the guiding instinct which make us grasp the sentence meaning and suggested meaning respectively. Both admit that *pratibhā* arises from traces and impressions left in this or in earlier existence. Both admit that *dhvani* is a mode of expression. According to Bhartṛhari, the relation between *dhvani* and *sphoṭa* is *vyaṅgyavyañjakabhāva* 'revealer-revealed'. The *sphoṭa,* according to Bhartṛhari, remains over and above the sounds at the distinctive level. The *dhvani* meaning according to Ānandavardhana remains over and above the constituent meaning at communicative level. The higher reality of *Brahman* is identified with the lower reality of *śabda.* Similarly, the higher reality of *Brahman* is identified with the lower reality of *rasadhvani.* Ānandavardhana admits that *rasadhvani* is inherent in language. The *dhvani* theory forms a province of language as a whole. Language plays a vital role in its capacity as an instrument of suggestive meaning. Just as according to Bhartṛhari *dhvani* and *sphoṭa* constitute the two components of language, so also, according to Ānandavardhana, *dhvani*-phonetics and *dhvani* semantics constitute the two components of language. According to Bhartṛhari, that which cannot be subjected to the expression of the articulated sound cannot be content (object) of thought and must therefore be regarded as illusion (*VP*.I.124). On the other hand, such things as 'sky flowers' and the sons of the barren women which have no external existence but can be subjected to the expression of articulated sound, are the contents of knowledge and by virtue thereof must be regarded as real. This articulated form gives the object existential status (*VP*.I.125).

Ānandavardhana maintains that *pratibhā* is the source of poetry, without it there can be no poetic creation. The *Pratibhā* establishes the relation betwen the mental image and the poetic statement. The point is that often poetic statement is more dependent on poetic creation than on actual observable fact. The *pratibhā* is an intellectual poetic power capable of producing novel objects *(apūrvavastunir-māṇakṣamatā)* which do not exist in outside world like 'sky flowers' and sons of barren women. In both the *VP* and the *Dhvanyāloka* the word meaning represents a mental image or conception of an external object (*VP*.II.132). It is not even necessary that the mental image must have a corresponding external object, it can have a non-existing objects too (*VP*.II.133). The world of literature is not an imitation of the real world. In the Pāṇinian tradition the grammarian's meta-language is very different from the ordinary Sanskrit which is their object language. From this wider notion, 'meta-communication' has been introduced in order to designate *dhvani* 'communication about communication'. The poetic expressions communicate emotion affective meanings etc.

Both Bhartṛhari and Ānandavardhana hold that two factors, namely context and speaker's intention are essential in understanding the meaning of sentence. The meaning of an utterance is fixed not only by words and sentences but by context and speaker's intention too. The words and sentences which are apart from their context have only artificial meaning. Between Bhartṛhari and Ānandavar-dhana there is no book in the school of grammar which deals specificially with the philosophy of language. Later Bhartṛhari's metaphysical and to some extent semantic contributions are quite forgottan. Bhartṛhari is often quoted for his contribution to grammar. But we find his influence on the *dhvani* theory, primarily as a semanticist and a philosopher of language. Bhartṛhari was the first author to elaborate the doctrine of *sphoṭa* and *pratibhā*. Bhartṛhari was the philosopher who maintained that the division of sentence into words and that of words into stems and suffixes is a fiction useful to students to understand the structure of language. Ānandavardhana accepted his philosophy and applied it to poetics. Still Ānandavardhana's contribution to Sanskrit poetics is of considerable value. What is new in the work of Ānandavar-dhana as opposed to that of Bhartṛhari is clarity of state-ments which give his analysis and arguments a great precision. He knows how to put arguments convincingly. His manner of presentation of arguments is highly pleasing and straight forward. The most important effect of Ānandavardhana's *dhvani* theory was in the realm of poetics, which is remarkably similar to the linguistic theory of Bhartṛhari. The *dhvanikāra* found out the parallelism between the formal features of grammar and the features of semantics. The extent to which Ānandavardhana was directly influenced by Bhartṛhari was not known to rhetoricians though his debt has been mentioned by the *dhvanikāra* himself. Later the *dhvani* theory has become the source from which the major developments in rhetorics have sprung. Ānandavardhana has firmly established the *dhvani* theory. Later on Abhinavagupta and Mammaṭa have unquestionably accepted that the *dhvani* element is the most important element in poetry.

Bibliography

(A) Sanskrit Texts and Translations

Abhidhāvṛttimātṛkā by Mukulabhaṭṭa, ed. Rewaprasad Dwivedi, Chowkhamba Vidyabhavan, Varanasi, 1973.

Alaṁkāramahodadhi by Narendraprabhā Sūri, ed. L.G. Pandit, GOS. XCV, Oriental Institute, Baroda, 1942.

Bharatārṇava by Nandikeśvara, ed. K. Vasudeva Shastri, Saraswati Mahal Library, Tanjore, 1954.

Dhvanyāloka by Ānandavardhana, ed. & translated into German by H. Jacobi, ZDMG. No. 56, Leipzig, F.A. Brockhaus, 1902. ed. with the *Locana* of Abhinavagupta by Durgaprasad Sastri, Kāvyamālā, 25, NSP, Bombay, 1911. tran. (with ten pages of the *Locana)* into English by N.Ram Pisharoti, *Indian Thought,* ix-x, 1917-18. With the *Locana, Uddyota,* iv, as 'The text of *Kāvyālokalocana',* ed. S.K.De, *JDL,* Calcutta University, Vol. ix, 1923. With a modern comm. *Avadhāna,* ed. Sri Madhusudan Mishra Sharman, Calcutta Sanskrit Series No. 25B, Calcutta, 1938. With the *Locana* and the *Bālapriyā* of Rāmasāraka, ed. Pattabhiram Sastri, 1940. With the *Locana* of Abhinava-gupta, the *Kaumudi* of Uttuṅgodaya and the *Upalocana* of the editor (first *Uddyota* only), ed. S.Kuppuswami Sastri assisted by T.V. Ramachandra Diksitar and T.R. Chintamani, Kuppuswami Sastri Research Institute, Madras, 1944. With a Hindi comm. of Acarya Viśveśvara, ed. Nagendra, Gyanamandal Ltd., Varanasi, 1952. With English tr., ed. K.Krishnamoorthy, Poona Oriental Series No. 92, Oriental Book Agency,

Poona, 1955; Karnatak University, Dharwar, 1974. With the *Locana* and Hindi tr. of both the texts by R.S.Tripathy, Motilal Banarsidas, Delhi, 1963. With the *Dīdhitī* comm. of Badrinath Sharma, Haridas Sanskrit Series No.66, Chowkhamba, Varanasi, 1964. With the *Locana* and Hindi translation of both the texts, ed. Jagannath Pathak, Vidya Bhawan Sanskrit Granthamala No.97, Chowkhamba, Varanasi, 1965. With the English tr. of Ist *Uddyota*, Bisnupada Bhattacharya, Firma K.L.M., Calcutta, revised 2nd ed., 1965. With the *Locana* and exposition in Bengali i, ii, ed. Bimalakanta Mukhopadhyaya, Pustakashree, Calcutta, 378 Sāl; by the same author, iii, iv, with *Locana* and exposition in Bengali, Burdnman University, 1983.

Dhvanyālokasāra, P.C.Caturveda, Haridas Sanskrit Granthamala, 249, Chowkhamaba, 1954.

Dhvanyāloka Saṁgraha, ed. K.K. Raja, Annals of Oriental Research, University of Madras, Vol. xxiv, part ii, 1973.

Dhvanigāthāpañjikā by Ratnākara of Kashmir, MSS. No.xii, 182, BORI.

Kāvyālaṁkāra by Bhāmaha, ed. Devendranath Sharma, Bihar Rastrabhasa Parisad, Patna, 1962.

Kāvyādarśa By Daṇḍin, ed. Dharmendra Kumar Gupta, Meherchand Lacchaman Dass, Delhi, 1973.

Kāvyālaṁkāra-Sāra-Saṁgraha by Udbhaṭa with the comm. *Laghuvṛtti* of *Indurāja,* ed. Narayana Daso Banhatti, BORO, Poona, 1925.

Kāvyālaṁkāra by Rudraṭa, ed. with Hidni Tr. Satyadev Choudhuri. Vasudev Prakashan, Delhi, 1965.

Kāvyamīmāṁsā by Rajasekhara, ed. Kedarnath Sharma, Bihar Rastra Bhasa Parisad, Patna, 1965.

Kāvyaprakāśa of Mammaṭa with the Comm. *Kāvyapradīpa* by Govinda Thakkura, and the sub.comm. *Pradīpoddyota* of Nageśa Bhaṭṭa, Ānandāśram a Sanskrit Series, 66, Poona, 1911, 1929. With the comm. *Saṁketa* by

Manikyagandra, ASS 89, Poona 1921. With the *Bālabodhinī* of V. Jhalakikara, BORI, Poona, 1965. - English tr. by M.M. Ganganath Jha, Bharatiya Vidya Prakasana, Varanasi, 1957. With *Rasaprakāśa* of Sri Kṛṣṇa Śarman, ed. S.N. Ghosal Śastri, Chowkhamba Sanskrit Samsthan, Varanasi, 1973. With *Bālacittānurañjanī of* Narahari Saraswati Tirtha, *Sārabodhinī* of Srivatsalanchana Bhattacharya, *Kāvyaprakāaadarpaṇa* of Viśvanātha Kavirāja, ed. by Goparaju Rama and Jagannath *Pathak,* Ganganath Jha Sanskrit University, Prayag, 1979. Ed. Sivaraja Kaundinyayana, Motilal Banarsidass, Delhi, 1980.

Kāvyānuśāsana by Hemacandra, ed. R.C. Parikh, Mahavir Jains Mahavidyalaya Bombay, 1938.

Kāvyānuśāsana by Vāgbhaṭa, ed. Pt. Sivadatta and K.P. Parab, Kāvyāmālā 93, NSP, Bombay, 19125

Kirātārjunīyam by Bhāravi, NSP, 1942.

Mahābhāṣya by Patañjali, ed. Kielhorn, BSS, (1880-85), Reprint, Third ed. BORI, Poona, 1962.

Mahābhāṣya Dīpikā by Bhartṛhari, ed. K.V. Abhyankar, V.P. Limaye, BORI, 1970.

Mīmāṁsā Śloka Vārtika by Kumārilabhaṭṭa, with Hindi tr. ed. Pt. Durgadhar Jha, Kameswar Singh Sanskrit University, Darbhanga, 1979.

Nātya Śāstra by Bharata, Vol. I, GOS, 1956, English tr. by Manmohan Ghosh, Manisha Granthalaya, Calcutta, 1967.

Nirukta by Yāska with Durgācārya's comm. ed. Pt. Mukunda Sharma, Meherchand Lachman Dass, New Delhi, 1982.

Nyāyasūtra-s of Gautama with the Bhāṣya by Vātsyāyana, ASS 91, Poona, 1922.

Nyāyavārttika by Uddyotakara, com, on the *Nyāyabhāṣya* BI. 113, Calcutta, 1887-1914.

Nyāyavārttikatātparyaṭīkā by Vācaspati Miśra KSS 24, Benaras, 1925.

NyāyaMañjarī by Jayantabhaṭṭa, Vol.I, II, ed. Pt. Suryanārāyan Sharma, Chowkhamba Sanskrit Series, 1936.

Nyāyakośa by Bhimacharia Jhalakikara, BORI, Poona, 1978.

Pañcadaśī by Vidyaranyamuni, Nirnaya Sagar Press, 1949.

Pradīpa by Kaiyata on *Vyākaraṇa Mahābhāṣya,* ed. Rudradhar Jha, Chowkhamba Sanskrit Series, Varanasi, 1954.

Pratāparudrīya by Vidyānātha with *Ratnāpaṇa* of Kumaraswamin, Sanskrit Education Society, Madras, 1970.

Rasagaṅgādhara by Panditarāja Jagannātha, Vol. I, ed. Madhusudan Sastri, BHU, 1963.

Raghuvaṁśa by Kālidāsa, Chowkhamba Sura Bharati, 1979.

Śābarabhāṣya on Jaiminī's *Mīmāmsā Sūtra-s,* ed. Yudhisthir *Mīmāṁsaka,* Hariyana, 1977.

Śastradīpikā by Parthasarathi Miśra, ed. Kishor Das Swami, Varanasi, 1977.

Siddhāntamuktāvali by Viśvanāthanyāyapañcānana, also called *Bhāṣāpariccheda, containing* kārikāvali and *muktāvali* with comm. *Dinakarī,* KSS 16, Banaras, 1951.

Sphoṭasiddhi by Maṇḍana Miśra, ed. with tr. and intro. by K.A. Subramania Iyer, Deccan College, Poona, 1966.

Sphoṭatattvanirūpana by Śeṣakṛṣṇa, The Gujarati Printing Press, Bombay, 1913.

Sphoṭavāda by Nāgeśabhaṭṭa, ALS 55, Madras, 1956.

Sphuṭanirṇayatantra by Achyuta, ed. K.V. Sharman, Viswesvarananda Viswabandhu Institute of Sanskrit and Indological studies, 1977.

Tarkasaṁgraha by Annaṁbhatta, ed. Narayan Chandra Goswami, Sanskrit Pustak Bhandar, Calcutta, year not mentioned.

Tattvasaṁgraha by Śāntarakṣita with comm. *Pañjikā* by Kamalśīla, GOS 30-1, Baroda, 1926.

Upaniṣadvākya Mahākośa, Vol. i, ii, ed. Sambhuputro Gajānana, Gujarati Printing Press, Bombay, 1940-41.

Vakroktijīvita by Kuntaka, ed. with trans, K.Krishnamoorthy, Karnatak University, Dharwed, 1977.

Vākyapadīya by Bhartrhari, ed.Raghunath Sharma, *Kāṇḍa i,* ii, Sampurnananda Sanskrit University, Varanasi, 1976-1980. - ed. K.V. Abhyankar and V.P. Limaye, University of Poona Sanskrit and Prakrit Series, Vol.II, Poona, 1965. With *vṛtti* and *paddhati* of Vṛṣabhadeva *kāṇḍa* I, ed. K.A. Subramania Iyer, Deccan College Monograph Series, 32, Poona, 1966. *Kāṇḍa* I with the comm. *Bhāvapradīpa* of Pt. Suryanarayan Sukla, Kashi Sanskrit Series, 124, Benares, 1937. *Kāṇḍa* I, English tran. by K.A. Subramania Iyer, Deccan College, 1965. *Kāṇḍa* II. English tran. by K.A. Subramaina Iyer, Motilala Banarasidass, Delhi, 1977. *Brahmakāṇḍa,* ed. Madeleine Biardeau, Editions E. De Boccard 1, Rue de Medicis, Paris, 1964. - ed. von Wilhelm Rau, Kommissionsverlag Franz Ṣteiner Gmbh, Wiesbaden, 1977. *Kāṇḍa* I, with author's own comm. ed. Charudeva Sastri, Ramlal Kapoor Trust, Lahore, 1934. *Kāṇḍa* I, with trillingual comm. by Satyakam Verma, Munishiram Manoharlal, New Delhi, 1970.

Vāgbhaṭālaṅkāra by Vagbhatta, with the comm. of Simhadeva Gaṇi, ed. Pt. Sivadatta and K.P. Parab, NSP, Bombay, 1913.

Vaiyākaraṇa Bhūṣaṇasāra of Kaundabhaṭṭa, Ch, XIV, ed. S.D. Joshi, in *Sphoṭa Nirṇaya,* Centre of Advanced Study in Sanskrit, University of Poonạ, Poona 7, 1967.

Vaiyākaraṇa Siddhānta Paramalaghu Mañjuṣā by Nāgeśa-bhaṭṭa, ed. Alakhadeva Sharma, Chowkhama Amara Bharati, Benaras, 1981. Ed. & tran. with critical notes by Kapildev Sastri, Kurukshetra Universịty, 1975.

Vaiyākaraṇa Siddhānta Laghu Mañjuṣā by Nāgeśabhaṭṭa, ed. Sabhapati Sharma Upadhyaya, Chowkhamba Sanskrit Series, Varanasi, 1973.

Veṇisaṁhāra by Bhaṭṭanārāyana, ed. G.V. Devasthali, Pub. D.M. Tilak, Bombay, 1953.

Vyaktiviveka by Mahimabhaṭṭa with the comm. of Ruyyaka and a Hindi comm. by the editor, ed. Rawaprasad Dvivedi, Kashi Sanskrit Series 121, Chowkhamba, Varanasi, 1964.

(B) Modern works Referred or Consulted

Vasudeva Sarana Agrawala, *Pāṇinikālīna Bhāratavarṣa,* Chowkhamba Vidya Bhavan, Varanasi, 1969. *India as known to Pāṇini,* Prithvi Prakasana, Varanasi, 1963.

Purosottamdass Agrawala, *Śabda Śakti,* Rosanlal Jain and Sons, Jaipur, 1970.

S.O. Akhmanova, Melchuk, M.R. Frumkina, V.E.Paducheva, *Exact Methods in linguistic Research,* tran. from Russian by Hays G. David, Mohr. V.Dolores, University of California Press, Los Angles, 1963.

Tate Allen (ed.), *The Language of poetry,* Princetion, 1942.

W. Gordon Allport, 'Attitudes', *Attitude theory and Measurements,* ed. Martin Fishbein, John Wiley and Sons, Inc, 1967.

Laśzlo Antal, *Content, Meaning and Understanding,* Mouton Co., The Hague, 1964.

B.R. Ashtikar, *Investigations into the contribution of Alaṁkārikas to the development of dhvani theory and its after effects,* Unpublished Ph.D.dissertation, Nagpur, 1974.

Brahma Mitra Avasthi, *Vākyārtha Mātṛkā,* Indu Prakashana, Delhi, 1978.

Amalendu Bagchi, 'Comparative Aesthetics and the Indian Stand point', *Our Heritage,* Calcuta, Vol. XXV, 1977, pp. 1-12.

Yevgeny Basin, *Semantic Philosophy of Art.* tran. from Russian by Christopher, Progress Publishers, Moscow, 1979.

Champa Bhattacharya, *An enquiry into the nature and significance of the empiricist conception of language*, Unpublished Ph.D. thesis, Visva Bharati University, Santiniketan.

Bisnupada Bhattacharya, 'Constitution of words, *sphoṭa* theory and its opponents', *Our Heritage*, Vol.iv, part ii, pp. 217-26, Calcutta, 1956.'The Riti school and Ānandavardhana's *dhvani* theory', *Journal of the Asiatic Society of Bengal*, Vol. XVII, No. 1,'Suggestion versus Inference in Sanskrit Aesthetics', *Indian Culture*, Vol.XIII, No. 1. *Sāhitya Mīmāṁsā* (Beng), Viśva Bharati Grantha Vibhag, Calcutta, 1975. *Kāvya Mīmāṁsā* (Beng), Jiñāsā, Calcutta, 1982.

G.N. Bhattacharya, *'A Study in the dialectics of sphoṭa'* JDL, XXIX, 1937.

Gopika Mohan Bhattacharya, 'On *saṁsargamaryādā* in *Navya Nyāya'*, PWISM. C.A.S.S., University of Poona, 1980. pp. 80-83.

J.V. Bhattacharya, *Nyāya Mañjarī*, Vol.I, eng. trans., Motilal Banarsidass, Delhi, 1978.

R.S. Bhattacharya, 'Some broad asopects of Indian grammar and the theory of *sphoṭa'*. *JGJRI*. Vol.15, 197-58.

R.K.Bhattacharya, *Śabdārthatatva* (Bengali), Pravartak Publishers, Calcutta, 1964.

Sadhankumar Bhattacharya, *Aristotaler poetics O Sāhitya tatva* (Beng.), De's Publishing, Calcutta, 1978. *Śilpadarśana O Sāhitya Samālocanā* (Beng.), Jātīya Sāhitya Pariṣad, Calcutta, 1970. *Crocer aesthetics O essence of aesthetics*, (Beng.), Jātīya Sāhitya Pariṣad, Calcutta, 1370 Sāl. *Śilpatatva paricaya* (Beng.) ibid., Calcutta, 1968.

G.N. Bhatta, *'krauñcavadha in Dhvanyāloka* and *Kāvya Mīmāṁsā'*, Baroda, Vol.ix, 1959.

N. Balasubrahmanya, 'The *ālaṁkārikas* and the semantics of suggestion', *Half yearly Journal of the Mysore University*, Vol. xvi, No.1.

MAX BLACK, *Models and Metaphors*, Cornell University

Press, Ithaca, Newyork, 1962; *Language and philosophy, Ibid.*, 1949.

Arthur L. Blumenthal, *Language and Psychology*, John wiley & Sons, Inc. New York, 1970.

John Brough, 'Theories of general linguistics in Sanskrit grammarians', *TPS*, 1951; 'Audumbarāyana's theory of language' *BSOAS*, Vol. xiv, 1952. 'Some Indian theories of meaning' *TPS*, 1953.

T. Burrow, 'Indian theories on the nature of meaning', *TPS*, 1936.

Helen S. Cairns & Charles K. Cairns: *Psycholinguistics- a cognitive view of language.* Holt, Rinehart and Winston, U.S., 1976.

Rudlof Carnap, *Introduction to Semantics*, Harvard University Press, Cambridge, 1948.

Ernst Cassirer, *The philosophy of symbolic forms*, Vo. i, Yale University Press, New Heaven, 1961.

Krishna Chaitanya: *Sanskrit Poetics - a Critical and Comparative study.* Asia Publishing House, Bombay, 1965. 'Poetic experience, Indian view', *Saṁskṛti*, A.N. Jha Commemoration Vol.ii, pp. 369-374, 1969.

Prabhatchandra Chakravorti, 'Linguistic speculation of the Hindus', JDL., Vol.xii, 1925.

Tarapada Chakravorti, *Indebtedness of ālaṁkārikas to the Vyākaraṇa*, Unpublished Ph.D. dissertation, Jadavpur University, 1970.

V.K. Chari, 'The concept of *rasa-dhvani* (emotive meaning)', ALB, XXXIX, 1975; 'Poetic emotions and poetic semantics', *Journal of Aesthetics and Art Criticism*, 34, pp. 287-99, 1976; 'The Indian theory of suggestion', Philosophy East and West, Vo., XXVII, pp,391-98, 1977.

Vaudeville Charlotte, 'A further note on *krauñcavadha* in the *Dhvanyāloka* and *kāvyamīmāṁsā*', JOI, Vol.XV, 1965.

K.K. Chatterji, *Words and meanings, a new perspective*, Chowkhamba orientalia, Varanasi, 1978.

Jagdish Chaturveti & Chakrovarti, *Padapadārtha-vibhāga pariśīlanam,* Kishor Vidya Niketan, Varanasi, 1980.

Isidor Chein, 'Behaviour theory and the behaviour of attitude, some critical comments', *Attitude theory and measurement,* ed. Martin Fishbein, John wiley and Sons, inc. New York, 1967.

Colins Cherry, *On Human Communication,* The technology press of Massachusetts Institute of technology and John Willey & Sons Inc. New York, 1957.

Noam Chomsky, *Aspects of the theory of syntax,* MIT Press, Massachusetts Institute of technology, Massachusetts, 1965: *Language and mind,* Harcourt, Brace & World, Inc. NewYork, 1968. *Reflections on language,* Fontana Collins, Great Britain, 1976.

P.J.Choudhuri: 'Studies in comparative aesthetics', *Visva Bharati Series* 18, Shantiniketan, 1953.

N.N. Choudhuri, *kāvyatatva samīkṣā,* Motilal Banarsidass, Delhi, 1959.

Mitreyi Choudhuri, *A critical and historical study of the function of vyañjanā,* Unpublished Ph.D. dissertation, Jadavpur Univesity, 1966.

Satyadev Choudhuri, *Śabdaśakti aur dhvanisiddhānta* (Hindi), Alaṁkāra Prakasan, Delhi, 1973; *Bhāratīya kāvya śāstra* (Hindi), *Ibid.* 1974.

Elizabeth Christie, 'Indian philosophers on poetic imagination *(Pratibhā), Journal of Indian philosophy,* Vol.7, No.2, June, D. Reidel publishing company, Dordrecht, pp. 153-207, 1979.

T.R. Cintamani, 'Bhaṭṭanāyaka on the confutation of *dhvani*', Journal of the Bombay University, Vol. XVII, part 2. 'Fragments from Mātṛguptācārya', JOR, No. 11, 1928. 'Fragments of Bhaṭṭanāyaka', JOR, Vol.I, 1927.

A.K. Coomaraswamy, 'Some pāli words for *vyañjanā* in pāli texts' Harvard Journal of Asiatic Studies, Vol.iv, 1939.

A.S. Dange, '*Sphoṭa,* a reapprisal' *PWISM,* C.A.S.S. Univesity of Poona, pp. 71-77, 1981.

Sudhir Kumar Dasgupta, *Kāvyāloka* (Beng), 4th edition, A.Mukherji & Co.Pvt.Ltd. Calcutta 1379 Śak.

S.N.Dasgupta & S.K.DK, *A history of Sanskrit literature*, University of Calcutta, 1962.

Amala A. Dass: *Philosophical implications of dhvani*, unpublished Ph.D. dissertation, Dept. of Sanskrit, Madras, University, 1980.

S.K.De, *History of Sanskrit poetics*, Firma, KLM, Calcutta, 1960. *Sanskrit poetics as a study of aesthetics*. University of California Press, Barkeley and Los Angles, 1963.

G.T.Deshpande, 'Contemporary background of *Dhvanyāloka*', *University Journal*, Vol.xvii, pp. 8-17, 1966.

Hemalata B. Deshpande, *Ānandavardhana and Kuntaka, Comparative Study*, unpublished Ph.D. thesis, Karnataka University, 1968.

Madhav Deshpande, 'Sentence cognition in Nyāya epistemology', Indo Iranian Journal, Vol.20, Nos. 314, October, 1978.

Indumati Nahar Dike, *The early beginnings of poetics in Ṛgveda*, unpublished Ph.D. thesis, Bombay University, 1953-59.

M.G. Dhadphale, '*Mīmāṁsā* and *Vyākaraṇa* on multiple meaning' PWISM, CASS, Poona University, pp. 61 ff, 1981.

Leonard W. Doob, 'The behaviour of attitude', *Attitude and Measurement*, John Willey and Sons, New York, 1967.

G. F. Droste, 'Intention, meaning, interpretation' *Lingua*, Vol. 21, North Holland Publishing Compamy, Amsterdam, 1968.

Kapildev Dvivedi, *Arthaviñāna aur vyākaraṇadarśana* (Hindi), Hindusthan Academy, Allahabad, 1951.

Franklein Edgerton, 'Indirect suggestion in poetry, a Hindu theory of literary aesthetics', Proceedings of the American Philosophical society, Vol. LXXVI (76), No. 5, Philadelphia, 1936.

Burtt Edwin, 'Intention of Eastern and Western Philosophy', *Philosophy East and West*, Honolulu University of Hawali Press, Vol. II, No. 4, January, 1953.

Willian Empson, *Seven types of ambiguity*, Chatto and Windus, London, 1963.

Pierre Filliojat, 'On the sementic use of the word *sphoṭa*' *Amṛtadhārā*, R. N. Dandakar's felicitation volume, Ajanta publications, Delhi, 1984.

J. R. Firth, 'The technique of semantics' *Papers in linguistics*, 1934-51, Oxford University Press, London, 1964.

Ivan Fonagy, 'Communication in poetry', *Word*, Vol. 17, Number-2, NewYork, 1961.

Roger Flower, *The languages of literature*, Routledge & kegan Paul, London, 1971.

Richard Muller Freienfels, *The evolution of modern psychology*, tra. W. Beran Wolfe, Third print, Yale University Press, New Haven, 1948.

Charles C. Fries, 'Meaning and linguistic analysis', *Language*, Vol. 30, 1954.

Alan Sir Gardinar, *The theory of speech and language*, Oxford, Clarendon Press, 1963.

Edwin Gerow, *A glossary of Indian figures of speech*. Near and Middle East studies, Columbia University Series, A. dvi, The Hague, Paris, Mouton, 1971. *Indian poetics*, (A history of Indian literature), ed. Jan Gonda, Vol, V, fase 3, Wiesbanden, Otto Harrasson Wits, 1977.

A.H. Gleason, *An introduction to descriptive linguistics*, Henry Holt and Company, New York, 1958.

V.K. Gokak, *The poetic approach to language*, Oxford University Press, 1952.

J. Gonda, *The vision of the Vedic poet*, Mounton and Co. The Hauge, 1963.

Louis H. Gray, *Foundation of language*, The Macmillan Company, New York, 1960.

Joseph H. Greenberg, *Essays in linguistics,* The university of Cicago Press, 1963.

Edward Hall, *The Silent language,* A Fawatt Premier book, 1959.

William A. Heffernan & James P. Deg, *Language and literature Reader,* Glenco press, California.

F.W.G. Hegel: *Aesthetics,* Vol. i, ii, Clarendon Press, Oxford, 1975.

Martin Heidegger, *Poetry language thought,* Harper Colophon Books, 1975.

Betty Heimann, *'Sphoṭa* and *artha'*, Frestschrift vol. of P.V. Kane, Oriental book agency, Poona, 1941.

A.L. Herman, *'Sphoṭa', JGJRI,* Vol.xix, Part i-4, 1962-63.

Thomas E. Hill, *The concept of meaning,* Humanitics Press, New York, 1971.

M.Hiriyanna, 'Vyādi and Vājapyāyana', IHQ, Vol.xiv, No. 2, 1938. *Art experience,* Kavyalaya publishers, Mysore, 1954.

Hans Hormann, *Psycholinguistics, An introduction to research and thory,* trans. from German by N.N. Stern, Springer, 1971.

Susan H. Houston, *A survery of Psaycholinguistics,* Mouton, The Hague, 1972.

K.A. Subramania Iyer, ' Who are *anityasphoṭavādinaḥ?'* POC, viii, Mysore, 1935. *'Pratibhā,* as meaning of a sentence', PAIOC, Tirupati, 1940-41. 'Originality and Sanskrit Poetics', JGJRI, Nov. 1943. 'The doctrine of *sphoṭa', JGJRI,* V. Part ii, Allahabad, 1948. 'Bhartṛhari on *dhvani', ABORI* Vol. XLVI, Poona, 1965. 'Bhartṛhari on the primary & secondary meanings of words', *S.M. Katre frestachrit Vol.* Deccan College, Poona, 1970. 'Bhartṛhari on sentence' *ALB,* K.K. Raja Felicitation, Vol. 44-45, 1980-81. *Bhartṛhari,* Deccan Collage, Poona, 1969.

Otto Jesperson, *The Philosophy of Grammar,* Georgs Allen and Unwin Ltd. London, (1924), 1963.

S.D. Joshi, *Sphoṭa Nirṇaya,* Poona University, 1967. 'Bhartṛhari's concept of *pratibhā,* a theory on the nature of language acquisition', *V.G. Paranjape commemoration Vol.* Ajanta publication, Delhi, 1977. 'Patañjali's definition of a word: an interpretation', BOCRI, 1966.

Dinabandhu Kar, *Samantic basis of the Aṣṭādhyāyī,* Unpublished Ph.D.thesis, Poona University, 1980.

M.M. Gopinath Kaviraj, 'The doctrine of *pratibhā* in Indian philosophy,' ABORI, Vol.V, part i, 1923-24.

Ruth M. Kempson, *Semantic Theory,* Cambridge University Press, Cambridge, 1977.

K. Krishnamoorthy, ' Ānanda's treatment of *rasa* in relation to *dhvani'*, *JOR.* xvii, 1947-48. 'Some critics of Ānandavardhana' a theory of *dhvani'*, Indian culture, V. 1948. 'Ānanda's treatment of *pratibhā, ABORI* xxxi, 1950. 'Bhaṭṭa Tauta's defence of poetry', Aryan path, Oct. 1960. *Essays in Sanskrit Criticism,* Karnataka University, Dharwar, 1964. *Some thoughts on Indian Aesthetics and Literary Criticism,* Mysore University, 1968. *'Dhvani* and *rasa'*, *Sri Venkateswar University Oriental Journal,* Vol. xv, part i, Tirupati, 1972. *Dhvanyāloka,* critical edition with introduction, English tr. and notes, Karnatak University, Dharwar, 1974 (also see in 'D', Section 'A' of the bibliography). *Studies in Indian aesthetics and criticism,* Mysore printing and publishing house, 1979. 'The nature of creative *pratibhā* according to Kuntaka', *Indologics Taurinensia,* Vol. viii-ix, Dr. Ludwik Sternback commoration Vol. Edizioni Jollygrafica, Tonino (Italy), 1980-81. *Dhvanyāloka and its critics.* Bharatiya Vidya Prakashan, Delhi, 1982.

V.M. Kulkarni, 'Sanskrit writers on Plagiarism' JOI, Vol. iii, 1954. 'The treatment of intonation *(kāku)* in Sanskrit poetics', *JOI,* Vol.xvi, No.1, 1966. 'A recent edition of *Dhvanyāloka', ABORI,* Vol. LVII, 1976.

F.W. Leopold, 'Semantic learning in infant language', word, Vol.iv, No.3, NewYork, 1948.

F.L.Lucas, *Literature and Psychology*, Ann Arbor Paperbacks, University of Michigan Press, 1957.

John Lyons, *Semantics*, Vol.i, ii, Cambridge University Press, Cambridge, 1978.

T.M.P. Mahadevan, *The Pañcadaśi of Bhāratītīrtha Vidyāraṇya, an exposition*, Centre of Advanced Study in philosophy, University of Madras, 1969. *The Philosophy of Advaita*, Arnold Heinemann, New Delhi, 1976.

Jaques Maritain, *Creative intuition in art and poetry*, Pantheon Books, 1953.

J.L. Masson, M. V. Patwardhan, *Śāntarasa and Abhinavagupta's Philosophy of aesthetics*, Bhandarkar Oriental Series, No. 9 Poona, BORI, 1969. *Aesthetic Rapture*, Vol. i, ii. (The *rasādhyāya* or *Nāṭya Śāstra)*, Deccan College, Poona 1970.

B.K. Matilal, 'Indian theorists on the nature of the sentence *(vākya)*', *Foundations of language*, Vol.2, Holland, 1966.

William Mcdougal, *An outline of Psychology*, Twelfth edition, 1948, first ed. 1923. Methuen and Co.Ltd. London.

David Mcneill, *The conceptual basis of language*, Lawrence Erlbaum Associates Publishers, New Jersey, 1979.

S. Meera, *Studies on Dhvanyāloka*, Unpublished Ph.D. thesis, Madra, 1978.

George A. Miller, *Language and Communication*, second ed. Mc Graw Hill Book Company Inc. New York, 1951. Ed. *Psychology and Communication*, Voice of America Forum Series, 1974.

Viswanath Mishra, '*Vaiyākaraṇa saṁpradāye* sphoṭa *paraṁparā*', *Ṛṣikalpanyāsa*, Bhārati Pariṣad, Prayag, 1972.

S. Mrusalgaunkar, '*Pratibhā Sādhana*', *Pattabhiram Śāstri Felicitation Vol.* Delhi, 1981.

M.S. Narayanmoorthy, 'Bhaṭṭoji Dīkṣita and Kauṇḍa Bhaṭṭa on the primary denotation'. Srivenkateswar University Journal, Vol. XV, part ii, Tirupati, 1972.

Srimannarayana Moorthy, 'Bhartṛhari on *svaṁ rūpam śabdasyāśabdasaṁjñā*' ALB, 44-45.

Ramaranjan Mukherji, *Literary criticism in ancient India*, Sanskrit Pustak Bhandar, Calcutta, 1966.

Siddheswar Mukhopadhyaya, 'Dhvani O tadīya virodhi saṁpradāya' (Beng). *OH*, Vol.iv, part i; Bulletin of the dept. of post graduate training and research. Sanskrit College, Calcutta, pp. 117-34, 1956.

Ravisankar Nagar, 'Indebtedness of Ānandavardhana to Bhartṛhari', *Indological Studies*, pp. 78-85, Delhi, 11, 1974. *Vyañjanā Vimarśaḥ*, Vandana Prakashan, Delhi, 1977.

P.S. Naidu, 'The concept of suggestion in Hindu aesthetics', *Frestschrift Vol.* P.V. Kane, Oriental Book Agency, Poona, 1941.

T.S. Nandi, *The origin and development of the theory of rasa and dhvani in Sanskrit poetics*, Gujrat University, Ahmedabad, 1973.

C.K.Ogden & I. A. Richards, *The meaning of meaning*, 10th ed. (fifth impression), Routledge & Kegan Paul Ltd., Landon, 1960.

K.C. Pandey, *Comparative Aesthetics*, Vol. i, ii, 1959, 1956. *Abhinavagupta*, Chowkhamba Sanskrit Series, 1963.

R. C. Pandey, *The problem of meaning in Indian Philosophy*, Motilal Banarsidass, Delhi, 1963.

Swaminath Pandey, *Comparative studies in greek and Sanskrit Literary criticism with special reference to Longinus and Ānandavardhana*, unpublished Ph.D. thesis, Jadavpur University, 1970.

G.H.R.Parkinson, ed. *The thoery of meaning*, Oxford University Press, London, 1968.

P.S.S.Pattar, *Studies in Dhvanyāloka or the reign of rasa in Sanskrit Criticism*, Trichur, 1938.

P.K.Narayan Pillai, 'Kālidāsa—an assessment by Ānandavardhana,' *BDCRI*, Silver Jubilee Vol. 1966.

V. Raghavan, 'Writers quoted in the *Abhinavabhāratī*', JOR, Vol. vi, 1932. *The number of rasas,* Adyar library research centre, xxvi, Madras, 1967.

K.K. Raja, 'Bhartṛhari's list of sentence definitions' *ALB.* xxvi, 1962. *Indian theories of meaning,* AIS 91, 1963 (Reprint 1977). 'Pāṇini's attitude towards *lakṣaṇā*', *ALB.* xxix, 1965. 'The *candrikā* commentary on the *Dhvanyāloka,*' *M. Hiriyanna birth centenary commemoration Vol.* Mysore, 1972. *'vyañjanā'*suggestive function of language', *AOR,* xxix, 1980.

Naraindas Ram, *Dhvani tatva samīkṣā,* unpublished D.Litt. thesis, Sampurnananda Sanskrit University, 1978.

V.S.Rao, *The Philosophy of a sentence and its parts,* Munshiram Manoharlal, New Delhi, 1969.

Krishan Rayan, *Suggestion and Statement in poerty,* London, 1972.

Louis Renou, 'Le dhvani dans la poetique sanskrit's' English tran. *ALB,* 18.

H.R. Robins, *A history of linguistic library, 1967.*

Gilbert Rype, *The concept of mind,* Penguin Books, England, 1973.

D.X.F.SA, *'Dhvani* as a method of interpretation, reading scripture the *dhvani* way', *Journal of Bible Bhāṣyam,* pp. 276-94, Poona, 1979.

Edward Sapir, *Language,* Harvest Books, Newyork, 1949.

A. Scharfe, *Kālidāsa lexicon,* Vol. iii, Index omnium verborum, Part i, Sanskrit pro manuscripts unpublished work, 1966.

K.A. Sankaran, 'Kuntaka's attitude towards *dhavni*', JOR, 1927.

S.C. Sengupta, *Towards a thoery of the imagination,* Oxford University Press, Calcutta, 1959. *Sāhityapāṭher bhūmikā* (Beng), Visva Bharrti Grantha vibhag, 1973.

S.N. Sengupta, *Saṁskrita śabda śāstrer mùlakathā* (Beng)., Frima KLM, Calcutta, 1957.

Bala Śastri, '*Sphoṭa vivechanam*', *Pattabhiram Sastri felicitation Vol.* pp. 56-59, Delhi, 1981.

Garuinath Sastri, 'The docrtine of *śabdabrahman*, a criticism by Jayantabhaṭṭa', IHQ. Vol.XV, 1939. *The philosophy of word and meaning*, Calcutta Sanskrit College research series No. V, 1959. *A study in the dialectics of sphoṭa*, Motilal Banarsidass, Delhi, 1980.

S.N. Ghosal Sastri: *Elements of Indian Aesthetics*, Vol. i, Chowkhamba Orientalia, Varanasi, 1978.

Peri Venkateswar Sastri, '*Pāṇinīyaśabdānuśāsane sphoṭa brahma nirūpaṇam*', *Ṛṣikalpanyāsa*, Ḅharatiya Parisad, Prayag, 1972.

Ramaswarup Shastri, '*Sabdadarśana*, Sarada Sadan Muzafer Nagar, 1972.

V.A. Ramaswami Shastri, '*Bhāvanā*, the leading concept of verbal cognition', *Bharatiya Vidya*, Bhāratiya Vidya Bhaban, Bombay, 1953. 'The doctrine of *sphoṭa*', Journal of Annamolai Uṇiversity, Vol.i, No.2, Annamolainagar, 1932.

S.S. Suryanarayan Shastri, 'Vācaspati's criticism of sphoṭavāda', *JOR*, Vol.vi, 1932.

Krusnakuar Sharma, *Dhavni siddhānta kā kāvya śāstrīya saundaryaśāstriya aur samājamanovaijñānika adhyayana*, Abhinavabharati, Allahabad, 1975.

Mukundamadhav Sharma, *Vyañjanā prapañca samīkṣā* Chowkhamba Orientalia, Varanasi, 1979. 'Creative art, genius and heredity'. Summaries of papers, AIOC, Jaipur Session, pp-191, 1982.

E.R. Shreekrishna Sharma, 'Sphoṭa and Saṁkara' *ALB*, Vol. 44-45, pp. 223-228, 1980-81.

P.C. Shukla, 'What Ānandavardhana meant by *dhvani*' JGJRI. xxii, 1965.

Nils. Simonsson, 'Audumbarāyana's theory of sounds', *OS*, Vol.x, Uppsala, Stockholm, 1962.

Jadunath Sihna, *A History of Indian Philosophy,* Vol. ii, Central book agency, Calcutta, 1952.

Kalpika Sinha, *A critical study of Ānandavardhana's Dhvanyāloka,* unpublished Ph.D. thesis, Visva Bharati University, Santiniketan, 1972.

V.V. Sovani, 'Pre-*dhvani* schools of *Alaṁkāra' R.G. Bhandarkar Commemoration* Vol. Nag Publishers, Dehli, 1977.

D. Danny Stenberg & Leon, A. Jakobovits, *Semantics.* Cambridge University Press, 1971.

Gustaf Stern, *Meaning and change of meaning,* University Press, Bloomington, 1965.

Ramsuresh Tripathy, *Saṁakrutavyākaraṇadarśana,* Rajkamal Prakeshan, Delhi, 1972. *'Pratibhāvākyāartha', Sārasvata Suṣamā,* 23rd year, 4th number, Varanasi Sanskrit University, Sambat-2025.

Siddheswar Verma, 'Analysis of meaning in Indian philosophy of language', *JRAS,* 1925. 'Analysis of meaning in Indian Semantics', *JDL,* Vol.xiii, 1926.

Satyakam Verma, *Bhāṣātatva aur vākyapadīya* (Hindi), Bharatiya Prakasana, New Delhi, 1971.

Bholasankar Vyasa, *Dhvani saṁpradāya aur uske siddhānta,* Vol. i, Kashi nagari Pracarini Sabha, Samvat 2013.